Early Praise for *Seven Obscure Languages in Seven Weeks*

One of the challenges that programmers face is that in the struggle to get today's work done while keeping up with what's coming next, we tend to neglect our history. In a real sense we are an industry with a present and a future but no past. By diving into seven lesser-known programming languages, Dmitry's book goes a long way to showing us how programming got this way, all in a witty and fun package.

➤ **Russ Olsen**
President, ROIV

Seven Obscure Languages in Seven Weeks takes readers on an intellectual journey through the early days of computer languages, when simplicity and efficiency were paramount. This book deserves a place on every shelf, offering a delightful exploration that brings a curious smile to one's face. It stands as a fascinating artifact of computer science history, documenting a past that risks fading into the fog of time.

➤ **Andrian Gorohovschi**
Software Engineering Senior Manager, Dassault Systèmes, SolidWorks Corporation

The books in the Seven in Seven series are among my very favorite computer science books of all——I return to them regularly for inspiration on how to approach a programming idea I'm mulling over with a fresh perspective. This new volume is a worthy addition to this series and will broaden your mind as you delve into some deeply interesting languages; you're probably aware of their existence but likely never programmed in them. Until now. Pick a chapter, install a compiler, and after following along with the examples, really dig in and write a whole new program of your own. While you may not keep the compiler in your toolkit, the Big Ideas in these languages will certainly elevate the way you approach programming after you've tried them!

➤ **Gary V. Vaughan**
Senior Software Engineer

Seven Obscure Languages in Seven Weeks

Rediscovering the Tools That Built the Future

Dmitry Zinoviev

The Pragmatic Bookshelf

Dallas, Texas

For our complete catalog of hands-on, practical, and Pragmatic content for software developers, please visit *https://pragprog.com*.

Contact *support@pragprog.com* for sales, volume licensing, and support.

For international rights, please contact *rights@pragprog.com*.

The team that produced this book includes:

Publisher:	Dave Thomas
COO:	Janet Furlow
Executive Editor:	Susannah Davidson
Development Editor:	Adaobi Obi Tulton
Copy Editor:	L. Sakhi MacMillan
Indexing:	Potomac Indexing, LLC
Layout:	Gilson Graphics

ISBN-13: 979-8-88865-063-9
Book version: P1.0—October 2024

To my wife, Anna, and my children, Eugenia and Roman, whose love and care made this book possible.

Contents

Acknowledgments

"This book is my fourth Pragmatic book produced in enjoyable cooperation with the outstanding editor Adaobi Obi Tulton. I can't stop admiring her helpfulness, mastery of the language, knowledge of the procedures, and willingness to understand the subject." I used the same phrase in my third book, but I do not mind repeating myself: Adaobi remains as helpful, knowledgeable, understanding, and outstanding as ever.

The book was inspired by Margaret Eldridge, Pragmatic's managing editor of online content and senior acquisitions editor. She heard the barely audible tune that I whistled on LinkedIn and swiftly transformed it into a book proposal before I knew it. This book would not exist without her.

The official technical reviewers did an incredible job improving the quality of the manuscript. My sincere thanks go to them, listed in alphabetical order by last name: Uberto Barbini, Paul Butcher, Fred Daoud, Daniel Duffy, Andrian Gorohovschi, Simon Hawkin, René Vincent Jansen, Russ Olsen, Nikolay Shulga, Karl Stolley, Adam Tornhill, and Gary V. Vaughan. My special thanks go to Nigel Karunaratne for help with debugging the Starset interpreter.

My beloved family—my wife, Anna; my daughter, Eugenia; my son, Roman; and my cats, Cesar and Susan—provided immense encouragement and emotional support, as always.

Thank you!

Preface

I was born in the USSR—a country that was at least twenty years technologically behind the West. It was a curse.

I got my first calculator when I was fifteen, and it was just a calculator, not a graphing one. I saw a computer for the first time as a college freshman, and it was not a PC but a mainframe console. I punched my FORTRAN (in all capital letters) programming labs on paper tapes—and I was lucky because my classmates couldn't negotiate tape punch access rights with the system administrator and had to finish their lab assignments on time without an option of saving them. Last but not least, we used a pirated version of IBM OS/360 with some missing bits and pieces.

However, looking back, it was a blessing. Locked out behind the Iron Curtain, the Soviet Union was a giant, continental-scale treasure trove of outdated hardware and software and, simultaneously, exciting testing grounds for groundbreaking and insane ideas and concepts deemed too impractical in the "capitalist West." On the one hand, I learned programming languages and used hardware not used anywhere else anymore. On the other hand, I witnessed the birth of Rapira (Rapier), a language designed to teach computer programming in schools, and Agat and Corvette personal computers. The Corvette was even developed by my teachers and classmates in my department at Moscow State University. The USSR was also the birthplace of the world's most modern ternary computer, the Setun, that used trits instead of bits, and a 48-bit supercomputer Elbrus-1 with ALGOL-68 as the system programming language. Not too bad for a country that was considered technologically backward.

So I was not a stranger to the world of "retro" languages (which didn't feel retro to me, since I didn't know any better). I rigorously collected translated books about APL, Algol, Forth, and PL/I, believing that in the late 1980s, those languages were popular abroad.

The last addition to my collection was a book about Starset. My relationship with Starset is very intimate. The language was developed by the branch of the Soviet Academy of Sciences located in my hometown, and I bought the book in Almaty while dating my future wife, Anna. Soon after we married, we emigrated to the United States, and that's when I learned that my precious knowledge of the "advanced" languages was obsolete. Alas.

Today, thirty years later, from the standpoint of a computer science professor interested in the history of computing, among other things, I realize that my experience with the "obscure" languages wasn't in vain. Many concepts found in modern programming languages are not so modern at all. They date back to the Golden Age of computer science, to the 1960s and 1970s, when they were either theoretically too advanced for their time or technologically infeasible. Some such concepts—objects, vectorized operations, message passing, pattern matching, and even indentation as an element of syntax—were rediscovered and successfully reimplemented in the 1980s and on. Other concepts were less fortunate; they are indeed forgotten. I consider it my duty to unearth the lore of the "obscure" programming languages and make it available to you—whether for use in your professional life or simply to satisfy your curiosity for arcane knowledge.

Dmitry Zinoviev
Professor of Computer Science and Data Science
dzinoviev@gmail.com
Boston, MA, Summer 2024

Introduction

The epigraph to this Introduction is taken from *The Canterbury Tales*, written by Geoffrey Chaucer around 1387. At first glance, it's written in English. At a second glance, it's not, for the number of misspelled words is enormous, and the grammar looks weird too. Indeed, the *Tales* are composed in Middle English, a language spoken and written in England in the fourteenth century but that gradually transitioned into Modern English from the late fifteenth century onward, joining the ranks of largely forgotten, and obscure for any practical purpose, *natural languages*, such as Akkadian, Ancient Egyptian, Old Norse, Latin, Aramaic, Manx, and Etruscan.

Natural languages originate (yes, even nowadays—Afrikaans in Dutch South Africa, Modern Hebrew in Israel, Tok Pisin in Papua New Guinea), evolve, and die. Programming languages are similar to them: they go through the same cycle but at a much faster rate. This book is about forgotten, obscure programming languages.

Why would one care about obscure languages? Well, for more than one reason!

- *Learning from history.* Studying older programming languages can provide insight into why modern languages are designed the way they are and why certain features exist.

- *Different paradigms.* Some obscure languages introduced programming paradigms that are still relevant today, even if the languages are not widely used anymore.

- *Problem-solving skills.* Programming languages are designed to solve particular problems efficiently. You can broaden your problem-solving skills and get new perspectives on tackling problems.

- *Improved code understanding.* Studying different programming languages improves your ability to understand code, making you more versatile.

- *Employability.* Knowledge in a obscure language can lead to unique and well-paying job opportunities in niche markets.

- *Maintaining legacy systems.* Much of today's code was written in older languages. Knowing these languages helps maintain and update these systems.

The rest of the Introduction explains the choice of languages, outlines the intended audience, and specifies the required software.

About the Languages

The Online Historical Encyclopaedia of Programming Languages lists approximately nine thousand languages arranged into two regnums (endogenous and exogenous), four phyla (algorithmic, functional, structural, and reflexive), twelve classes (conversational, imperative, spatially algorithmic, operation-oriented, expression-oriented, state/flow, lambda calculus, structural generic, structural specific, phenomenological, simulating, and close mapping), and forty orders (too many to list).[1] Regardless of whether we take this classification as ground truth, the variety of coding paradigms is astonishing.

Most of the languages mentioned by hopl.info are dead languages. Some of them were popular at creation but went out of favor later. Some were "stillborn"—created but never having caught the momentum. The others lived a long, respectable life and retired, superseded by more advanced tools.

The surviving languages could be grouped by their popularity among programmers. The position of a language on the TIOBE Index is an acceptable proxy for popularity.[2] The languages like Python, C, Java, and C++ are broadly used in industry and academia and cover the full development stack: front end, back end, and databases. They are loved and remembered—even Fortran, the oldest coding language.

TIOBE individually rates the next thirty languages, including COBOL, Perl, Objective-C, Ada, Lua, Lisp, Haskel, Kotlin, Scala, and Prolog. They're not forgotten either. However, TIOBE lumps the next fifty languages together: their popularity is low and barely above the statistical margins of error (ActionScript, BCPL, Erlang/Elixir, Forth, J, Occam, PL/I, Scheme, Smalltalk, Tcl, and VHDL are in this group). And this is where things become intriguing.

A vast amount of literature exists on Erlang and Elixir (including Pragmatic's own *Programming Erlang [Arm13]* and *Modern Erlang for Beginners [Ost18]*). Scheme is popular in higher education for teaching organization of programming languages and similar topics. COBOL is a niche language: the entire

---

1.   https://hopl.info
2.   https://www.tiobe.com/tiobe-index

financial and insurance industries run on it, but outside coders couldn't care less. Haskel and Lua are confined to their niches too. Kotlin (2011) is relatively new in the field; let's give it a couple of years to shine in its full glory (or not). Every language in this and the following groups has a story of success and eventual failure—the story that almost nobody remembers. These are the languages that I call "obscure."

The format of this book allows me to tell you only seven obscure language stories. Painful as it was, I had to choose those seven. I wanted the selection to be diverse and include feature-rich, bizarre, and promising languages, even if their promises would fail to be fulfilled.

As a result, I picked Forth, Occam, APL, Simula, SNOBOL, Starset, and m4. They feature, among other things, pattern matching, computer simulation, array and stack processing, macroprogramming, message passing, and set programming. Only m4 needs an explanation. It's not obscure because it was once known—it's "obscure" because it was never exposed to most software developers. Heavily used today by various system configuration tools, it deserves much more credit as a practical, Turing-complete language.

You can see the rise and fall of the "obscure" languages in the table below. The introduction years are taken from Wikipedia. The peak and decline years have been inferred from the Google Books Ngram Viewer, which is imperfect yet gives some ballpark estimates of what was hot and what was not.

	Introduced	Peaked	Declined
APL	1962–1966	1981	1995
SNOBOL	1962–1967	1972, 1982	1990
Simula	1962–1967	1985	2007
Forth	1968	1988	2013
m4	1977	n/a	active
Occam	1983	1989	1995
Starset	1991	n/a	n/a

From this point on, I will not put the word *obscure* in quotation marks. I hope we agree on its meaning: the obscure languages are not truly forgotten. They are in the dark. Together, we can bring them back to daylight.

About the Tips

This book is peppered with tips highlighting critical conceptual connections between the obscure languages and those currently in active use. Such subtle connections are not only a tribute to the groundbreaking ideas from the glorious past but the pulling ropes that could take the obscure languages out of obscurity, and those connections could reveal the rainbows pointing to pots of software development gold waiting to be rediscovered.

A Helpful Tip

 The function foobar() in an obscure language loosely resembles the function barfoo() in a popular existing language.

Think of these tips as a way to build and reinforce associations between obscure languages and popular existing languages. The generative power of a network of associations is in its density. The denser the network, the more associations and creative ideas it generates in the reader, which is one of the reasons for reading this book.

About You

This book is intended for software developers seeking new, unorthodox, inspirational ideas to better their coding skills and theoretical understanding of computer language organization. However, it's also a crucial resource for IT managers and team leads. Understanding the older languages enables them to make informed decisions about legacy system maintenance, staff training, and system integration. Additionally, tech enthusiasts and software historians will find this book captivating, offering a deep dive into the evolutionary layers of coding languages. Whether you're hands-on with code or overseeing teams and projects, this book provides invaluable insights into obscure programming.

I hope that you, the reader, will see the connections between the concepts in the past and their implementations today (for example, the first OOP language was designed for computer simulation; digital humanities date back to the early 1970s; indentation as a syntax feature is forty years old). Finally, you will know how living in a world of specialized programming languages rather than the general-purpose C, C++, Java, and Python could feel.

About the Software

In my youthful days, amid the stark realities of the former Soviet Union—known today as Russia—my only way of learning a new programming language was to imagine myself being that language interpreter and interpreting the code written on paper. In the twenty-first century, you have better options. Any programming language, with few exceptions, has been eventually brought to life, one way or another—even Starset, the most obscure of the seven. The question is not whether an interpreter or a compiler of a language exists but where to find one. Being a devoted Linux user, I'll advise you on how to get a grip on Linux versions of the interpreters if they exist.

The luckiest of the obscure languages, m4, is not truly forgotten. Rather, it's obscured by more specialized tools that are unfamiliar to the users and even programmers. I know a good programmer who believes that m4 is no more. However, m4 is alive and kicking and at the heart of the GNU Autoconf system, sendmail (a popular mail transfer agent), and Ratfor (a structured version of Fortran 66). As such, it's a part of any good Linux distribution; even if it's not, you'd have no trouble installing it.

For unknown reasons, but most likely not because of their exceptional practical significance, three more languages made it into the GNU ecosystem: APL, Forth, and Simula. Their implementations became known as GNU APL, GNU Forth (gforth), and GNU Simula (cim), and they are reasonably well maintained.

Phil Budne's free CSNOBOL4 (snobol4), a port of Macro SNOBOL4, supports full SNOBOL4 language plus SPITBOL and other extensions. You'll have to compile it yourself.

KRoC is the Kent Retargetable occam Compiler developed at the University of Kent. It is open source but works only with 32-bit architectures. KRoC implements Occam-pi—a modern flavor of Occam 2.5 with some elements of π-calculus.

Finally, a Starset interpreter, christened "Suffolk Starset" or s3, is developed and maintained by the team at my own Suffolk University. Its GitHub repository will be made public as soon as we release the first fully functional version.

The following list shows links to the obscure development tools' repositories at the time of writing this book.

- *Forth.* GNU Forth (gforth; for best results, install gforth-0.7.9; many examples fail to compile with earlier versions)[3]

- *Occam.* Kent Retargetable occam Compiler (KRoC in Docker)[4]

- *APL.* GNU APL (apl),[5] Dyalog APL/S (dyalog, proprietary, but free for non-commercial use)[6]

---

3.   https://www.gnu.org/software/gforth/
4.   https://github.com/omegahm/kroc
5.   https://www.gnu.org/software/apl/
6.   https://www.dyalog.com/products.htm

- *Simula.* GNU Simula (cim)[7]

- *SNOBOL.* CSNOBOL4 (snobol4)[8] for any operating system with a C89 compiler

- *Starset.* Suffolk Starset (s3)[9]

- *m4.* GNU m4 (m4)[10]

An obligatory note—while every effort has been made to ensure that a functional compiler or interpreter of each obscure language exists for at least one popular platform (macOS, Linux, or Windows), this idyllic situation is hard to preserve due to the very definition of "being forgotten." If you want to enjoy this book thoroughly, get the software previously mentioned while you can!

Writing Something Big

Forgotten or not, any programming language claiming a right to exist must be good at least for something beyond printing "Hello, world!" The second-to-last section of each chapter is called "Writing Something Big." It presents a moderately sized (a page or two), relatively practical, and self-contained example of the chapter's language use. If the example feels offensively incomprehensible, you can safely skip it and proceed to the next chapter.

Further Reading

Each chapter concludes with a section titled "Further Reading" (just like this one). That section contains a curated list of further suggested reading on the subject.

One cannot expect to achieve a complete mastery of seven such diverse languages in seven weeks, and not only are they diverse, but each is a mind-breaker. Fortunately, many reference books and textbooks on most of these languages have been published during their peak popularity. To save you the effort of searching for these materials, I've compiled a comprehensive list of books for each chapter. Please note, some of these resources may be hard to find, some only exist in scanned format, and a few are only available in Russian due to the absence of English translations.

However, if a particular language captivates you, say, like Starset on page 173, you will hopefully appreciate my cataloging effort made to support your

---

7.   https://www.gnu.org/software/cim/
8.   https://www.regressive.org/snobol4/csnobol4/curr/
9.   https://github.com/dzinoviev/starset
10. https://www.gnu.org/software/m4/

learning journey. The books are listed chronologically to illuminate the flows and ebbs of the language popularity.

Online Resources

This book has a dedicated web page,[11] where you can access all the accompanying code. On the site, you'll also find a community forum where you can ask questions, share comments, and submit errata (registration on DevTalk is required).[12] If you've purchased the ebook, clicking the gray box above the code extracts will allow you to download them directly.

What to Do Next?

Choose the first obscure language to explore. Download and install its interpreter or compiler, or grab a pencil and sheet of paper. Start reading and coding in awe.

---

11. https://pragprog.com/book/dzseven
12. https://devtalk.com/books/seven-obscure-languages-in-seven-weeks/

Simplicity is the ultimate sophistication.

      Leonardo da Vinci, Italian polymath

CHAPTER 1

Mastering Stack-Based Computing with Forth

In this chapter, you'll learn to build efficient programs using stacks in the Forth programming language instead of variables, ideal for resource-constrained settings. Mastering Forth gives you a specialized understanding of stack-based computing, making you more effective in low-resource and hardware-specific environments, and broadens your problem-solving techniques.

Forth was designed as a hardware-friendly language. It's so adaptable that it can be used without an operating system or even replace it. For example, a Forth system at Sun Microsystems was used to diagnose and develop hardware, eventually evolving and being standardized into Open Firmware (1994–2005).

In Forth, the basic unit of computation is a word on a stack. The stack is the core computational unit. So, what is a stack?

Understanding Stack Essentials

A *stack* is a LIFO (last in, first out) linear data structure. In my head, a "classical" stack is an array-like collection of *cells* that supports only three operations:

- push(item). Push the item onto the stack, making it the top item of the stack ("last in").

- pop(). Remove the top item from the stack ("first out").

- empty(). Check if the stack is empty (whether it has the top item).

Stacks as data structures have been known before their software implementations. Stack automata and stack-based pushdown automata play an essential role in the theory of computation. The pushdown automaton was introduced by Allen Newell in 1959 and mentioned in the context of theoretical computer science by Edsger Dijkstra in 1960. However, the stack itself can be traced to 1947 (Alan Turing), and some elements can be found in the U.S. tax laws in 1939! (See *A Brief History of the Stack [Hen09]*.)

In addition to being elementary abstract data structures, stacks are, at the same time, some of the simplest hardware components. A hardware implementation of a stack was supposed to be used in the PERM II computer in 1955 (unfortunately, it was never built). Most modern computer architectures provide a hardware stack, which is one of the reasons for Forth's existence.

When Forth appeared in 1968, designed by Charlie "Chuck" Moore, the new language was expected to use hardware stacks wherever available. Eventually, software stacks became mainstream, but of all the languages illuminated in this book, Forth still has the most intimate connection to computer hardware. And that's why we start our journey through the land of obscure languages with Forth.

Writing Comments and "Hello, World!"

Many programming languages use a stack (as a matter of fact, any language that supports recursive function calls, such as C or Java, probably uses a stack). The extraordinary feature of Forth is that it uses not one stack but two: one for data (the *data stack*) and one for control (the *return stack*). And, unlike the stacks in C or Java, which are invisible to the programmer, the Forth stacks can and should be manipulated explicitly.

Before you see the stacks in action, I must say a word or two about the typing convention, comments, and the "Hello, world!" program in Forth.

Forth supports several commenting styles:

- \ text (backslash followed by at least one space) comments the remainder of the current line.

- (text) (an opening parenthesis, followed by at least one space) comments the following text up to the first closing parenthesis; this type of comment is also used to define command parameters and return values—see Word Documentation, on page 7.

- .(text) (a period, followed by an opening parenthesis, followed by at least one space) comments the following text up to the first closing parenthesis but also displays the commented text on the command line—say, for debugging.

- In some versions, { text} (an opening brace followed by at least one space) comments the following text up to the first closing brace; this notation allows one to comment parentheses.

The reason for having a space after the commenting symbol is that, unlike other languages, Forth treats comments as commands (words) and requires a separator between them and the commented content. The following code fragment illustrates all three commenting styles.

forth/helloworld.fs

```
\ Hello World in Forth
( Hello World in Forth )
.( Hello World in Forth )
CR
s" Hello World" TYPE CR
BYE
```

You'll see two output lines if you execute this code fragment in gforth as a script:

```
/home/dzseven> gforth code/forth/helloworld.fs
Hello World in Forth
Hello World
```

The first line is the output of the dot-parenthesis comment followed by a CR ("carriage return," also known as line break). CR is a Forth word whose purpose is just to break the current line. All Forth words, including CR, are case-insensitive.

Carriage Return

 The word CR loosely corresponds to the functions print() in Python and puts("") in C or expression std::cout<<std::endl in C++.

The second line is the combined output of the words TYPE and another CR. Note that the word parameter "Hello World" is placed in front of the word. The section Reverse Polish Notation, on page 5, explains why.

In the interactive mode, Forth prints the output of the most recently executed word on the same line. If the execution is successful, the output is followed by the word ok and by the current depth of the data stack unless the stack is empty. In the rest of the chapter, the character ↵ represents the keystroke Enter . The character itself isn't a Forth character, and everything after the character is the output of Gforth. Let's look at a small example. Note how the data stack grows with each entered word.

```
1↵  ok 1
2↵  ok 2
"Hello"↵  ok 4
'W'↵  ok 5
BYE↵
```

The word BYE terminates the Forth session.

You may wonder why the stack grows by two words when you enter a string. These two words represent the string's length and the address of the character array, as will be explained later on page 7.

Learning Predefined Forth Words

The Forth programming language makes every attempt to pretend that it's a human language. It has words; the words are stored in a *dictionary*; to "speak" Forth fluently, you must learn the dictionary words and understand their meaning. As a Forth programmer, you are only as good as your combined knowledge of the dictionary.

All Forth words fall into several groups based on their level of standardization and purpose.

Word Types

The most popular Forth standards are FORTH-79 (superseded by FORTH-83) and fig-Forth (1978, replaced by ANS Forth in 1994). Gforth, used in this book, is a free implementation of the latter. Depending on adherence to a standard (for example, FORTH-79), words belong to required, extension, reference, and user-defined sets:

- The required word set is expected to be implemented by all Forth systems. It includes words for the following:
  - Arithmetic operations
  - Stack manipulation
  - Flow control
  - Memory operation.
  - Device control
  - Other operations

- The extension word set supports semi-standardized extensions, such as double numbers and assembler.

- The reference word set contains words that have not been standardized but are informally widely used and expected to become a part of the standard in the future.

- Finally, you are free to (and usually have to) define specific words to solve your specific problems.

Reverse Polish Notation

Stacks go side by side with Reverse Polish Notation (RPN)—a *postfix* notation in which operators (words) follow their operands. For example, the sum of two numbers in Forth is written as 1 2 +. Compare RPN to Normal Polish Notation (NPN)—a *prefix* notation in which operators precede their operands. NPN is used in Lisp, where the same expression is written as (+ 1 2). RPN is the soul of Forth, as NPN is of Lisp. The other soulless programming languages use the *infix* notation with a binary operator between the operands—1+2. Could we care less about them in this chapter?

One exciting property of RPN is that it naturally obviates operator precedence. No need to remember what goes first—addition or multiplication. Simply push the operators and operands onto the stack in the [reverse] order in which you want them executed.

RPN and HP

 You might know Reverse Polish Notation (RPN) if you've used Hewlett-Packard (HP) calculators. Several HP models, such as the HP-19C, HP-20b, HP-28C, HP-29C, HP-30b, HP-35s, and HP Prime, effectively let you program in a style similar to Forth, though Forth was not explicitly mentioned.

To get a better sense of RPM, imagine the numeric operands in the expression 1 2 3 4 + + + . being *stacked* on the floor in the natural order. 1 is put right on the floor, 2 goes on top of 1, 3 goes on top of 2, and 4 goes on top of 3. When the operator + "arrives," it takes the two top operands (4 and 3), adds them up, and puts the result (7) back on the top. The second + extracts 7 and 2 and leaves their sum, 9, on the stack. ("Leave on the stack" is Forth programmers' shorthand for "put at the top of the stack.") The third + extracts 9 and 1 and leaves their sum, 10. Now, 10 is on the floor alone. The word . ("dot") extracts and displays the final result. The stack is empty again (see the figure on page 6).

In another example, the expression 1 2 * 3 * 4 * .s calculates and displays the product of the first four natural numbers (the factorial of 4). The word .s shows the value on the top of the stack without removing it.

1	2	3	4	+	+	+	.
			4				
		3	3	7			
	2	2	2	2	9		
1	1	1	1	1	1	10	

Data Types

All cells in both data and return stacks are the same size (usually the size of the machine word). Initially, each cell was meant to hold one value—a signed or unsigned integer number, further denoted as n or u. Later, Forth extensions added support for double precision numbers (DPNs) occupying two consecutive words each (d and ud, respectively). Don't confuse Forth DPNs with double floating-point numbers in C, C++, and Java. DPNs are still integer numbers consisting of the most significant word (MSW, closer to the top of the stack) and the least significant word (LSW) in the following position.

As an example, consider the top two words of the stack in the middle of the image on page 6—4 and 3. You can treat them as two single-precision words at face value or as the LSW and MSW parts of a DPN, whose value is (4*0x10000000000000000)+(3), which is $MSW*2^{64}+LSW$.

Underscores In Numbers

 Forth numbers, like Python numbers, can contain underscores. 1_234_567 is 1234567 in both languages.

To enter a DPN in a program or on the command line, either type the LSW followed by the MSW or insert a period *anywhere* in the number, as in the following code fragment. Note how the stack depth increased by two after entering the "pseudo-π."

```
3.14159↩  ok 2
.↩ 0  ok 1 \ The MSW
.↩ 314159  ok \ The LSW
```

The code fragment on page 34 and the follow-up explanation have more DPN examples.

Remember, *the period does not make that number a floating-point number!* But what about floating-point numbers? The "classical" Forth doesn't have them (but Gforth does). Use rational numbers if you should.

Forth treats characters in single quotation marks as integer numbers. The words TRUE and FALSE represent Boolean values (flag data type); they're numerically equal to -1 and 0.

```
'A' .↵ 65  ok
TRUE .↵ -1  ok
FALSE .↵ 0  ok
```

A character string in double quotation marks is converted to a pointer to the character array of type addr. The array is not NULL-terminated (as in C) and does not store its length (as in Java/Python/Pascal). It's your responsibility to remember the length, but Forth is trying to be helpful: when you enter a string on the command line, its address and length are both left on the stack.

```
"Hello, world"↵  ok 2
.↵ 12  ok 1 \ length
.↵ 93900026360080  ok \ character array address
```

You'll see one more data type in Demystifying Vectored Execution, on page 26, but that's all. Forth doesn't have too many data types—not as few as the B language but not even remotely as many as Python or Java.

Word Documentation

Forth words depend much on the stacks, especially the data stack (they take operands from it and store the results in it). Forth designers provided a mechanism for documenting the effect of words on the stacks—a comment that describes the expected state of the stack before and after the execution of the word. The comment is placed in parentheses. It uses the type notation developed in the previous section, with an addition of the symbol x that denotes a cell of any type.

For example, the word / ("divide") expects the dividend n1 and divisor n2 in the stack and leaves the quotient n on the stack:

```
10 2 / .↵  5  ok
```

You can describe its behavior as (n1 n2 – n), which means pop n1 from the stack, pop n2 from the stack, execute the operation, and push the result n back to the stack. The string literal in the code fragment on page 7 behaves as (– len addr): pop nothing, execute the operation, and push the length len and the address addr to the stack.

Word Documentation

 Forth word documentation loosely corresponds to function proto-
types in C.

Just like any other documentation, word documentation in Forth isn't required
but is strongly encouraged.

Arithmetic Operations

Forth arithmetic operations behave as expected, as long as your expectations
are based on understanding data types: signed vs. unsigned and single vs.
double precision. The words +, D+, M+, -, D-, *, / or MOD add (single, DPN, or
mixed), subtract (single and DPN), multiply, divide, and calculate the
remainder, respectively. The result has the same type as the operands unless
the operands have different types.

The words UM* (u1 u2 -- ud), M* (n1 n2 -- d), UM/MOD (ud u -- urem uquot) multiply and
divide with an appropriate upgrade (from single to DPN) and downgrade (from
DPN to single).

```
10000000000000 -10000000000000 * .↩  -2537764290115403776  ok
10000000000000 -10000000000000 M* . .↩ -5421011 2537764290115403776  ok
10000000000000 -10000000000000 UM* . .↩  9999994578989 2537764290115403776 ok
```

The first and the last expressions in the preceding example produce incorrect
results because Forth does not check for signedness and overflows.

The middle result is correct: (10000000000000 × -10000000000000) mod 2^{64} (which
equals 2537764290115403776) fits into the least significant 64-bit word, and
(10000000000000 × -10000000000000) ÷ 2^{64} (which equals -5421011) fits into the next,
most significant one.

The lack of "classical" floating-point numbers necessitates extensive use of
rational numbers. As a result, multiplication by a rational number (that is,
multiplication by its numerator followed by division by the denominator)
becomes an operation on its own: */ (n num den -- quot) for single precision
numbers and M*/ (d num uden -- dquot) for DPNs. The operation uses extra-wide
storage for the intermediate product to avoid overflow. Here's how Forth programmers calculate the circumference of a circle with a diameter of 10,000:

```
10000↩  ok 1 \ Push the diameter
355 113↩  ok 3 \ Push the π as a rational number
*/ .↩ 31415  ok
```

The sidebar on page 9 explains why 355/113 is the best π your money can buy.

Know Your π's!

π, one of the best-known numbers in mathematics, is transcendental: it's not a root of any polynomial with rational coefficients. π has infinitely many digits and must be approximated for practical use. (Another such value is e, the base of natural logarithms.) The two most popular approximations are 3.14159 and 22/7, which are 2.65e-06 and 0.0013 off, respectively. 355/113 is an even better approximation. As a ratio of two whole numbers, it's particularly suited for Forth and differs from π by no more than 2.67e-07.

The words 1+, 1-, 2*, and 2/ simplify indexing operations involving increments, decrements, doubling, and halving. These words are boring but handy.

The last group of arithmetic words of interest is NEGATE, DNEGATE, MAX, DMAX, MIN, DMIN, and ABS and DABS. They do what they say they do.

Stack Manipulation

You may have noticed that the comments in the code fragment on page 8 mention pushing values onto the [data] stack, but nothing in the code looks like a push() word. So who actually pushes the values? It's you—or whoever types the program.

Any word representing a value—such as a numeric or character literal, a variable, or a constant—gets pushed onto the stack. The value stays on the stack until extracted by a word representing an operation, like an arithmetic function. As for popping values from the stack, you're already familiar with the words . ("dot") and .s introduced on page 5.

The stacks have a dedicated word set you should master to understand the language. The set includes words for juggling single numbers and DPNs in both stacks.

The most straightforward words are DUP (x -- x x), DROP (x --), and their two-word counterparts 2DUP and 2DROP. They duplicate or remove the top item. DROP and . are different: the former doesn't display the removed item but simply discards it. For example, consider calculating the square of the number of characters in the sacred phrase "Hello, world!" (Because why not?)

```
"Hello, world!"↵  ok 2 \ Stack: the length and the pointer
DUP↵  ok 3 \ Stack: two copies of the length and the pointer
*↵  ok 2 \ Stack: squared length and the pointer
.↵  169  ok 1 \ Print the squared length
DROP↵  ok \ Clean the stack: drop the pointer
```

The stacks are your workspace. You must keep them clean. If you leave unused items on a stack, they'll pile up and eventually cause a memory shortage.

Let's rewrite the code fragment on the same line, except for the string:

```
"Hello, world!"↩  ok 2
DUP * . DROP↩ 169   ok
```

The code fragment expects that the user or another operation will provide the string (essentially, the parameter) at the top of the stack. That's the Forth way!

The next group of words shuffles the data stack:

- SWAP (x1 x2 -- x2 x1) and 2SWAP swap the top two items. For example, you can use it to access the pointer to a literal string in the most recent code fragment.

- ROT (x1 x2 x3 -- x2 x3 x1) and 2ROT rotate the top three items so that the second item moves to the top, the third becomes the second, and the former top item submerges into the third position. ROT is a three-item version of SWAP. -ROT (x1 x2 x3 -- x3 x1 x2) rotates the stack in the opposite direction. There is no -2ROT!

- OVER (x1 x2 -- x1 x2 x1) and 2OVER leave a copy of the second item on the stack. You can define this word in terms of the other more elementary words. Compare these two fragments:

```
1 2↩  ok 2
OVER↩  ok 3
. . .↩ 1 2 1   ok
```

and

```
1 2↩  ok 2
SWAP DUP -ROT↩ ok 3
. . .↩ 1 2 1   ok
```

The two code fragments accomplish the same goal, but the first one is more concise and efficient. Forth is a "Lego-like" language. It gives you a set of "blocks" and encourages you to assemble them into bigger blocks that make programming easy and fun.

- The word PICK (u pos -- x) (available only in FORTH-79) leaves the nposth item on the stack. This operation is against the spirit of an abstract stack, as explained on page 1. However, Forth is a pragmatic language—it cares more about goals than the means.

Finally, three more words and their DPN cousins let you move items between the two stacks. In some versions of Forth, they're available only in word definitions, but Gforth is more permissive and allows one to use them anywhere.

- The words >R (x -- R:x) and 2>R move the top item from the data stack to the return stack denoted as R: in the word description.

- The words R> (R:x -- x) and 2R> move the top item from the return stack to the data stack.

- The words R@ (-- x ; R: x -- x) 2R@ copy the top item from the return stack to the data stack. The documentation shows the states of both stacks separated by a semicolon.

You would use the return stack as auxiliary storage for the items ("two heads are better than one") and, rarely, to implement customized control structures. No matter what, ensure that the state of the stack before and after any operation doesn't change, because that's what a Forth system expects.

Defining New Words

The code fragment on page 10 and the paragraph that followed had a barely hidden message: as a Forth programmer, you can and should create new words, and Forth provides the wordsmithing mechanisms and tools.

A word consists of a name and a definition. For now, you can think of a word as a *macro* that, when used, expands into a set of adequately arranged words. Some would prefer to see that expansion as a function call.

Forth stores words in a dictionary—an opaque data structure resembling Python dicts and C++ maps. Word names are the dictionary keys; their definitions are dictionary values.

You can define new words, redefine existing words (please don't!), and remove unnecessary words. A new word definition and an existing word redefinition begin with the word : ("colon"). When you type this word, Forth switches from the default *interpret mode* (interactive mode) to the *compile mode*; it doesn't execute the code immediately but stores it in the dictionary for future use.

The new word name follows the colon. Forth allows *any* characters in a name except spaces, backspace, CR (carriage return), and DEL (delete). So ^, h*********!, and even %#?*& would be legal word names. I strongly advise you to use this feature responsibly.

The body of the word follows its name. The body is the code fragment executed when the word is expanded; it can be empty. A semicolon ; concludes the definition. The following examples illustrate a silly DO-NOTHING word, a word that displays "Hello World", another word that squares a number, and another word that raises a number to the fourth degree by reusing the previously defined word.

```
: DO-NOTHING ( -- ) ;↵  ok
DO-NOTHING↵  ok

: HELLO! ( -- ) "Hello World" TYPE CR ;↵  ok
HELLO!↵ Hello World
 ok

: SQ ( n -- n ) DUP * ;↵   ok
32 SQ .↵ 1024  ok

: FOURTH-DEGREE ( n -- n ) SQ SQ ;↵   ok
16 FOURTH-DEGREE .↵ 65536  ok
```

With the mastery of arithmetic operations, and stack and dictionary control, you can use Forth as a calculator. Now let's make it a computer.

Dissecting Flow Control

Flow control is about controlling the execution of the individual program statements (in our case, words). The "natural" flow control is sequential: the next statement in the program text is the next to be executed. Any other execution pattern requires some combination of unconditional jumps, conditional branches, and loops.

Theoretically, loops are not needed. Some languages don't support loops directly. Assembly languages survive with jumps and branches. Erlang and Prolog implement looping behavior with *tail recursion*. Python list comprehensions and NumPy vectorized operations are also loops in disguise.

Forth has a set of predefined words to jump, branch, loop, go recursive, and handle *exceptions* (two more ways to control program execution). It also allows you to define your control structures. But first, let's find out how to calculate *flags* that control the control structures.

Relational and Logical Operations

A flag is a Boolean result (TRUE or FALSE) of a relational or logical operation. Relational operators compare numbers for equality and non-equality and all other objects for equality. Forth has a bunch of them.

- The words 0<, 0<=, 0>, 0>=, 0=, and 0<>, and their DPN counterparts like D0= compare a number to zero.

- The words <, <=, =, <>, >, >=, and their DPN and unsigned cousins like D< and U> compare two numbers.
- The word WITHIN (n1 n2 n3 -- flag) checks if n2≤n1<n3.

Logical operators traditionally combine Boolean results based on their truth tables. In Forth, however, they're implemented as bitwise operators and operate on individual bits. Nothing's wrong with this arrangement; the result of a pure Boolean logical operation is a special case of a bitwise operation on the same operands. Simply remember that 100 99 AND numerically is 96, which is still true because only 0 is false.

Forth logical/bitwise operators are AND, OR, XOR, and INVERT. Some versions also have a pure Boolean NOT.

Let's pretend that XOR is unavailable and implement it as a new word using the mathematical definition $X \oplus Y \equiv X \cdot (\sim Y) + (\sim X) \cdot Y$. The following code fragment shows the original built-in XOR, the "mathematical" XOR step by step, and the "mathematical" XOR defined as a new word MY-XOR.

```
77 15 XOR .↵ 66  ok

77 15↵  ok 2
2DUP↵  ok 4 \ Stack: 77 15 77 15
INVERT AND↵  ok 3 \ Stack: 77 15 64
-ROT SWAP↵  ok 3 \ Stack: 64 15 77
INVERT AND↵  ok 2 \ Stack: 64 2
OR .↵ 66  ok

: MY-XOR ( n n -- n ) 2DUP INVERT AND -ROT SWAP INVERT AND OR ;↵  ok
77 15 MY-XOR .↵  66  ok
```

Aren't stacks cool?

Conditionals

The simplest conditional word is ?DUP: it duplicates the top item if it's true. The reason for its existence is not trivial. Why not just compare the top item as a flag and duplicate it if it's true? The problem is that any comparison operator (for example, 0=) irreversibly consumes the item from the stack. If the item happens to be true, it cannot be duplicated. A way around this is to duplicate the top item unconditionally, then check the condition and duplicate the item again if it's not zero. Sure. Or just use ?DUP. By the way, you can print the whole stack with the word .S.

```
99 ?DUP↵  ok 2
.S↵ <2> 99 99  ok 2
0 ?DUP↵  ok 3
.S↵ <3> 99 99 0  ok 3
```

Now let's look at the more familiar operation—the if-then-else statement. In Forth, it has two flavors:

- The IFTRUE-OTHERWISE-IFEND form exists only in some rare language versions and cannot be nested (it cannot have another IFTRUE-OTHERWISE-IFEND inside).

- The IF-ELSE-THEN form in FORTH-79 is probably more familiar, except it's written in Reverse Polish Notation.

The word IF checks the Boolean condition (the flag) on the stack, removes it, and selects the action. If the flag is logically true, Forth executes the words between IF and ELSE; otherwise, it executes the words between ELSE and THEN.

```
: SAY ( flag -- ) IF ." Hello" ELSE ." Goodbye" THEN ;↵   ok
TRUE SAY↵ Hello ok
FALSE SAY↵ Goodbye ok
```

If the statement doesn't have the "else" branch, it doesn't use the word ELSE. You can use this statement only in the compile mode. Your friendly Forth software will remind you if you forget.

You can nest IF-ELSE-THEN statements. The following example implements a toy traffic light sensor for *Toysla*—a fictitious self-driving car. The sensor "transforms" numeric traffic line signals into car "actions" by checking sequentially if the value on the stack equals one of the predefined constants.

```
forth/traffic.fs
\ Traffic light "sensor" via IF
\ Valid signals: 0 - red, 1 - yellow, 2 - green
0 CONSTANT RED-TL
1 CONSTANT YELLOW-TL
2 CONSTANT GREEN-TL
: TL ( n -- )
  DUP \ Duplication needed to enable further comparisons
  RED-TL = IF
    ." STOP"
  ELSE
    DUP \ Same here
    YELLOW-TL = IF
      ." WAIT"
    ELSE
      GREEN-TL = IF
        ." GO"
      ELSE
        ." ERROR"
      THEN
    THEN
  THEN ;
```

Note the new word CONSTANT that, together with its DPN cousin 2CONSTANT, defines a constant value. You can also use the words VALUE to define a "changeable" constant (a pseudo-constant) and TO to redefine it:

```
314 CONSTANT MY-PI-CONST↵  ok
314 VALUE MY-PI-VAL↵  ok
3 TO MY-PI-VAL↵  ok \ MY-PI-VAL=3
MY-PI-VAL .↵ 3  ok
3 TO MY-PI-CONST↵
,*the terminal*:5:6: error: Argument type mismatch
```

Do Not Redefine Colors!

Do not redefine Gforth words RED, YELLOW, GREEN, and the like as variables or constants! They're already defined to denote ASCII terminal colors. Some Forth implementations also define PI. Stay away from redefining it too.

Testing the code doesn't reveal any suprises. The sensor works as expected:

```
INCLUDE code/forth/traffic.fs↵  ok
0 TL↵ STOP ok 1
1 TL↵ WAIT ok 2
2 TL↵ GO ok 2
32 TL↵ ERROR ok 2
```

The testing fragment introduces another new word, INCLUDE. It includes verbatim and interprets an external Forth source file, mainly to reuse code fragments between projects.

Constants

Forth CONSTANTs loosely correspond to C/C++ preprocessor macros without parameters, introduced via #define. In the same spirit, Forth INCLUDE loosely corresponds to C/C++ preprocessor directive #include.

The example on page 14 works well for a few choices, but it quickly becomes hard to read and maintain as the number of options increases.

Help comes from the CASE statement. The CASE statement in Forth corresponds to the switch statement in C/C++/Java. It collects the top stack item and compares it repeatedly without duplication to each of the case markers. When a marker matches the item, Forth executes the corresponding code. If a match is not found, Forth executes the default code. The CASE-based traffic sensor implementation is elegant and easily extendable:

```
forth/traffic.fs
\ Traffic light "sensor" via CASE
: TL-1 ( n -- )
  CASE RED-TL    OF ." STOP" ENDOF
       YELLOW-TL OF ." WAIT" ENDOF
       GREEN-TL  OF ." GO"   ENDOF
       ." ERROR" ENDCASE ; \ default code
```

You'll find it enlightening to test the second version of the sensor yourself.

Loops

You're now ready to do what differentiates a computer from a non-programmable calculator—automatically repeat an operation several times or indefinitely. Just like many other languages, Forth has a concept of a loop and implements it in four ways: loops that don't stop (infinite loops), loops that terminate after no more than a fixed number of iterations, and loops that terminate before or after a specific condition is met.

Infinite Loops

You may have been advised by your programming teacher, mentor, or book to avoid infinite loops. After all, the purpose of any program is to deliver results, and if a loop never ends, it will never produce a result, will it? This logic is correct at first glance but flawed in general. First, there are ways to terminate a loop even if it pretends to be infinite (see Exiting Loops, on page 19). It's often easier to write an infinite loop with an explicit exit statement than an equivalent finite loop, and that can be later converted to a proper finite loop. Second, some loops are meant to be infinite. Their goal is not to provide the final result but to process data and signals as they arrive—for example, a database server or our sensor developed in the code fragment on page 14.

So, infinite loops have a niche, and Forth lets you organize them with the words BEGIN and AGAIN (both can be used only in compile mode). This example is toyish:

```
: AND-NEVER-COME-BACK BEGIN ." Leave now" CR AGAIN ; \ Do not execute!
```

But the following example of a server is realistic, assuming that the words RECEIVE, PROCESS, and SEND are adequately defined:

```
: RECEIVE ( -- n) ;↵ ok
: PROCESS ( n -- n) ;↵ ok
: SEND ( n -- ) ;↵ ok
: SERVER ( -- )
  BEGIN
```

```
RECEIVE PROCESS SEND
   AGAIN ; ↵  ok
SERVER      \ And never comes back...
```

You can nest loops the same way you nest conditionals. You can also have conditionals in loops and loops in conditionals. The coding best practice is to have up to three levels of nesting.

Post-testing Loops

A post-testing loop terminates after some condition represented by the item at the top of the stack becomes logically true. The condition is tested after executing at least one loop iteration (hence the name); the loop runs at least once. The assumption is that the condition results from the execution of the words in the loop's body.

The loop is defined with BEGIN for starting the loop and UNTIL (or END in some dialects) for checking the flag. Incidentally, AGAIN equals 0 UNTIL (compare while(0) in C/C++/Java).

Let's code the famous *Heron's method* for calculating the square root of a number N. The method assumes that $\sqrt{N}=S≈1$ (odd!) and then rectifies the result iteratively as $S=(N/S+S)/2$ until the difference between the two consecutive iterations becomes zero (for integer numbers) or arbitrarily small.

forth/sqrt.fs
```
Line 1  \ Calculate Result=sqrt(Num) as Result[0]=1;
   -    \ Result[i+1]=(Num/Result[i]+Result[i])/2
   -    : SQRT ( u -- u )
   -      1 \ Result[0] = 1
   5      BEGIN
   -        OVER 0 2 PICK \ Make Result a DPN
   -        UM/MOD \ Num/Result
   -        SWAP DROP \ Drop the remainder
   -        OVER + 0 \ (Num/Result)+Result
  10        2 UM/MOD \ ((Num/Result)+Result)/2
   -        SWAP DROP \ Drop the remainder
   -        SWAP OVER = \ The new flag
   -      UNTIL
   -      SWAP DROP ; \ Drop the Num
```

Note how the new flag is calculated on line 12.

Pre-testing Loops

As opposed to a post-testing loop, a pre-testing loop checks the flag before executing the body. It has the form BEGIN code1 WHILE code 2 REPEAT. code1 is executed first and leaves the flag on the stack. code2 is executed as long as the flag is true. A loop will be skipped if the flag is initially false.

The following code imitates driving a Toysla car (from the subsection Conditionals, on page 13):

```
: DRIVE-TOYSLA ( u -- u )
  CR
  BEGIN
    ?DUP \ Make a copy of the distance
  WHILE
    ." Going... " 1- \ Update the flag: decrement the distance
  REPEAT
  ." Gone!" ;↵ ok
5 CONSTANT DISTANCE-2-CLIFF↵ ok
DISTANCE-2-CLIFF DRIVE-TOYSLA↵
Going... Going... Going... Going... Going... Gone! ok
```

While an excellent toy example, this code would look conceptually better as a finite loop because the number of iterations is known beforehand—and Forth has that too.

Finite Loops

The number of finite loop iterations is limited by the item in the second position on the stack. (You can still break the loop earlier.) The top of the stack is initially occupied by the loop index—an integer number that's incremented automatically after each iteration. The loop has the form DO (n1 n2 --) code LOOP. A copy of the index is provided by executing the word I, which is a tribute to the for loops in Fortran—their loop variables were usually called I, J, or K. Forth has J and K too—they're the indices of the first and second outer loops, if any. It's not considered good practice to nest more than three levels of loops.

A trivial first example of a finite loop is a numeric range printer (compare Python print(range(n))):

```
: PRINT-RANGE ( n -- ) 0 DO I . LOOP ;↵ ok
5 PRINT-RANGE↵ 0 1 2 3 4  ok
```

Forth checks the termination condition after the execution of the first iteration. If the limit is already equal to the limit, the loop becomes infinite and crashes the program. You can use another word, ?DO, that skips the loop if there's nothing to do.

Would you rather iterate with a non-unit step? The word +LOOP (n --) adds a specified number to the loop index. The number can be different from one but could be one too. The following code shows a subset of the multiplication table for the odd numbers. It also illustrates nested loops.

```
: M2-TABLE ( -- )
10 1 DO
  10 1 DO
    I J * .
  LOOP
  CR \ End of a row
2 +LOOP ;↵  ok

CR M2-TABLE↵
 1 2 3 4 5 6 7 8 9
 3 6 9 12 15 18 21 24 27
 5 10 15 20 25 30 35 40 45
 7 14 21 28 35 42 49 56 63
 9 18 27 36 45 54 63 72 81
 ok
```

The table doesn't look particularly neat. You can use pictured output, explained on page 35, to tidy it.

Loops

 Infinite loops in Forth correspond to infinite loops (LOOP) in Lisp. Finite loops resemble for loops in Fortran and BASIC and loosely correspond to the namesake loops in C/C++/Java. Pre-testing loops correspond to while loops in C, Java, Python, and many other languages. Post-testing loops correspond to do-while loops in C/C++/Java.

Exiting Loops

A nontrivial program may need to exit a loop and proceed to the succeeding words before the loop condition is met or the loop index reaches the limit. No matter how you terminate a loop, ensure that any changes to the return stack you made in the loop are undone. Forth keeps loop-related information (such as the current value of the loop index) in the return stack and expects it to be in order. Messing up the return stack guarantees a problem.

Forth is a language of choices. Often there's more than one way to do things right. Terminating loops isn't an exception.

The word LEAVE instantly terminates the loop—however, the loop must be finite (DO-LOOP). The reason for this restriction is that LEAVE also discards the limit and index from the return stack. The other three types of loops do not use them, which causes LEAVE to fail.

```
: DO-TEST 10 0 DO          LEAVE LOOP ; \ Do this
: AGAIN-TEST BEGIN         LEAVE AGAIN ; \ Do NOT do this!
: REPEAT-TEST BEGIN 1 WHILE LEAVE REPEAT ; \ Do NOT do this!
: UNTIL-TEST  BEGIN        LEAVE 1 UNTIL ; \ Do NOT do this!
```

The word EXIT has no such restriction and is even more potent than LEAVE. It terminates the current loop and the execution of the current word. This behavior poses a dilemma: how do you end, say, only an infinite loop if it's part of another word? One option is to create a new word that encloses the infinite loop.

Leave vs. Exit

 The words LEAVE and EXIT loosely correspond to break in C/C++, Java, and Python.

When breaking the loop, EXIT doesn't clean up the data stack. If the loop body changed the state of the stack (for example, by executing DUP), those changes would not be undone.

Lastly, EXIT can exit finite loops but does not discard the limit and index from the return stack. Rather than trying to locate and extract them, use the word UNLOOP which does precisely that. The word was designed to be used with EXIT and doesn't seem to serve any other purpose.

```
: DO-TEST 10 0 DO     UNLOOP EXIT LOOP ; \ Do this
: AGAIN-TEST  BEGIN          EXIT AGAIN ; \ Do this
: REPEAT-TEST BEGIN 1 WHILE EXIT REPEAT ; \ Do this
: UNTIL-TEST  BEGIN          EXIT 1 UNTIL ; \ Do this
```

Discovering Recursion

Forth has a return stack and four types of loops. But does Forth have recursion? It depends on whom you ask. "Clean" FORTH-79 doesn't directly support recursion. However, you can implement recursion yourself with the help of R>, >R, and similar words. It sounds like a cool do-it-yourself project. If you're not much into DIY, consider using fig-Forth with the word RECUR (in some dialects, MYSELF)—or, better, revert to Gforth with RECURSIVE.

The word RECURSIVE immediately follows the name in a new word definition. It creates a temporary entry in the dictionary, to which the rest of the definition can refer. If you provide no such entry, attempting to use a word within its definition will cause an Undefined word error.

An obligatory recursive factorial example illustrates the concept. Also, for your reference, 25! is the largest factorial that a 64-bit CPU can calculate.

```
: FACTORIAL ( n -- n ) RECURSIVE
  ?DUP 0= IF
    1 \ 0! = 1; The base case
  ELSE
```

```
    DUP 1- FACTORIAL * \ n! = n*(n-1)!; The recursive case
  THEN ;↵  ok
```

25 FACTORIAL .↵ *7034535277573963776 ok*

As a rule, avoid recursion when possible, whether you code in Forth, C, Python, or Java. Recursion is theoretically elegant but practically hard to debug and often leads to poor performance unless it's tail recursion. A recursive solution may cause devastating damage to the execution time (consider, for example, calculating Fibonacci numbers via fib[i+1]=fib[i]+fib[i-1]).

Arriving to Memory Operations

Isn't it amazing that you read twenty pages of the Forth story without seeing a word about variables or arrays? Forth works great without variables and arrays. But it's even better with them.

Variables

Forth variables are named memory locations. You must create them explicitly and initialize them after or at the time of creation (the latter option works only in fig-Forth). The location consists of one or two cells (a *2-variable*). In some dialects of Forth, single-byte variables exist. A 2-variable can be accessed piecewise, one cell at a time.

The name of a variable resolves into its address in memory. To create a variable, use the words VARIABLE or 2VARIABLE, followed by the variable name. (Compare constant creation on page 15.) All variables, constants, and words in Forth are, by default, global. You can restrict their visibility by placing them on *word lists*, but word lists are beyond the scope of this chapter.

You can use and modify the value of an existing variable with the words "fetch" @ (addr -- x), "store" ! (x addr --), and "add" +! (x addr --). Fetching and storing are also available for 2-variables as 2@ and 2!.

```
VARIABLE AGE↵  ok \ Create
50 AGE !↵  ok \ Initialize/Store
1 AGE +!↵  ok \ Increment
AGE @ .↵ 51 ok \ Fetch
```

Variables in Forth don't enjoy the same level of appreciation as in other procedural languages. They're great for "long-term" storage, but you should try to put transient, especially single-use values, on the stack.

As you already know, a variable name is interpreted as the address of the memory cell(s). Thus, you can treat a 2-variable as a rudimentary two-cell array. (Don't worry—Forth has real arrays! You'll meet them in the next subsection.) This code fragment stores two ages in the two consecutive cells of a 2-variable.

```
2VARIABLE AGES↵  ok \ Create
50 AGES !↵  ok \ Store into one cell
45 AGES CELL+ !↵  ok \ Store into the other cell
AGES 2@ . .↵ 50 45 ok \ Fetch both cells
```

The word CELL+ (addr1 -- addr2) is a member of the address arithmetic subset. It takes the address at the top of the stack (the address of the variable AGES in the example) and adds the size of one cell to it. The latter is usually 8 bytes for a 64-bit CPU (one machine word), but don't make this assumption, or your program won't be portable. The word CELL- (addr1 -- addr2), naturally, subtracts a cell size.

Since Forth prefers the stack to variables, it undeservedly neglects them. One operation that's notably missing from Forth is copying variables. You cannot simply write a=b in Forth; Python's famous simultaneous assignment statement a,b=b,a is totally out of the question. That's not to say that you cannot copy variables—you just have to write a new word for it:

```
: COPY ( src dest -- ) SWAP @ SWAP ! ;↵  ok
VARIABLE AGE1↵  ok
VARIABLE AGE2↵  ok
45 AGE1 !↵  ok
AGE1 AGE2 COPY↵   ok
AGE1 @ .↵ 45  ok
AGE2 @ .↵ 45  ok
```

You can even copy one cell of a 2-variable into the other:

```
AGES 2@ . .↵ 50 55  ok
AGES AGES CELL+ COPY↵  ok
AGES 2@ . .↵ 50 50  ok
```

Can you write a word that swaps two variables (executes simultaneous assignment)?

Since CELL+ and CELL- were already mentioned, it would be unfair not to mention the words CHAR+ (addr1 -- addrs2), CELLS (u1 -- u2), CELL (-- u), and CHARS (u1 -- u2). The first adds the size of one character to the address on the stack. For any practical purpose and according to C/C++ standards, the size of one character is 1 byte. However, C/C++ standards are not directly applicable to Forth. One can imagine an implementation where a character requires more than 1 byte (did I say "Unicode"?) or less than 1 byte. Better to be safe than sorry and use CHAR+ and CHAR-.

To add another level of portability, the words CELLS, CELL, and CHARS leave on the stack the size of n cells, one cell, and n characters, respectively.

How Many Bits Are in a Byte?

If the answer were "eight," I would not ask this question. The correct answer is "a byte typically consists of eight bits." The word "typically" makes the difference. The term traditionally described a group of bits used to encode a single character, and the size could vary depending on the system and context. In some computer systems, a byte could be 4 bits (Intel 4004), 6 bits (UNIVAC 1100/2200), 7 bits (IBM 1401, Minsk-32), 9 bits (PDP-10), 10 bits (CDC 160A, PDP-5), or some other size.

With the knowledge of variables and address arithmetic you can proceed to explore real arrays.

Arrays

If you are, for instance, a C/C++ or Fortran programmer, you know that an array is a homogeneous collection of contiguous memory cells. Other languages have arrays, too, and some (notably, APL on page 77) have virtually nothing but arrays. Forth isn't an exception—it supports arrays, which are indispensable for any realistic project.

Arrays in Forth are not variables. They are declared, allocated, and accessed differently. They're essentially pointers to the storage space (after the space is allocated), and they don't "remember" their size; you have to store the size in a separate variable. The latter may be an unpleasant surprise for Java and Python programmers accustomed to the fact that someone keeps track of their arrays.

Arrays

 Forth arrays loosely correspond to one-dimensional arrays in C created dynamically with malloc().

You can create an array two ways: standard (declare with CREATE, allocate with ALLOT) and nonstandard but convenient (declare and allocate with BUFFER:— yes, with a colon at the end of the word).

- CREATE ("name" --) creates an object called name but does not allocate memory.

- ALLOT (u --) allocates u bytes (not cells!) if u is positive. Otherwise, it deallocates -u bytes. Forth treats memory as one continuous block. Your program is responsible for memorizing the beginning addresses and lengths. From Forth's point of view, it's permissible to allocate 100 bytes and then deallocate (free) 95 bytes. But is it what you want?

- BUFFER: (u "name" --) creates an object called name and allocates u bytes. The following two constructs behave almost identically:

```
CREATE GRADES 100 CELLS ALLOT
100 CELLS BUFFER: GRADES
```

Now, the value of GRADES is the address of the new array—a pointer to it, using the C/C++ terminology.

- HERE (-- addr) and UNUSED (-- u) report the address of the next available byte of memory and the amount of available, nonallocated memory.

- ERASE (addr u --), BLANK (addr u --), and FILL (addr u char --) fill the first u bytes of the array with zeros, white spaces ("blanks"), and any other characters, respectively. They do not check array boundaries (nobody does except you).

- DUMP (addr u --) displays the array or a portion of it (for debugging).

Note that the last four words expect to find two array attributes on the top of the stack: a pointer to the first element and length. The section Exploring Character and String Operations, on page 31, shows that strings follow the same calling convention.

In Forth and other languages with similarly organized arrays and finite loops (Fortran, C), the two go hand in hand. It's time to practice them by defining a set of words that calculate the mean of all array elements. The first word, SUM, adds all elements. The second word, MEAN, executes SUM and divides the result by the array size. The mean is scaled up by 100 to compensate for the lack of floating-point numbers. Alternatively, you could return it as a rational number.

forth/mean.fs
```
\ Calculate the sum of array elements
: SUM ( addr n -- n1 )
  0 SWAP \ Initialize the accumulator
  0 DO
    OVER I CELLS + @ + \ Calculate the index, fetch, add
  LOOP
  SWAP DROP ; \ Drop the array pointer to clean the stack

\ Calculate the mean of array elements
: MEAN ( addr n -- n1 )
  DUP -ROT \ Make a copy of "n"
  SUM SWAP
  100 SWAP */ ; \ Multiply by 100 to get better accuracy
```

You need an initialized array to test the new words. In real life, the array is produced by another word or comes from a file, but you can also create it by hand using the "comma" word ,. Such an array of constants is called a *table*. Once constructed, a table doesn't differ from an "ordinary" array. By the way, the calculated mean is correct!

```
CREATE GRADES 4 , 2 , 3 , 2 , 4 , 1 , 3 , 2 ,↵ ok
GRADES 8 MEAN . 262↵ ok
```

Tables

Forth tables loosely correspond to one-dimensional arrays with an initializer list in C/C++/Java: int grades[] = {4, 2, 3, 2, 4, 1, 3, 2}. In the latter case, the last comma and spaces before the commas are optional.

You can use a similar notation to create initialized character arrays, except the comma becomes a "C-comma" C,. A character array is actually a character string. The dump shows its address, the hexadecimal codes of all characters, and printable representation. Each character consumes a byte of memory, not a cell.

```
CREATE HELLO 'H' C, 'e' C, 'l' C, 'l' C, 'o' C,↵ ok
HELLO 5 DUMP↵
,7FCEC96E2140: 48 65 6C 6C  6F                -              Hello
, ok
```

Let's go over one more example to grasp loops and arrays even better. Suppose the array VALID is *parallel* to GRADES; for each element in GRADES, the matching element of VALID (true or false) defines whether the grade is valid. You want to replace invalid grades with a -1.

The auxiliary word FIX checks the flag and leaves on the stack either the old grade or -1. The word FILTER applies FIX in a loop to each Ith pair of elements.

```
: FIX ( n flag -- n1 ) INVERT IF DROP -1 THEN ;
: FILTER ( addr1 addr2 u -- )
  0 DO
    DUP I CELLS + @ ROT \ Access the original grade
    DUP I CELLS + @ ROT \ Access the validity flag
    SWAP FIX
ROT DUP -ROT \ Bring the new grade
    I CELLS + ! \ Update the grade
  LOOP
  DROP DROP ; \ Clean the stack

CREATE VALID TRUE , FALSE , FALSE , TRUE , TRUE , FALSE , TRUE , TRUE ,↵ ok
VALID GRADES 8 FILTER↵ ok
```

Demystifying Vectored Execution

From the modern-day terminology perspective, vectored execution in Forth is neither vectored nor execution, yet it exists, and it's a unique feature in Forth. In the core of vectored execution lies an *execution token* (previously promised on page 7).

An execution token (xt) is a fragment of compiled Forth code—a compiled word. Forth enters compile mode when you type a colon : and leaves when you type a semicolon ;. Everything between : and ;, except the word name, is converted into a token. Then the token is combined with the name and stored in the dictionary. In this previously presented example, INVERT IF DROP -1 THEN becomes an execution token, and FIX becomes its dictionary name:

```
: FIX ( n flag -- n1 ) INVERT IF DROP -1 THEN ;
```

When you activate a word by typing it on the console or invoking it indirectly in another activated word, Forth locates and extracts the execution token associated with the word and executes it. It works straightforwardly and seamlessly if you know which word to activate. But what if you don't? What if the action depends on a condition?

A non-Forth programmer would have to use conditionals on page 13. But a C programmer could build an array of pointers to functions for each occasion and call a function by address, and a Python programmer could resort to a list of lambdas. Incidentally, both techniques resemble vectored execution.

Vectored Execution

 Vectored execution loosely corresponds to calling functions by address in C and lambdas in Python.

To enjoy vectored execution, you must first separate a word and its execution token and store the token in a variable (named) or on the stack (nameless). The words "quote" ' (-- xt) and "quote in brackets" ['] (-- xt) separate the execution token from a word in interpret and compile modes.

Second, there must be a way to execute the token. The word EXECUTE (xt --) is doing just that. Since the execution token is often fetched from a variable with @, the two words can be lumped into @EXECUTE (addr --). We can summarize as follows:

1. Convert a word to an execution token.
2. Assign the token to a variable or push it onto the stack.
3. Execute the token any time later. This type of execution is also known as deferred execution.

You can assign different tokens to the same variable and execute the most recently assigned token later. Consider our Toysla car from the subsection Conditionals, on page 13. In the following example, it responds to three commands: DRIVE, HALT, and SLOW DOWN. The execution token of the next command is stored in the namesake variable NEXT-COMMAND by the car controller and executed as needed.

```
\ Three options:
: DRIVE ." Driving" CR ; ↩  ok
: HALT ." Halting" CR ; ↩  ok
: SLOWDOWN ." Slowing down" CR ; ↩  ok

VARIABLE NEXT-COMMAND ↩  ok
' DRIVE NEXT-COMMAND ! ↩  ok \ Prepare to act: store the command
NEXT-COMMAND @EXECUTE ↩ Driving
.ok 1 \ Act!
```

Storing one execution token in a variable doesn't look like a life changer. Let's put all possible tokens in an array! The array must be of a particular kind—an *execution vector* created with the word DEFER ("name" --) and populated with the word IS (xt "name" --). DEFER creates a new execution vector named "name". The vector is dynamic and grows as needed. Once the vector is ready, add elements to it with IS. This word inserts an execution token into a vector like a word definition inserts a word into the dictionary.

```
DEFER NEXT-COMMAND
: DRIVE     ' CR ." Driving"      IS NEXT-COMMAND ;
: HALT      ' CR ." Halting"      IS NEXT-COMMAND ;
: SLOWDOWN  ' CR ." Slowing down" IS NEXT-COMMAND ;

: COMPLEX-ACTION ( stuff ) ; \ Two-step example
: FOOBAR ['] COMPLEX-ACTION IS NEXT-COMMAND ;
```

To execute a token, leave it on the stack and activate the vector by name. The vector acts as if it were @EXECUTE.

```
HALT NEXT-COMMAND ↩
.Halting ok
SLOWDOWN NEXT-COMMAND ↩
.Slowing down ok
DRIVE NEXT-COMMAND ↩
.Driving ok
```

Handling Errors and Exceptions

Runtime errors are inevitable in real-world programs. The signals from the real world (keystrokes, mouse events, network packets, sounds of speech, and videos, to name a few) are often unpredictable, untimely, noisy, and inconsistent. To build dependable software, you should anticipate their imperfect nature and write code that can handle errors. Forth assists this noble goal by providing two levels of error handling.

he "higher-level" commands aim to bring the unruly program under control by returning to the command line interpreter. The higher-level commands are ABORT, ABORT" (yes, with a quotation mark as a part of the word), and QUIT.

- The word ABORT stops the execution of the enclosing word, empties both stacks, and *silently* returns to the console. If you're interested in the reason for the termination, you must display an error message before aborting.

- The word ABORT" <text>" (flag --) is more intelligent. It starts by checking the flag. If the flag is false, the word is *silently* ignored. Otherwise, the word displays the text embedded into a standard Forth error message, empties both stacks, and returns to the console like its quote-less friend. This word is compile-only.

- Finally, QUIT empties the return stack and *silently* returns to the console. This word does not clear the data stack, allowing you to inspect it for debugging.

None of the higher-level error handling commands terminates the interpreter. For that, you should use BYE.

The following example illustrates the behavior of all four higher-level error handlers. The first code block defines four almost identical testing words.

```
: ERROR-1 1 2 3 4 ABORT 5 6 ;
: ERROR-2 1 2 3 4 QUIT 5 6 ;
: ERROR-3 1 2 3 4 ABORT" Ignore me" 5 6 ;
: ERROR-4 1 2 3 0 ABORT" Ignore me" 5 6 ;
```

The second block executes them. Note the state of the data stack after each attempt.

```
ERROR-1↵
.S↵ <0>  ok \ Empty stack
ERROR-2↵
.S↵ <4> 1 2 3 4  ok 4 \ Stack not empty
```

```
ERROR-3 ↵
 *the terminal*:49:1: error: Ignore me
 >>>ERROR-3<<<
«...more gforth output...» \ Empty stack
ERROR-4↵  ok 5
.S↵ <5> 1 2 3 5 6  ok 5 \ Stack not empty
```

The "lower-level" commands deal with exceptions; they throw and catch them. Forth exception handling mechanism is different from C++, Java, and Python but uses similar words: THROW and CATCH.

The section Writing Comments and "Hello, World!", on page 2, suggests that Forth "uses not one stack but two." My apologies; that was a lie. Forth uses not two stacks but three. The third one is for exception frames—data structures that memorize the last known safe state of the program. As a programmer, you don't control this stack; it squarely belongs to the Forth runtime.

When you're about to execute a word that may cause a problem, you should use CATCH (xt -- n). CATCH saves the program's current state (the stacks, in the first place) as an exception frame and then executes the execution token of the "scary" word with EXECUTE, as explained on page 26. If the word was executed successfully, CATCH leaves 0 on the stack. Otherwise, it leaves on the stack the error code produced by THROW.

The word THROW (n -- | n) generates an exception. As a reminder, the vertical bar in the word documentation means that the format of the result depends on the input. If n is zero, THROW takes it as an indication of success and does nothing. If n is nonzero, THROW pops the most recent exception frame from the exception stack, restores the program's state, and transfers control to the following word after CATCH ("throws an exception"). Exceptions can be nested; THROW always takes you back to the most recent CATCH (that's why the exception stack is needed).

You can use exceptions two ways: as a means of controlled recovery from an error and to return from a deeply nested word to the high level (such as the command-line interpreter). As an illustration of the first scenario, let's write the word AREA that calculates the area of a rectangle, provided that both sides are nonnegative.

```
: AREA ( n1 n2 -- n3)
  DUP 0< IF 314 THROW THEN SWAP \ Is n1 < 0?
  DUP 0< IF 314 THROW THEN SWAP \ Is n2 < 0?
  * ;
```

While testing, the word throws an exception number 314 when either side is negative. However, wrapping the calculation with a CATCH prevents the crash.

```
10 10 AREA .↵ 100  ok
10 -10 AREA .↵
.*the terminal*:2:15: error: error #314
: TRY-IT ['] AREA CATCH IF CR ." The area was not calculated" THEN ;↵  ok
-10 10 TRY-IT↵
.The area was not calculated ok 2
.S↵ <2> -10 10  ok 2
```

The offensive cells are still on the stack, ready to be interrogated.

In the other scenario, suppose you have a word that executes another word that executes another word, and so on. Eventually, the most recent word may conclude that the operation should be canceled. It may return the cancellation status to the previous word, then to the previous word, and all the way to the top—or throw an exception and let the top-level word catch it. In the following example, the word COMMAND imitates random cancellations. The word TAKE-COMMAND emulates a high-level controller that initiates the commands.

```
REQUIRE random.fs
999 CONSTANT CANCEL
: COMMAND ( -- )
  10 RANDOM 2 MOD IF \ Flip a coin!
    CANCEL THROW
  THEN ;
: TAKE-COMMAND ( -- )
  ['] COMMAND CATCH CR
  CASE      0 OF   ." Done!"            ENDOF
        CANCEL OF   ." Command canceled" ENDOF
        ( default ) ." Command failed"   ENDCASE ;
```

Note the word REQUIRE at the top of the code block: it includes and interprets another source Forth file if it hasn't been included yet. The file random.fs provides the word RANDOM (n1 -- n2), which generates a random number from 0 to n1-1. The commands are now safe to execute.

```
TAKE-COMMAND↵
.Command canceled ok
TAKE-COMMAND↵
.Command canceled ok
TAKE-COMMAND↵
.Done! ok
TAKE-COMMAND↵
.Done! ok
```

The coding best practice is to have a highest-level, catch-all CATCH word that handles all exceptions not addressed explicitly.

Exploring Character and String Operations

Following the tradition of the C language, a Forth character is simply an integer number optionally represented as a single-quoted literal. Characters can be subtracted, incremented, and compared, which is helpful, but they can also be added, divided, and multiplied, which is not. Forth giveth you a lot of power over characters—use it wisely. For instance, you can define a word to check if a character represents a decimal digit:

```
: ?DIGIT ( c -- flag ) [CHAR] 0 [CHAR] 9 1+ WITHIN ;
'a' ?DIGIT .↵ 0   ok
'7' ?DIGIT .↵ -1  ok \ True
BL ?DIGIT .↵ 0   ok
```

In this example, the word [CHAR] ("name" -- n) converts a literal into an integer number, according to the current character encoding. The same word in interpret mode doesn't need the square brackets (CHAR). The built-in word BL represents a blank—a white space, a character with code 32. You can create other constants for other characters if you wish (for example, 27 CONSTANT ESC for Escape); see also the definition of CR on page 3.

A string is simply an array of characters. Earlier dialects of Forth supported counted strings. The first byte of a counted string stores the number of characters in the string, and that's why a string could be no longer than 255 characters. "Modern" strings don't "remember" their length, but they're not NULL-terminated either (as in C). Your program must remember their lengths.

Counted Strings

Counted strings in Forth correspond to strings in Pascal (procedural programming language inspired by ALGOL 60 and designed by Niklaus Wirth mainly for teaching purposes in 1970); both are character arrays that store the length in the first byte.

A string can be entered as a literal in the program or read from an input device (keyboard or file). String literals begin with the words S" ("name" -- addr u), C" ("name" -- addr) (compile-only), or ." ("name" --). There must be a space between any of these words and the rest of the literal. You can also enter a string in double quotation marks, which is equivalent to using S". Forth transforms a literal string into two cells, one of which contains the address of the string and the other holds its length. The combination (addr u --) is what all other string-related functions expect.

- S" ("name" -- addr u) reads a string from the input stream (the console or the script) and compiles it.

- C" ("name" -- addr) acts like S" but does not leave the length on the stack.

- ." reads, compiles, and outputs the string when the enclosing word is executed.

To get ready for experimenting with strings, you need two more words:

- TYPE (addr u --) displays the string identified by the address and string on the output device (screen).

- ACCEPT (addr u1 -- u2) pauses the program and waits until the user enters up to u1 characters into the buffer designated by the addr. The word fills in the buffer until the user presses Enter or exceeds the character allowance, and then leaves the actual character count on the stack. The exceeding characters are discarded.

The word ACCEPT does not allocate the buffer—you should create a character array, as explained in the section Arrays, on page 23, or use the scratchpad.

The Accept Word

 The word ACCEPT loosely corresponds to the fgets() function in the C standard library. It's more secure than gets() because it monitors the number of typed characters.

Putting it all together, the word GREET asks you to enter your name into a preallocated buffer and then displays a three-piece greeting.

```
: GREET ( addr u -- )
  SWAP DUP ROT \ Duplicate the address
  CR ." Enter your name: " ACCEPT \ Leaves new length on the stack
  CR ." Welcome, " TYPE ." !" ;
```

To test the word, create a temporary buffer and pass its address and size to GREET.

```
50 CONSTANT BUFF-SIZE↵
BUFF-SIZE BUFFER: TEMP↵  ok
TEMP BUFF-SIZE GREET↵
Enter your name: Dmitry ↵
Welcome, Dmitry! ok
```

What makes this word awkward is its reliance on external temporary storage. This dependence would be justified if the word were used elsewhere and needed to be kept for the future, but it seems transient and not worthy of a dedicated buffer. Instead, you should use a recyclable built-in buffer called the *scratchpad*.

The scratchpad is an elastic buffer—a working area of indefinite size for temporary string manipulations. Its location is given by the word PAD (-- addr). With the scratchpad, the new version of the GREET word doesn't need to worry about storage—but it still needs to know the maximum input size.

```
: GREET ( u -- )
  PAD SWAP
  CR ." Enter your name: " ACCEPT
  PAD SWAP \ Leaves new length on the stack
  CR ." Welcome, " TYPE ." !" ;
```

The scratchpad is yours to use, but don't forget that there's only one scratchpad. If you start using it and then execute a word that also uses it, you'll inherit a mess.

It's common for users to add, intentionally or not, a couple of blanks at the end of input, especially if the input comes from a file. These white spaces ruin formatting and make exact comparisons impossible. Forth has a word for trimming the trailing whitespaces: -TRAILING (addr u1 -- addr u2). The trimmed string stays at the same address, but its size may change. You may want to insert this word in the definition of the greeting word.

The word /STRING (addr1 u1 n -- addr2 u2) is another string-trimming word. It trims the first n characters at the beginning of a string (this operation is called *adjustment*).

Here are some more string-specific words for your toolset:

- The word MOVE (addr1 addr2 u --) copies u characters from the address addr1 to addr2. The word knows how to handle the source and destination overlap correctly.

- The words CMOVE and CMOVE> do the same thing but copy the characters from left to right or from right to left. They're somewhat more efficient than MOVE.

- The word COMPARE (addr1 u1 addr2 u2 -- n) compares two strings lexicographically. If the strings are identical, the word leaves 0 on the stack. Otherwise, it leaves 1 or -1.

- The word SEARCH (addr1 u1 addr2 u2 -- addr3 u3 flag) searches the first string ("the haystack") for the first occurrence of the second string ("the needle"). The Boolean flag indicates if the needle is found. If it is, it begins at addr3 and has length u3.

Compare vs. Search

 The words COMPARE and SEARCH loosely correspond to the functions strncmp() and strstr() from the standard C library.

The preceding list of string-processing words is far from complete, but even with it, you can develop something exciting and nontrivial, such as COLLECT-WORDS. This word prompts the user to enter any text ("end" to exit), concatenates the fragments, and stores the result in the scratchpad.

forth/collect.fs
```
"end" 2CONSTANT SENTINEL \ The stopword: address and size
CREATE TEMP 100 ALLOT     \ Temporary space for input words

: COLLECT-WORDS ( -- u )
  0 \ The offset in the scratchpad
  BEGIN
    CR ." > " TEMP 100 ACCEPT \ Prompt and read, leave the length
    DUP TEMP SWAP SENTINEL COMPARE \ Is it the stopword?
    0= IF QUIT THEN \ If so, break the loop
    DUP TEMP
    PAD 4 PICK CHARS + \ Concatenate
    ROT MOVE
    + \ Adjust the offset
  AGAIN ;
```

COLLECT-WORDS leaves on the stack the result size that can be used to display the concatenated fragments.

```
COLLECT-WORDS ↵
> hello↵
>  ↵
> world↵
> . ↵
> end↵
+ PAD SWAP TYPE↵ hello world. ok
```

Forth has some good words for turning numbers into strings and back, without which the string story will be incomplete. The word >NUMBER (d1 addr1 u1 -- d2 addr2 u2) attempts to convert a string to a double number. You must drop a DPN zero into the stack before passing the string. >NUMBER uses that zero as an accumulator. After the termination of the word, that cell holds the result. In addition, >NUMBER leaves on the stack the part of the string that it failed to convert. >NUMBER is very straightforward and cannot convert negative numbers.

```
0 0 "3.14" >NUMBER↵  ok 4 \ 4 cells hold the result
TYPE↵ .14 ok 2 \ Failed to convert, two more cells left
D.↵ 3  ok
```

The last line of the code fragment is an example of a numeric output word. The word D. (d --) displays a signed DPN. The following example illustrates how other words from the same set display unsigned numbers (U.), right-justified numbers (.R), and various combinations of them.

```
-45       .↵ -45  ok
-45     U.↵ 18446744073709551571  ok
-45 0  D.↵ 18446744073709551571  ok
-45 0 UD.↵ 18446744073709551571  ok
45   7  .R↵        45 ok \ 7 positions
45   7  U.R↵       45 ok
45 0 7  D.R↵       45 ok
45 0 7 UD.R↵       45 ok
```

For the number-to-string conversion (the opposite of >NUMBER), you should use *pictured output,* nowadays known as formatted output. It begins and ends with the words <# and #>. The word #S (d --) represents all digits (or, rather, all remaining digits) of an unsigned number. The word # inserts one decimal digit at a time. The word SIGN (d --) inserts a negative sign into the pictured numeric output string if d is negative (must be executed after all digits are converted).

Converting numbers to strings is not much fun in Forth. See for yourself!

```
-45↵  ok 1
DUP ABS 0↵  ok 3 \ Prepare the number and its absolute value
<# #S ROT SIGN #>↵  ok 2
\ The result is a string!
TYPE↵ -45 ok
```

This section started as a conversation about characters and strings but got unintentionally, though briefly, pivoted into the area of general input/output. In the next section, let's look at the more advanced I/O words.

Performing Input/Output Operations

As an interface to the rest of the world, with all its diversity and uncertainty, an input/output subsystem is often one of the most challenging parts of a programming language. Historically, Forth has several different I/O layers, two explained in this section and one more in Forth Meets BASIC, on page 38.

Low-Level I/O

You're already familiar with the word TYPE (addr u --) that displays a string. You should use the word EMIT (char --) to display just a single character. You could reimplement TYPE with EMIT, but please don't, for the sake of performance.

```
: MYTYPE ( addr u -- ) 0 DO DUP I CHARS + @ EMIT LOOP ;↵  ok
"Hello" MYTYPE↵  Hello ok 1
```

The following four words enable interactive character-based input. They're the workhorses enabling ACCEPT and EXPECT. KEY (-- char) and EKEY (-- u) read a character and a keyboard event (the latter includes characters, function keys, arrows, and so forth). These words are blocking; they don't finish the execution until a key is pressed. If you only want to know if a key has been pressed, use the Boolean words KEY? (-- flag) and EKEY? (-- flag). They're nonblocking and execute instantly. You can use them for programming video games or other interactive environments.

File I/O

Older Forth systems relied on their own disk data organization and stored information as numbered 1024-byte blocks (for data) and numbered 1024-byte screens (for programs). The words for managing blocks, screens, and memory buffers, such as SCR, EMPTY-BUFFERS, SAVE-BUFFERS, and LOAD, still exist, but primarily for backward compatibility.

Your modern Forth assumes that the operating system manages files. In particular, Forth isn't concerned with file and directory names as long as they're character strings.

Forth has two sets of file-related words. In the following descriptions, ior is a one-cell *input/output result* (zero for success, nonzero for failure), fam is a one-cell *file access method* (R/O for read-only access, W/O for write-only access, and W/R for reading and writing), and sts is OS-specific file status. The first set works with files without opening them:

- FILE-STATUS (name len -- sts ior)
- CREATE-FILE (name len fam -- fid ior)
- OPEN-FILE (name len fam -- fid ior)
- RENAME-FILE (name1 len1 name2 len2 -- ior)
- DELETE-FILE (name len -- ior)

The words CREATE-FILE and OPEN-FILE also produce fid—an opaque file identifier used by the second word set. This set contains the words that work with the file contents.

- FILE-POSITION (fid -- ud ior). Report the current position within a file.

- FILE-SIZE (fid -- ud ior). Report the open file size.

- RESIZE-FILE (len fid -- ior). Change the length of an open file.

- FLUSH-FILE (fid -- ior). Flush an open file (synchronize the file buffers with the secondary storage).

- CLOSE-FILE (fid -- ior) . Close an open file.

- READ-FILE (addr u1 fid -- u2 ior). Read at most u1 bytes from an open file, and report the actual count.

- READ-LINE (addr u1 fid -- u2 flag ior). Read a line of at most u1 bytes from an open file, and report the actual count and the end-of-file flag.

- WRITE-FILE (addr u fid -- ior). Write u bytes to an open file.

- WRITE-LINE (addr u fid -- ior). Write a line of u bytes to an open file.

File Access Words

 The words READ-FILE, READ-LINE, WRITE-FILE, and WRITE-LINE loosely correspond to the functions read(), readline(), write(), and writeline() in Python.

To practice the newly learned skills, you can write a word for copying a "small" (with the size fitting into a single precision number) file. Note how it uses the return stack to store the address of the temporary data buffer to minimize the data stack joggling.

forth/copyfile.fs
```
\ Testing example:
\ "foobar" "foobar.bak" COPY-FILE

: COPY-FILE ( src-name1 u1 dest-name2 u2 -- )
  2SWAP R/O OPEN-FILE THROW \ src-name1 u1 src
  -ROT W/O CREATE-FILE THROW \ src dest
  DUP ROT DUP DUP FILE-SIZE THROW \ dest dest src src size0 size1
  THROW \ File too large!

  HERE >R DUP ALLOT \ Allocate the buffer and save its address

  R> DUP >R SWAP ROT READ-FILE THROW
  SWAP CLOSE-FILE THROW
  SWAP R> -ROT OVER >R WRITE-FILE THROW
  CLOSE-FILE THROW

  R> NEGATE ALLOT \ Deallocate the buffer
;
```

The word checks for all possible I/O mistakes and correctly deallocates the data buffer.

> ## Forth Meets BASIC
>
> It's not typical for programming languages to crossbreed. Languages often share concepts and features (as illustrated by the numerous tips in this book), but sharing complete subsystems is rare. Only three migration examples readily come to mind:
>
> - Turtle graphics—from the Logo language through NetLogo to Python.
> - Tk graphical user interface—from Tcl/Tk to Python and Erlang.
> - BASIC plotting and I/O extensions in Forth.
>
> BASIC was the de facto standard built-in programming language in the early days of personal computers. In 1982, Jupiter Cantab[a] challenged the status quo and designed a Forth-driven *Jupiter ACE (Automatic Computing Engine) [Vic17]*. The computer had 3kB of RAM, 8kB of ROM, 2kB of video memory, and a Z80A CPU with a peak performance of fewer than 1,000 ops.
>
> A unique feature of Jupiter ACE Forth was its interface to the output device (a TV set) and the secondary storage device (a tape recorder). Both interfaces were borrowed from the traditional BASIC and included such words as these:
>
> - BEEP (pitch length --) for beeping
> - LOAD, SAVE, and VERIFY for tape operations
> - PLOT, CLS ("clear screen"), DRAW, INVIS, and VIS for drawing pseudographics. The output was black-and-white.
>
> Unlike Turtle graphics and Tk, BASIC words didn't help Jupiter ACE. With fewer than five thousand sets sold, it was discontinued in 1984. Apparently, integrating Forth and BASIC was *an error*.
>
> ───────────
>
> a.   https://jupiter-ace.com/jupiterace/

Writing Something Big

Everybody loves toys and games. Most people love "toy" games too. To conclude this chapter, you'll develop a toy game called Hangman.[1] Honestly, it's not a game (though it will be playable and even enjoyable) but a prototype—nothing fancy, just the core functionality. And you need to go over one more word set.

Terminal Control

Forth provides a tiny collection of words that control the terminal. You can use them to create rudimentary text-based user interfaces, including text-based games.

───────────────

1.   https://en.wikipedia.org/wiki/Hangman_(game)

The first word in the set, PAGE (--), clears the page and places the cursor in the upper-left corner.

The word FORM (-- u1 u2) reports the height and width of the terminal (the number of rows and columns). Knowing these two numbers ensures your game stays within bounds.

The sister words AT-XY (u1 u2 --) and GET-XY (-- u1 u2) position the cursor at the specific row in the specific column and report the cursor's position. Once the cursor is positioned, you can use EMIT and TYPE to show characters and strings.

Let the game begin!

The Hangman

The game prototype will display a hidden "secret" string of characters (limited to letters and spaces) called SECRET and let the player enter up to N letters to reveal the secret. The value of N is your choice—for now, it's equal to the secret string's length.

The secret string is currently hardcoded but should come from a file or be autogenerated. You have all the necessary tools to make this happen.

Oh, and there are no actual gallows or the hangman. Forth is a language of creation, not destruction!

First, let's define some constants (such as the game layout parameters) and buffers (for the hidden secret string and its visible representation) and copy the secret into the hidden buffer.

```
forth/hangman.fs
"FORTH RULEZZ" 2CONSTANT SECRET \ Comes from elsewhere

10 CONSTANT X-MARG
10 CONSTANT WORD-LINE
15 CONSTANT LETTER-LINE
SECRET CONSTANT LENGTH DROP
LENGTH CONSTANT ROUNDS
LENGTH BUFFER: HIDDEN
LENGTH BUFFER: VISIBLE

SECRET HIDDEN SWAP MOVE
```

The following three words—GET-LETTER, UPDATE-VISIBLE, and PLAY-ONCE—make it possible to play one round of the game. GET-LETTER waits for a keystroke, converts the key code to uppercase, and checks if the code corresponds to a letter. UPDATE-VISIBLE loops in parallel through the hidden and visible buffers and replaces the characters in the latter (initially set to asterisks) with actual letters if there's a match. PLAY-ONCE gets a single letter and updates the visible buffer (but doesn't redraw it).

```
forth/hangman.fs
: GET-LETTER ( -- u flag ) KEY TOUPPER DUP [CHAR] A [CHAR] Z 1+ WITHIN ;

: UPDATE-VISIBLE ( u -- )
  LENGTH 0 DO
    DUP HIDDEN I + C@ DUP ROT =
    IF
      VISIBLE I + C!
    ELSE
      DROP
    THEN
  LOOP
  DROP
;

: PLAY-ONCE ( -- ) GET-LETTER SWAP DUP ROT 0<> IF UPDATE-VISIBLE THEN ;
```

The word PLAY-ROUNDS allows the player to play multiple rounds (as many as it takes to win or fail). It starts by leaving a Boolean FALSE flag on the stack, assuming the player will fail—not a nice assumption, but easy to implement. The word loops through the available attempts, letting the player play one round at a time. After each round, it updates the visible representation on the screen and checks if any more secret letters are left (by searching for "*"). If not, the game is over, the player is a winner, and the flag changes to TRUE. Otherwise, the game continues until all attempts are used.

```
forth/hangman.fs
: PLAY-ROUNDS ( -- flag )
  FALSE \ Assume failure
  ROUNDS 0 DO
    PLAY-ONCE
    X-MARG WORD-LINE AT-XY VISIBLE LENGTH TYPE
    X-MARG I + LETTER-LINE AT-XY EMIT
    VISIBLE LENGTH "*" SEARCH ROT DROP SWAP DROP 0= IF
      DROP TRUE \ Change our mind
      LEAVE
    THEN
  LOOP
;
```

The culmination of the code is the word PLAY. It (re)initializes the visible buffer, clears the screen (the "page"), updates the controls, and executes PLAY-ROUNDS. Finally, it displays the results of the game and concludes.

```
forth/hangman.fs
: PLAY ( -- )
  VISIBLE LENGTH '*' FILL
  PAD ROUNDS '_' FILL

  BL UPDATE-VISIBLE \ "Blanks" are not to be guessed
  PAGE
  X-MARG WORD-LINE AT-XY VISIBLE LENGTH TYPE
  X-MARG LETTER-LINE AT-XY PAD ROUNDS TYPE
  X-MARG LETTER-LINE AT-XY

  PLAY-ROUNDS

  FORM DROP 0 SWAP 4 - AT-XY
  IF "Success!" ELSE "You failed..." THEN TYPE CR
  "Press any key to exit" TYPE CR
  KEY DROP
;
```

This concludes the chapter too. Enjoy the game! If you want to learn more about the role of Forth the Obscure Language, *read about Postscript [Hol92]*. Otherwise, your journey takes you to another hardware-oriented language—Occam.

Further Reading

- *BREAKFORTH Into FORTH!* [MM80]

- *The Jupiter ACE Manual—35th Anniversary Edition: Forth Programming* [Vic17] (This is a reprint of a book originally published in 1982.)

- *FORTH programming* [Sca82]

- *Starting Forth: An Introduction to the Forth Language and Operating System for Beginners and Professionals [Bro87]*

- *The Evolution of Forth [RCM93]*

- *Thinking Forth [Bro04]*

- *Forth Programmer's Handbook [RC07]*

- *Forth Application Techniques [Rat08]*

- *Programming Forth [Pel11]*

Entia non sunt multiplicanda praeter necessitatem.

> Attributed to William of Ockham, fourteenth-century
> English philosopher and theologian

CHAPTER 2

Appreciating Concurrent Computing with Occam

The Earth boasts two renowned entities famous for their *canali*: the Italian city of Venice (canals) and the programming language Occam (channels). For travel tips to Venice, your local travel agent is your best bet. But for a deep dive into the universe of Occam (also spelled "occam" or "OCCAM"), I'm here to guide you. You'll learn to build applications using communicating sequential processes, which are crucial for crafting efficient and responsive software.

Paying Tribute to Transputer

Many programming languages have been designed for specific purposes:

- Fortran for number crunching
- Lisp for artificial intelligence
- Ada for military applications
- SNOBOL on page 147 for what is now termed digital humanities

In contrast, until very recently, there are a mere handful of languages designed for specific hardware platforms:

- Numerous assembly languages, usually one for every architecture
- The B language, a Bell Labs systems programming language for DEC PDP-7
- Occam, the language of and for transputers[1]

Transputers, such as T212, T414, and T800, are the brainchildren of Inmos, a now-defunct British company. Devised between 1983 and 1984, they were intended to serve as building blocks for future massively parallel computing

---

1.   www.transputer.net/

systems. Each transputer comprised a CPU with a minimal local microcode memory and external hardware links (*channels*). The channels allowed a transputer chip to connect with up to four other transputers or I/O devices, thereby enabling the creation of a systolic array or any other distributed system.

Transputers had a minimalistic instruction set architecture, though not reduced instruction set computer (RISC) architecture: most instructions were translated to microcode, a common complex instruction set computer (CISC) characteristic. The programming language Occam added a proverbial cherry on top. It was optimized for concurrency, parallelism, and transputer hardware. Some argue that Occam was intended to serve as the assembly language for transputers (see *Introduction to occam 2 on the Transputer [BS89]*).

Theoretically, Occam draws from the principles of *communicating sequential processes [Hoa78]*—a formal language for describing communications between concurrent processes. This positioning situates Occam between the relatively low-level Forth on page 1 and the more abstract, high-level APL on page 77, both in terms of taxonomy and in the context of this book.

Greeting in Occam and KRoC

In this chapter, you'll primarily use KRoC—the Kent Retargetable occam Compiler (note the official spelling!) from the University of Kent. The KRoC implements Occam-π, a modern version of Occam 2.5 infused with some elements of π-calculus.

π-calculus

π-calculus is a theoretical model for concurrent computing, developed by Robin Milner in 1992 as an extension of his work on the calculus of communicating systems (CCS). π-calculus provides a framework for understanding and analyzing the behaviors of concurrent systems, where multiple processes operate simultaneously and interact. A key feature of π-calculus is its ability to describe dynamic topology, meaning that the connections between processes can change over time. This flexibility is achieved through the concept of "channel mobility," where the names of communication channels can be passed between processes, allowing for flexible and evolving communication structures. π-calculus is highly abstract and mathematical, but it has significantly influenced computer science and theoretical informatics, particularly in designing and analyzing distributed systems, communication protocols, and mobile computing.

A significant difference exists between the highly optimized, industrial-grade KRoC and the "classical" Occam of David May and Tony Hoare. Out of respect for its originators, this chapter will guide you through classical Occam, providing specific notes to address the disparities between the two dialects as necessary.

So here's the standard greeting in Occam, illustrated in two ways. (This code doesn't run with KRoC.) One immediate observation is that comments begin with two dashes and continue until the end of the line.

occam/hello-classical.occ
```
-- Display "Hello, world!"
CHAN([BYTE]BYTE) output:
output ! "Hello,*sworld!*n"
```

The peculiar markers *s and *n denote a space and a line break, respectively. You can substitute *s with a literal space, but *n cannot be replaced with the familiar \n.

Next, KRoC employs a preprocessor akin to CPP, the C/C++ preprocessor, except the directives are composed in uppercase letters. The directive #INCLUDE "course.module" includes the file course.module verbatim. The file contains the KRoC standard library, a feature absent in classical Occam.

occam/hello.occ
```
-- Display "Hello, world!"
#INCLUDE "course.module"
PROC hello (CHAN BYTE out!)
  out.string ("Hello, world!*n", 0, out!)
:
```

Lastly, be mindful of the colon at the end of the second example. Usually placed on a separate line, it signifies the end of a definition (in this case, the end of the procedure).

You'll learn about other features used in these examples in the subsequent sections.

Studying Variables and Data Types

In the spirit of Occam's razor and in the spirit of being essentially a glorified assembly language, Occam offers a limited set of numerical data types. Three primary types are mandatory, with some allowing further specifications:

- INT. Required, equal in size to the computer's machine word; INT16, INT32, INT64 are optional extensions.

- BYTE. Required, comprising eight bits; also represents characters.

- BOOL. Required, can be TRUE or FALSE.

- REAL32, REAL64. Both are optional extensions.

Simple Data Types

Occam's palette of simple data types, especially the absence of required floating point data types, resembles one of Forth, explained on page 6. It almost feels like all assembly-like languages are the same, no matter how disguised.

Other simple data types denote Occam-specific objects, such as timers and channels. If you need an equivalent of a C structure of a C++ class, use declarations RECORD in combination with DATA TYPE. In the example that follows (highlighted), the former defines a new data structure with two REAL32 fields, x and y. The latter incorporates the data structure into Occam's type system. Consequently, you can generate variables of this data type and access their fields through square bracket notation.

occam/testrecord.occ
```
PROC test.record ()
➤  DATA TYPE xy.point
➤    RECORD
➤      REAL32 x :
➤      REAL32 y :
➤  :
   -- In "classical" Occam:
   -- RECORD xy.point IS (REAL32, REAL32):
   -- Declare a 2D point
   xy.point center :

   SEQ
     -- Initialize the point coordinates
     center := [2.0 (REAL32), 3.0 (REAL32)]
     -- Translate the point by 1,-1
     center[x] := center[x] + 1.0
     center[y] := center[y] - 1.0
:
```

Records

Occam RECORDs loosely correspond to the C language structs or to the attributes (but not methods) of the C++ language class. The declaration DATA TYPE loosely corresponds to the C language operator typedef.

Occam doesn't support implicit type conversion. You must explicitly convert a value to a matching type using either of two methods: by prefacing the new type name before the value (without parentheses, known as pre-casting) or after the value (in parentheses, referred to as post-casting).

```
INT big.dog: -- An integer variable
BYTE am.potat: -- A byte-sized variable
```

```
SEQ -- Disregard!
  big.dog := (INT TRUE) + '0' (INT)
  am.potat := BYTE big.dog
```

Take note of a few things: a variable declaration ends with a colon; a block of code (SEQ, Sequential Processes, on page 50) is indented by two spaces; pre-casting can be used with constants and variables, whereas post-casting only applies to constants; if an operand of an arithmetic expression is a pre-cast, it must be parenthesized.

From the previous code example, you've been subtly introduced to identifiers. Occam identifiers are case-sensitive. They must begin with a letter and can include only letters, digits, and periods. All variables used in a process need to be declared in the specification section; their scope remains local to the specified process and all processes depending on it.

Processes cannot share variables, as two processes may be executed by separate transputers with no shared memory! The sole method to interchange values between processes is via channels.

A declaration doesn't initialize the variable. Hence, you must initialize each variable prior to its first usage.

In addition to variables, Occam also supports constants. The combination of keywords VAL (or CONST in some dialects) and IS defines a constant. If the constant's data type can be inferred, you don't have to declare it. In classical Occam, several variables of the same data type can be declared on the same line, separated by commas.

```
VAL INT year IS 365:
VAL leap.year IS year + 1:
VAL ESC IS 27 (BYTE):
```

Navigating Channels

When life gives you no global variables, use *message passing*, the other data-sharing mechanism. Message passing in Occam happens through channels.

- Channels are unidirectional. If you send a message through a channel within a process, you're prohibited from receiving a message from that same channel and vice versa.

- Channels are exclusive, allowing for one-to-one communication. Multiple processes cannot send or receive from the same channel simultaneously.

- Channels are synchronous, meaning the sending and receiving processes must have started the send() and receive() operations, respectively, before the communication can take place.

- Channels are semi-structured, enabling you to send individual bytes or more complex data structures by defining protocols. This will be discussed further in Crafting Channel Protocols, on page 59.

Like any other variable, you need to declare a channel in the process specification, using the keyword CHAN. The following code snippet outlines the declaration of an unstructured channel (capable of carrying bytes) named data.feed:

```
CHAN BYTE data.feed: -- KRoC
CHAN[BYTE] data.feed: -- "Classical" Occam
```

Now, let's shift our focus to processes, the workhorses of Occam.

Exploring Processes

An Occam process is a fundamental unit of computation and concurrency. Processes, in their simpler forms, serve as building blocks for more complex ones. A process can either function as an application or form a part of a larger process.

An Occam process differs from an operating system process, which is an instance of an application executed by one or more threads. This is because, firstly, an Occam process forms part of an application rather than being a standalone application, and secondly, Occam isn't dependent on an operating system but was designed to act as the operating system itself.

An Occam process is more akin to a statement in other programming languages, hence why Occam lacks traditional statements. This distinction is not merely linguistic: a programming statement is presumed to be part of an application, whereas an Occam process can, but doesn't necessarily have to, be a part. From here on, let's refer to Occam processes simply as "processes."

With a few exceptions, processes start, perform an action, and finish (although some might not). They can be categorized into one of the following classes: special, action, or construction.

Special Processes

Occam features two types of special processes—SKIP and STOP. Remember Occam is case sensitive; while SKIP and STOP are reserved words, skip and stop are not. Also, by Occam's own rules, OCCAM ≠ Occam ≠ occam, whatever it means.

A SKIP process starts, does nothing, and immediately finishes. It's typically used as a placeholder for future development or in instances where Occam's grammar necessitates the mention of a process but there's nothing to mention. The following is the shortest KRoC program. If it were written in Occam, only the word SKIP itself would be needed.

occam/minimal.occ
```
-- The shortest program in Occam
PROC minimal ()
  SKIP
:
```

A STOP process starts, fails (by displaying the message "KRoC: application error, stopped."), and never finishes. You can use it to mimic faulty code fragments but not to terminate an application gracefully.

The Skip Process

A SKIP process loosely corresponds to the pass statement in Python. Both exist because the indentation is a part of the languages' grammar that doesn't allow to represent an empty indented block as a pair of curly braces {} or a begin–end construct. A STOP process loosely corresponds to the abort() function in the C standard library.

One critical reason to avoid using STOP, beyond aesthetics, is that it doesn't terminate the application; it merely halts the enclosing process. If the enclosing process is sequential (Sequential Processes, on page 50), stopping the process and terminating the application are effectively the same. However, in a concurrent application (Parallel Processes, on page 51) which comprises several semi-independent processes, stopping one doesn't affect the others. You'll learn how to terminate a concurrent application later on page 68.

Action Processes

In Occam, action or primitive processes form the smallest building blocks of applications. An action process can be an assignment, input, or output process.

You've already encountered assignment processes. Such a process (known in other languages as an assignment statement) assigns a new value to an existing variable. A key point to remember here is that the data types of the variable on the left-hand side and the expression on the right-hand side must match. Multiple assignments are also permissible:

```
a, b := b, a - b
```

An input process receives an item from a predeclared channel and assigns it to a predeclared variable. Similarly, an output process sends the value of a constant or a predeclared and initialized variable to a predeclared channel. The data types of the channel and the value must match.

```
CHAN BYTE in, out:
BYTE item:
SEQ
  in ? item -- "What?" Read/receive a byte from channel 'in'
  out ! item -- "Bang!" Write/send a byte to channel 'out'
```

A process gets blocked if it attempts to receive from a channel with no incoming message. Similarly, if a process attempts to send a message that no other process wants to receive, the sender is blocked. Synchronous communications demand full cooperation!

Taming Construction Processes

Suppose you are crafting your first nontrivial Occam application which divides two floating-point numbers. The application receives the numbers from two incoming channels (two input processes), calculates and stores the quotient (an assignment process), and sends it to the outgoing channel (an output process). You possess the necessary components, but how do you assemble them?

You need containers to pack primitive processes. Such containers are called construction processes.

Sequential Processes

Most well-known programming languages adhere to the sequential execution paradigm, where a sequential application starts with the first statement, followed by the second, and so on, until the last statement is executed, and the application terminates. The next executed statement is always the subsequent textual statement, destination of a conditional branch or unconditional jump.

You can create a sequential application in Occam using a sequential process, defined with the keyword SEQ. The body of the process must be indented by two additional spaces relative to the keyword. The procedure divide() in the subsequent code fragment is sequential, comprising a body (the highlighted block) and a specification (the first three lines). The final procedure in a file represents the application's "main" procedure.

```
occam/divide.occ
PROC divide ()
  CHAN REAL64 in1, in2, out :
  REAL64 quotient, m1, m2 :
```

```
➤   SEQ
➤     in1 ? m1
➤     in2 ? m2
➤     quotient := m1 / m2
➤     out ! quotient
    :
```

The colon at the end of a definition indicates it forms part of the specification of what follows. In the same vein, the procedure divide() also forms part of the specification of the following empty process (the runtime).

Sequential processes can be nested, although there's typically no need to do so. They can also be empty. An empty SEQ is equivalent to a do-nothing SKIP. KRoC amusingly notes when it encounters an empty SEQ: "Empty SEQ process? Equivalent to SKIP…"

Parallel Processes

Occam sets itself apart from other programming languages through its intrinsic support for parallelism at the syntax level.

Consider the two input processes highlighted in the previous code fragment on page 50; both await values from their respective channels, but the notation suggests that m1 arrives first, followed by m2. Unless we have specific knowledge about the order of arrival, this assumption holds true only half the time. What if each number needs preprocessing before division, and that preprocessing takes considerable time? It would be advantageous to receive the first arriving number and start processing it while waiting for the second.

Occam facilitates concurrency via a parallel process defined with the keyword PAR. A parallel process (highlighted in the following code fragment) consists of one or more parallel or sequential subprocesses, executed concurrently.

```
occam/divide-par.occ
PROC main ()
  CHAN REAL64 in1, in2, out :
  REAL64 quotient, m1, m2 :
  SEQ -- SEQ0
➤   PAR
➤     SEQ -- SEQ1
➤       in1 ? m1
➤       -- preprocess m1 here
➤     SEQ -- SEQ2
➤       in2 ? m2
➤       -- preprocess m2 here
    quotient := m1 / m2
    out ! quotient
  :
```

If Occam has access to more than one transputer, SEQ1 and SEQ2 truly run simultaneously. Otherwise, the order of execution is determined by the runtime *scheduler*. The resulting quotient should not depend on the execution order. If it does, it means SEQ1 and SEQ2 are not independent and shouldn't be parallelized.

Parallel execution isn't unique to Occam. It's supported by many languages such as Ada, Concurrent Pascal, Modula-2, Java threads, C++ threads, Python, Go, Erlang, Rust, Kotlin, and Elixir, among others. However, Occam was the pioneer in this regard—another reason to remember it.

Developing concurrent and parallel software is challenging for several reasons, a few of which are named here:

- Future software developers are seldom instructed in concurrent programming, which relies on different concepts, tools, and best practices, including debugging and testing techniques. Advanced concurrency topics are outside this story's scope, but help yourself by reading some good Erlang books (such as *Modern Erlang for Beginners [Ost18]*).

- Because of synchronization and coordination issues, parallel processes cannot share global variables.

- In the world of concurrency, the *deadlock* is the evil king.

A deadlock is a condition where two or more parallel processes are waiting for input from one another, and thus neither can continue, as in the following example:

```
PAR
  SEQ -- SEQ1
    chan1 ? x
    chan2 ! y
  SEQ -- SEQ2
    chan2 ? x
    chan1 ! y
```

Here, SEQ1 is waiting to read a value from channel 1, which should be written by SEQ2, after reading another value from channel 2, which SEQ1 should write but will not. Phew. By the way, an empty PAR is also equivalent to a do-nothing SKIP. Read more about deadlocks in Revisiting Deadlocks, on page 57.

Repetitive Processes

Occam features repetitive processes, essentially loop statements, that begin with the keyword WHILE, followed by a Boolean expression and the loop body.

Boolean expressions can be constants (TRUE or FALSE), relational expressions (=, <>, >, <, >=, or <=), or logical combinations thereof (AND, OR, or NOT). This syntax will be familiar to those who have experience programming in Python.

Repetitive Processes

 Occam repetitive processes and logical operators correspond to Python while loops and logical operators.

You can surely recognize the highlighted code as the procedure that estimates how many times one can divide an integer number by 2 before it becomes zero. (The quantity is known as the binary logarithm of the number.)

```
occam/while.occ
PROC main (CHAN BYTE keyboard, screen)
  INT x, count:
  BYTE in:
  SEQ
    count := 0
    -- Prepare the input
    keyboard ? in
    x := INT in
➤   WHILE x <> 0
➤     SEQ
➤       x := x / 2
➤       count := count + 1
    -- Display the result
    screen ! BYTE (count + '0')
    screen ! '*n'
:
```

One thing to note about classical Occam—it doesn't conceptually recognize standard input and output. Instead, it uses virtual channels, which can connect to a variety of hardware devices as long as they can send or receive bytes (a serial port, a parallel port, or even a phone line). Connections to the hardware are expected to be made at the configuration stage, explained on page 69. Meanwhile, the application is supposed to work correctly, no matter how connected.

The KRoC Occam recognizes the need for the standard I/O and allows to pass CHAN BYTE parameters to the main procedure and recognizes them based on their names. For example, it treats screen and out as the standard output, and keyboard as the standard input.

While we're on the expressions page, let me show you some arithmetic operators. They look and act as expected: +, -, /, *. The remainder can be written as \ or REM (in different dialects). The bitwise operators are BITNOT (or ~), BITAND (or /\), BITOR (or \/), >< (XOR), <<, and >> (left and right shift). Somewhat unusual are the operators PLUS, MINUS, and TIMES. They calculate the sum, the difference, and the product modulo $2^{\#INT}$, where #INT is the number of bits in an integer number. These modulo operators are particularly useful when working with time.

One peculiarity of Occam is the absence of operation precedence. All operators are executed from left to right. The value of 10+10/2 is (10+10)/2=10, not 15. Use parentheses to enforce your desired operation order.

Conditional Processes

The next class of construction processes is conditional processes (if and switch statements for non-Occam speakers).

An IF process is closer to a C/C++/Java switch statement. Like a switch, it allows multiple outcomes. However, the desired outcome is chosen based not on equality but on the sequential evaluation of general Boolean conditions, including TRUE (always matches) and FALSE (never matches). If an IF process does not have any matching conditions, it stops (as if by execution of a STOP process) and reports an error. Add a TRUE SKIP clause at the end to avoid such errors.

Remember the Toysla electric car on page 14? The following toy example implements communications between a Toysla engine controller (begins on line 9) and the "driver" (the other SEQ process), running in parallel. The one-way communication channel is called toysla. Lines from 20 to the end of the file illustrate an IF process.

```
occam/conditional.occ
Line 1  #INCLUDE "course.module"
        PROC toysla (CHAN BYTE in, out)
          VAL LEFT.TURN IS 0 (BYTE):
          VAL RIGHT.TURN IS 1 (BYTE):
     5    VAL STOP.AND.QUIT IS MOSTPOS BYTE: --
          BYTE command, execute:
          CHAN OF BYTE toysla:
          PAR
            SEQ -- The car engine controller --
    10        toysla ? execute
            SEQ -- The "driver"
              out.string ("Enter a command:*n", 0, out!)
              in ? command
            -- Check command validity
    15        CASE command  --
                'L','R','F','B','Q'
```

```
        SKIP
      ELSE
        STOP
20    IF --
      command = 'L'
        toysla ! LEFT.TURN
      command = 'R'
        toysla ! RIGHT.TURN
25    command = 'Q'
        toysla ! STOP.AND.QUIT
      TRUE
      -- Undefined command
        SKIP
30  :
```

Line 5 has another treat for you: it shows the operator MOSTPOS that evaluates to the largest (most positive) number for the specified data type. Likewise, MOSTNEG evaluates to the smallest number.

Newer Occams add one more tool for constructing conditional processes—CASE (line 15 of the same code sample). It checks the parameter (which must be an integer number, or possibly a character) against lists of constant numbers and executes the matching process.

Alternative Processes and Timers

A problem arises with a conditional process if the conditions require receiving from multiple channels. An input process is blocking: once you start executing it, it doesn't terminate until something is received, which precludes the application from checking the other channels. An alternative process allows you to monitor several channels simultaneously and respond to the first that is ready to receive.

The concept of simultaneity is intimately related to measuring time. For that, Occam has *timers*. Once you define a timer with the namesake keyword TIMER, you can use it as a channel in an input process. A timer emits integer numbers—typically, Unix timestamps.

You can also use a timer to introduce a delay with the operator AFTER. The operator forces the input process to wait until the value of the timer equals the operand. The operand can be a constant, a variable, or an expression involving the current time and a delay. Use PLUS to calculate the wake-up time from the current time and the delay, not +, to avoid numerical overflows.

In some dialects of Occam, a timer is a built-in singleton object accessible as an input channel TIME, for example, via TIME ? now.

An application with multiple external input channels doesn't know which input arrives first or whether it arrives at all. Alternative channels address the problem of blocking selection, and timers solve the problem of timeouts.

The following example illustrates how timers complement alternative processes to handle input uncertainty. This application waits for the user to enter a key. If the user doesn't respond in two seconds, the application crashes. The highlighted alternative process monitors the delay timer clock and the keyboard kbd.

```
occam/timed-key.occ
#INCLUDE "course.module"
PROC main (CHAN BYTE kbd, scr)
  VAL delay IS 2000000: -- 2 sec
  INT now:
  TIMER clock:
  SEQ
    out.string ("Enter your key:*n", 0, scr)
    clock ? now
    BYTE key:
➤   ALT
➤     clock ? AFTER (now PLUS delay)
➤       STOP -- Too late!
➤     kbd ? key
➤       out.string ("Welcome!*n", 0, scr)
  :
```

You can add Boolean *guards* to any or all ALT conditions. Receiving from a channel will be attempted only if the corresponding guard is true. Here's an implementation of a gated multiplexor, a process that receives messages from four incoming channels, src0, src1, src2, and src3, and forwards them to a single outgoing channel dest:

```
CHAN INT src0, src1, src2, src3, dest:
BOOL enabled0, enabled1, enabled2, enabled3:
INT x:
ALT
  enabled0 & src0 ? x
    dest ! x
  enabled1 & src1 ? x
    dest ! x
  enabled2 & src2 ? x
    dest ! x
  enabled3 & src3 ? x
    dest ! x
```

You may feel disappointed that almost the same code block is repeated in the previous example four times. What if you want to multiplex 128 channels?

Should you copy the block 128 times? Not at all—see Introducing Arrays, on page 57, and Replicating Processes, on page 64.

Alternative Processes

 An alternative process is a loose equivalent of the select() function in the standard C library.

Revisiting Deadlocks

There used to be two good friends, Alice and Bob. Once, they had a bitter argument over different dialects of Occam. Chuck, who happened to be their mutual friend and a go-between, told Alice that Bob would send her a text message, but only after she texted him first. Then he told Bob that Alice would send him a text message, but only after he texted her first. The two never spoke to each other again.

The following example translates the drama into Occam:

```
occam/deadlock.occ
PROC deadlock ()
  VAL hello IS 'H':
  CHAN OF BYTE alice.to.bob, bob.to.alice:
  PAR
    BYTE text.msg:
    SEQ -- Alice: text me, then I text you
      bob.to.alice ? text.msg
      alice.to.bob ! hello

    BYTE text.msg:
    SEQ -- Bob: text me, then I text you
      alice.to.bob ? text.msg
      bob.to.alice ! hello
:
-- KRoC: deadlock: no valid processes found in workspace(s)
-- KRoC: program deadlocked (no processes to run)
```

Deadlocks are real and dangerous; deadlocks are very hard to detect and debug. Deadlocks are outside this book's scope, but if you plan to do serious distributed programming in Occam or another language, you should consult a good operating system book (for example, *Operating System Concepts* [SGG11]), especially a chapter on concurrent programming.

Introducing Arrays

Any respectable programming language has arrays or array-like collections (tuples, lists, vectors, matrices, you name it). Occam is not an exception.

Occam arrays are homogeneous, have fixed sizes, and are created uninitialized. To create an array, specify its size, data type, name, and, optionally, values:

```
[4]BOOL enabled: -- An array of four Boolean values
VAL trues IS [TRUE, TRUE, TRUE, TRUE]: -- An array of constants (a table)
[8][8]BYTE board: -- An 8x8 array of bytes (a checkerboard)
```

When describing an array or a table as a procedure parameter, don't mention the size. Operator SIZE on line 6 of the next example will calculate it for you.

occam/array-with-loop.occ
```
Line 1  -- Define the initializing procedure
    -   PROC make.true ([]BOOL array)
    -     INT i:
    -     SEQ
    5       i := 0
    -       WHILE i < (SIZE array) --
    -         SEQ
    -           array[i] := TRUE
    -           i := i + 1
    10  :
    -
    -   PROC main ()
    -     -- Call the initializing procedure
    -     [4]BOOL enabled:
    15    make.true (enabled)
    -   :
```

The body of make.true() appears to be a poor man's attempt to reimplement a for loop using a while loop, which it is. Replicating Processes, on page 64, will provide a better solution.

You can assign a table to an array from a literal or a variable. Once assigned, the array elements become editable:

```
enable := [TRUE, TRUE, TRUE, TRUE]
```

Segments

A segment, which loosely correspond to list slices in Python, is a contiguous subarray of an array starting at the position p and consisting of n items:

```
segment := [enable FROM p FOR n] -- In KRoC
segment := enable[FROM p FOR n] -- In some dialects
```

Segments on the right-hand side are copies of the original arrays, not views. If you modify a segment, the original array won't change, and vice versa. On the contrary, segments on the left-hand side are views of the original array. Assignment to a segment modifies the original array:

```
[5]INT data, copy:
data := [1,2,3,4,5]
copy := [data FROM 0 FOR (SIZE data)]
copy[0] := 0 -- data[0] is still 1
[data FROM 0 FOR 2] := [0,0] -- data is now [0,0,3,4,5]
```

Strings

Occam wasn't designed as a string-friendly language. In the spirit of Erlang, a string in Occam is just an array of printable bytes. The double quotation mark notation is the *syntactic sugar*: it makes strings easier to read and type but doesn't affect their internal representation:

```
VAL []BYTE literal.string IS "Hello World!":
[SIZE literal.string]BYTE string.var:
string.var := literal.string -- Copying
```

Crafting Channel Protocols

Occam channels may be semi-structured connectors, as claimed in Navigating Channels, on page 47, but some structure never hurts. It's in your power to make them fully structured. Simply attach protocols.

A *protocol* is a scheme that allows a channel to carry typed or mixed-type data. Protocols can be simple, sequential, array, or variant (case).

Simple Protocols

A simple protocol mandates that all transferrable items belong to one data type. In the classical Occam, you would supply the data type in the parentheses after the CHAN. KRoC uses the CHAN OF notation:

```
-- "classical"
CHAN(INT) int.channel:
-- KRoC
CHAN OF INT int.channel:
```

A process may receive or send only items whose data type matches the channel protocol. Sometimes it may be necessary to specify a protocol where the format of the protocol cannot be defined. Such a protocol is called anarchic and is introduced with the keyword ANY:

```
CHAN OF ANY alien.device:
```

Array Protocols

Array protocols are a subclass of simple protocols. They allow you to send and receive arrays of known or unknown length. An array whose length is stored in the first item is called a counted array (compare counted strings in Forth on page 31). A counted array is easy to send but hard to receive.

In the following example, two channels, text.in and text.out, are formatted for counted byte arrays (strings). The size of an array is an INT16 value separated from the array body with a double colon (::). When you send a counted array, Occam first sends its size and then its body:

```
CHAN OF INT16::[]BYTE text.in, text.out:
INT16 size:
[100]BYTE buffer:
text.out ! 13::"Hello, world!"
text.in ? size::buffer
```

Sequential Protocols

You can define complex protocols separately from channels by naming them with the keyword PROTOCOL. Separate definitions are easier to read, are reusable, and enforce code consistency:

```
PROTOCOL ID.PROTO IS INT16:
CHAN OF ID.PROTO id.channel:
```

A sequential protocol is an example of a complex protocol. Use it when you have a sequential, record-style (records were introduced on page 46) communications pattern. However, if a record data type has already been created (xy.point), there's no reason to define a matching sequential protocol. You can use a simple protocol with a complex data type!

```
PROTOCOL POINT.2D IS REAL32; REAL32:
CHAN OF POINT.2D point.data:
-- Alternatively:
CHAN OF xy.point point.data:
```

Variant (Case) and Tag-Only Protocols

A variant protocol is an advanced form of a sequential protocol in which the first item serves as a tag and defines the format of the rest of the message.

In classical Occam, a variant channel requires a manual assignment of numerical values to the tags and receiving through a specialized IF process:

```
CHAN(1; INT OR
     2; REAL32; REAL32 OR
     3; [BYTE]BYTE OR
     4) in, out:
out ! 1; 100 -- Send the tag and the matching content
SEQ
  in ? tag -- Receive the tag
```

```
IF -- Inspect the tag, receive the leftover
  tag = 1
    in ? x
  tag = 2
    in ? y; z
  ...
```

KRoC introduced autodefined tags and a CASE structure consistent with other modifications in this Occam dialect.

```
PROTOCOL things
  CASE
    word; INT
    point; REAL32; REAL32
    message; BYTE::[]BYTE
    sync
    :
CHAN OF things in, out:
out ! word; 100 -- Send a "thing"
SEQ
  in ? CASE
    word; n -- receive a word
      action1 (n)
    point; x; y -- receive a 2D point
      action2 (x, y)
    message; len::buffer -- Receive a string
      action3 (len, buffer)
    sync -- Receive a tag alone
      action4 ()
```

Note that the tag sync is not followed by any other items. It represents a subclass of variant protocols called tag-only protocols.

Tag-Only Protocols

 Messages in tag-only protocols loosely correspond to POSIX signals, except they are user-defined and sent by processes, not by the operating system.

You may also have seen function-like objects on the highlighted lines in the previous example. They are indeed Occam functions, and Functions, on page 62, explains how to use them.

Arranging Code in Compilation Units

Classical Occam allows you to define processes as top-level, first-class statements. According to KRoC, a process must be a part of a compilation unit—a procedure or a function. An Occam file may contain data type and constant definitions and any number of compilation units, including no units at all.

Procedures

You've already seen procedures in this chapter, though they weren't the focus of discussion but mere wrappers around the code of interest. Let's look at them closely.

A procedure, also known as a *named process* in the classical Occam, has a name, optional parameters, and optional local variables. Syntactically, a procedure starts with the keyword PROC and ends with a colon : (not a semicolon ; !). The smallest and arguably the least practical procedure takes no parameters and does nothing.

```
PROC does.nothing ()
  SKIP -- Must be a process
:
```

Unless otherwise requested, Occam passes procedure parameters by reference. You can modify their values if necessary. If you want to pass a parameter by value, mark it as a VAL.

The main procedure of an application is the last procedure of the application code file. The name of that procedure is irrelevant, but it is limited in what parameters it can take. They all must be of type CHAN OF BYTE. The number can be from zero to three. The first channel, if present, is a link to the application's standard input (usually the keyboard). The second channel, if present, is a link to the standard output (usually the screen). The third one links to the standard error output. A simplified version of the Unix/Linux tee utility that reads from standard input and writes to standard output can be implemented as a seven-line Occam program.

```
occam/tee.occ
PROC tee (CHAN OF BYTE stdin, stdout, stderr)
  BYTE x:
  WHILE TRUE
    SEQ
      stdin ? x
      stdout ! x
:
```

Functions

A function is a more lightweight object than a procedure. It is intended to perform calculations that don't involve channel input/output, parallelism, or parameter modification.

A function consists of a return type declaration, a name, an optional parameter list, and an expression or a *value process*. Occam passes parameters by value—a function cannot change them. A function may return comma-separated multiple values but must return at least one.

A simple one-line function without local variables is a wrapper around an expression. The value of the expression is the value of the function. In the example, function BOOL is.lower(VAL BYTE ch) returns TRUE if byte ch is a lowercase letter and FALSE otherwise. (Note the VAL modifier!)

occam/toupper.occ
```
-- Check if ch is a lowercase letter
BOOL FUNCTION is.lower (VAL BYTE ch) IS (ch >= 'a') AND (ch <= 'z') :
```

A more typical function is a value process—a process producing a value. The process still cannot contain input, output, parallel, or alternative subprocesses but can define local variables. A value process begins with the keyword VALOF and ends with RESULT, followed by the list of return values.

Function BYTE to.upper(VAL BYTE ch) in the example returns a byte converted to uppercase, but only if it's a lowercase character, which is determined by calling is.lower().

occam/toupper.occ
```
VAL not.found IS -1:
-- Convert a lowercase letter ch to uppercase
BYTE FUNCTION to.upper (VAL BYTE ch)
  BYTE upper.char:
  VALOF
    IF
      is.lower (ch)
        upper.char := ch BITAND #DF
      TRUE
        upper.char := ch
    RESULT upper.char
:
```

Procedures and Functions

Procedures and functions in Occam loosely correspond to procedures and functions in Starset. Procedures in both languages do not return values and, by default, pass parameters by reference. Functions in both languages return values and pass parameters by value.

Functions and procedures are essential code structuring and reuse tools in Occam and most other languages. They make code easier to write, read, maintain, and recycle.

Replicating Processes

Occam processes are fantastic; Occam arrays are fabulous. Why don't we combine them and get something even better—arrays of processes? Occam supports them via *process replication.*

Let's look again at the code example on page 56 and revisit the problem, "What if you want to multiplex N=128 channels? Should you copy the block N=128 times?" No, you should instruct Occam to replicate the highlighted block N times:

```
ALt
➤     enabled.i & src.i ? x
➤        dest ! x
➤  ...
```

The result is a process replication (also highlighted in the following example):

```
occam/mux.occ
VAL N IS 128:
PROC mux ()
  CHAN OF INT dest:
  [N]CHAN OF INT src:
  [N]BOOL enabled:
  INT x:

  WHILE TRUE
    -- The replicated part
➤   ALT i=0 FOR N
➤     enabled[i] & src[i] ? x
➤        dest ! x
  :
```

The segment-like structure i=0 FOR N implicitly creates an integer loop variable i and N instances of the body. The value of i in each instance is different (from 0 to N-1). The procedure mux() multiplexes N input channels []src into one output channel dest. The Boolean array []enabled selects the channels to multiplex.

When you compile the example, you'll get a warning message:

```
/home/dzseven> kroc mux.occ
Warning-occ21-mux.occ(11)- variable `enabled[..]' is undefined here
```

The message means that the Boolean flags have never been initialized. Assuming that initially you want to combine all inputs and do some tuning later, you should set all the array bits to TRUE. If the array were short, this operation would be a matter of executing several assignment processes. But not only is it not short, its size is actually not fixed. You need an array of assignment processes—a sequence replicator:

```
[N]BOOL enabled:
SEQ i=0 FOR N
  enabled[i] := TRUE
```

The replicator implicitly creates N assignment processes with different values of i executed strictly one after another. It's hard not to see a good old for loop here!

Sequential Process Replicators

 A sequential process replicator loosely corresponds to a for loop in C/C++ and similar languages.

The new multiplexor is much more robust:

occam/mux-new.occ
```
Line 1  VAL N IS 128:
        PROC mux ()
          CHAN OF INT dest:
          [N]CHAN OF INT src:
     5    [N]BOOL enabled:
          INT x:

          SEQ
            -- Initialization
    10      SEQ i=0 FOR N
              enabled[i] := TRUE

            -- Multiplexing
            WHILE TRUE --
    15        ALT i=0 FOR N
                enabled[i] & src[i] ? x
                  dest ! x
        :
```

What are conditional process replicators good for? For starters, you can write a character search procedure.

The procedure find.1st() takes three parameters. The first is an immutable string haystack to be searched (see the sidebar Haystacks and Needles, on page 66 if intrigued!). The second is a character needle to be found. The last one is the position of the first found character or a constant not.found:

```
occam/search.occ
#INCLUDE "toupper.occ"

-- The search procedure
PROC find.1st (VAL []BYTE haystack, VAL BYTE needle, INT pos)
  IF
    IF i=0 FOR SIZE haystack
      to.upper (haystack[i]) = to.upper (needle)
        pos := i
    TRUE
      pos := not.found
  :
```

The highlighted part of the code is a replicated conditional process. It compares the ith character of the haystack to the needle (both characters are converted to uppercase to provide case-insensitive search). If the needle is in the haystack, the comparisons stop at the first match. It's crucial to understand that the conditional processes are not executed in parallel. They're sequential. In a sense, a replicated conditional process is a sequential loop of conditional processes. Parallelization is possible but well outside of this book's scope.

Haystacks and Needles

The function strstr() in the C language library, and similar functions in other languages, takes two arguments: a haystack and a needle. This metaphor is derived from the idiom "finding a needle in a haystack," which refers to the difficulty of finding a small, specific item in an ample, cluttered space. The metaphor provides an intuitive understanding of what the function does, making it easier for programmers to remember and use.

Parallel process replicators have the same structure as the other replicators: they consist of the keyword PAR, a FOR counter, and the body. A parallel process replicator creates a loop variable and several identical parallel processes. The number of processes must be a compile-time constant (it cannot be a variable, as in the other three types of replicators, due to placement concerns addressed in Hardware Placement, on page 70).

Parallel replicators are often used in homogeneous pipelines: applications that pass data through a sequence of simple identical or nearly identical filters. For example, you can implement a pipeline that takes a stream of numbers from a channel and collects the biggest N of them. The application may consist of four types of processes, as shown in the code that follows. The comparator() procedure reads a number from a channel and compares it to the stored number. If the new number is bigger, it replaces the stored number and forwards the latter to the next stage. Otherwise, it forwards the new number. This algorithm is known as *bubble sort*.

The drain() and feed() processes remove the unused numbers from the pipeline and feed random numbers to be sorted into the pipeline. Each of the first three processes handles exactly COUNT numbers and then terminates. They are fully sequential and do not use parallel process replicators:

occam/topN.occ

```
VAL COUNT IS 25 :
-- "Bubble sort" comparison
-- largest = number > largest ? number : largest
PROC comparator (CHAN OF INT in, out)
  INT number, largest, i:
  SEQ
    largest := MOSTNEG INT -- Nothing can be smaller
    i := COUNT
    WHILE i > 0
      SEQ
        in ? number
        IF
          number > largest
            SEQ
              out ! largest
              largest := number
          TRUE
            out ! number
        i := i - 1
:

-- Remove smaller items from the pipeline
PROC drain (CHAN OF INT in)
  INT x:
  SEQ i=0 FOR COUNT
    in ? x
:

-- Insert items to be sorted into the pipeline
#INCLUDE "course.module" -- for random()
PROC feed (CHAN OF INT out)
  INT seed, number:
  SEQ
    seed := 0
    SEQ i=0 FOR COUNT
      SEQ
        number, seed := random ((MOSTPOS INT) - 1, seed)
        out ! (number + 1)
:
```

Magic happens in the sort() procedure. Here, you start a feeder, a drainer, and N parallel comparators (highlighted). Each comparator takes input from the previous (or the feeder) and forwards it to the next (or the drainer). The bigger numbers settle in one of the comparators, while the smaller numbers are drained:

```
occam/topN.occ
VAL N IS 5 :
PROC sort ()
  [N+1]CHAN OF INT slot:
  PAR
    -- Feed random numbers
    feed (slot[0])
    -- Sort
    PAR i=0 FOR N
      comparator (slot[i], slot[i+1])
    -- Drain the leftovers
    drain (slot[N])
  :
```

What if you want to process more than 25 numbers? What if you don't want to expose your application to an input sequence of any specific length? The following section explains how to avoid the limitation.

Terminating a Distributed Application

You'll see a WHILE TRUE loop on line 14 of the multiplexor example on page 65 and several similar loops in the bubble sorter on page 67. A WHILE TRUE loop doesn't terminate, nor does any process enclosing it. How would you gracefully terminate such a perpetual application?

Distributed termination involves the termination of every constituent process. It's very tempting to declare a global Boolean variable whose value would be checked by every repetitive process in the system before starting the next iteration. When the value of the variable changes, the processes will stop at once. Sadly, Occam doesn't allow global variables.

Another distributed termination option is to connect each parallel process to a central control process via control channels. Each parallel process would use ALT to listen to termination instructions and stop when one arrives. This solution requires a superabundance of rarely used channels and input processes, making code hard to develop and maintain.

Lastly, as in the following example, you can integrate data and control messages and send them through the same channels formatted according to a case protocol:

occam/mux-term.occ

```
DATA TYPE Payload IS INT:
PROTOCOL mux.proto
  CASE
    data; Payload
    terminate -- Control
:

VAL N IS 128:
PROC mux ()
  CHAN OF mux.proto dest:
  [N]CHAN OF mux.proto src:
  BOOL continue:
  Payload x:

  SEQ
    -- Initialization
    continue := TRUE

    -- Multiplexing
    WHILE continue
      ALT i=0 FOR N
        src[i] ? CASE
          data; x
            SEQ
              dest ! data; x
          terminate
            SEQ
              continue := FALSE
              dest ! terminate
:
```

The terminate message is called a marker. It's sent after the last data item and "bleeds" data out of communication channels. Generally, it's incorrect to terminate a repetitive process immediately after receiving a marker. This simple solution works only in the absence of looping and parallel channels data paths in the application. Consult a distributed systems book (for example, *Distributed Systems [vT23]*) for more ideas.

Configuring Occam Programs

Your Occam application is written, debugged, and found correct. (The latter is an exaggeration. It takes some nerve to claim that a distributed application is correct.) The last stage of the project is the configuration—tuning the application parameters.

Prioritization

Alternative Processes and Timers, on page 55, introduced alternative processes executed based on the availability of inputs. It didn't say what happens if two or more inputs become available simultaneously. It's up to the Occam runtime scheduler to decide which process to execute first. Fair enough, the runtime scheduler is clever, but you may want to have a say—in other words, assign higher or lower priorities to the channels.

Prioritization is a blessing and a curse. On the bright side, it optimizes the performance of critical processes and improves resource utilization. On the dark side, it causes starvation of lower-priority channels and may lead to undesirable scenarios if not done correctly.

Prioritization in Occam is easy: simply put the keyword PRI before the ALT that you want to prioritize. Now the constituent processes will be executed in the textual order. This multiplexor favors lower-number channels, consistent with typical priority assignment schemas:

```
occam/mux-pri.occ
VAL N IS 128:
PROC mux.with.prios ()
  CHAN OF INT dest:
  [N]CHAN OF INT src:
  INT x:

  WHILE TRUE
    PRI ALT i=0 FOR N
      src[i] ? x
        dest ! x
:
```

The same prioritization mechanism can be used to discriminate parallel processes. You are still responsible for choosing the correct order!

Hardware Placement

Being an "assembly language for transputers," Occam allows you to access computer hardware directly.

First, you can request that a parallel process is executed by ("placed on") a processor/core of your choice. Use the keyword PLACED before the PAR and keyword PROCESSOR, followed by the processor/core number, before each constituent process. KRoC doesn't currently support processor placement:

```
PLACED PAR
  PROCESSOR 1
    in ? char
  PROCESSOR 2
    out ! char
```

With proper permissions, an Occam application can access hardware ports. The keyword PORT creates an abstraction that behaves like a channel but retrieves items from a port and sends them to a port. An Occam port must be placed to a specific bus address:

```
INT16 status:
PORT OF INT16 uart.status:
PLACE uart.status AT #16000004:
uart.status ? status
```

Finally, you can map an Occam array to the physical RAM (including video RAM and device RAM):

```
VAL screenstart IS #B800:
[32000]BYTE screen:
PLACE screen AT screenstart:
screen[10] := #76 -- "Draw a pixel"
```

Cool as it is, further configuration story belongs to a different book.

Writing Something Big

What could be a better tribute to William of Ockham, fourteenth-century English philosopher and theologian, than an exotic programming language named after him? Only one thing could be better—a simulation of the problem of dining philosophers in Occam.

Rumor has it that five learned men ("the philosophers") sit around a table somewhere in the universe and think. Now and then, at random times, they get hungry. Luckily, there is a massive dish of pasta on the table. Sadly, being philosophers, they are poor and can afford only one fork per person, but they need two each to enjoy the pasta. As shown in the figure on page 72, each philosopher (P in the figure) grabs the fork (F in the figure) on the left and the fork on the right, dines, and puts the forks back for his hungry neighbors to use. (Yes, they share utensils!)

Food for thought—what happens if all men become hungry simultaneously and pick up their left forks?

Jokes aside, the problem concerns communications, deadlocks, and resource allocation in distributed systems. It's worth solving.

You can represent each philosopher and each fork by one parallel process. A philosopher has two incoming and three outgoing channels: Boolean left.rq and right.rq for requesting and releasing the namesake forks, Boolean left.ok and right.ok for receiving the acknowledgments, and a byte-formatted report for reporting the condition.

Philosophers have a timer and spend some random time thinking about the intricacies of Occam programming. When the timers expire, the philosophers report that they are hungry (literally, for your information), request their left fork from the fork itself, wait for permission to use it, and then repeat for the right fork. Once both forks are in order, the philosophers dine, release the forks, and continue thinking. The process repeats forever. You are welcome to terminate it, say, by limiting the amount of pasta:

occam/philosophers.occ

```
#INCLUDE "course.module" -- for random()

VAL GOT.IT IS TRUE: -- Some useful constants
VAL PICKUP IS TRUE:
VAL PUTDOWN IS FALSE:

PROC philosopher (CHAN OF BOOL left.rq, right.rq, left.ok, right.ok,
                  CHAN OF BYTE report, VAL BYTE id)
  BOOL any:
  TIMER clock:
  VAL eat IS 100000:
  INT seed, think:
  SEQ
    think, seed := random (10 * eat, (INT id) + 1)
    WHILE TRUE
      INT now:
      SEQ
        -- Think
        clock ? now
```

```
clock ? AFTER (now PLUS think)
think, seed := random (10 * eat, seed)
-- Get hungry
report ! id

left.rq ! PICKUP
left.ok ? any
right.rq ! PICKUP
right.ok ? any
-- Eat
clock ? now
clock ? AFTER (now PLUS eat)
PAR
  left.rq ! PUTDOWN
  right.rq ! PUTDOWN
-- Think again
:
```

A fork process uses the same four data channels (but not the reporter). A fork is initially not used. When it receives a request from a philosopher, it sends an acknowledgment to the corresponding channel and marks itself as used. The fork becomes available again if a putdown message comes from the matching side. If a putdown message comes from the wrong side, the application crashes, which should never happen. If a used fork receives a request from a philosopher, it puts that request on hold. (Doesn't this paragraph sound like *Alice in Wonderland* or some other fantasy tale?)

occam/philosophers.occ
```
PROC fork (CHAN OF BOOL left.rq, right.rq, left.ok, right.ok)
  VAL NOT.USED IS 0(BYTE):
  VAL LEFT.USED IS 1(BYTE):
  VAL RIGHT.USED IS 2(BYTE):
  BYTE used:
  SEQ
    used := NOT.USED -- not used
    WHILE TRUE
      BOOL rq:
      ALT
        used = NOT.USED & left.rq ? rq
          IF
            rq = PICKUP
              SEQ
                used := LEFT.USED
                left.ok ! GOT.IT
        used = NOT.USED & right.rq ? rq
          IF
            rq = PICKUP
              SEQ
                used := RIGHT.USED
                right.ok ! GOT.IT
```

```
        used = LEFT.USED & left.rq ? rq
          IF
            rq = PUTDOWN
              used := NOT.USED
        used = RIGHT.USED & right.rq ? rq
          IF
            rq = PUTDOWN
              used := NOT.USED
  :
```

The reporter procedure is a trivial multiplexor that collects the reports from the philosophers and displays them on the screen. Occam doesn't allow more than one process to use the screen.

The main procedure defines the 25 channels and starts the reporter, five forks, and five philosophers as 11 parallel processes. Once the parts find each other, the simulation begins:

occam/philosophers.occ

```
-- Essentially a multiplexor
PROC reporter ([]CHAN OF BYTE in, CHAN OF BYTE out)
  WHILE TRUE
    BYTE x:
    ALT i=0 FOR (SIZE in)
      in[i] ? x
        SEQ
          out ! x
          out ! '*n'
  :

PROC dining.philosophers (CHAN OF BYTE out!)
  VAL N IS 5:
  [N]CHAN OF BOOL left.rq, right.rq:
  [N]CHAN OF BOOL left.ok, right.ok:
  [N]CHAN OF BYTE reports:

  PAR
    reporter (reports, out)
    PAR i=0 FOR N
      fork (right.rq[i], left.rq[(i+1) REM N],
            right.ok[i], left.ok[(i+1) REM N])
    PAR i=0 FOR N
      philosopher (left.rq[i], right.rq[i],
                   left.ok[i], right.ok[i], reports[i],
                   (BYTE i) + 'A')
  :
```

It all runs smoothly for a while, possibly for a long while, but eventually the application deadlocks because all five stubborn philosophers pick up their left forks and never put them down again.

You don't need to wait for the end of the party. Philosophy and pasta are great, but mathematics and arrays are better. APL, an array processing language, is your next destination.

Further Reading

- *Communicating Sequential Processes [Hoa78]*
- *Occam Programming Manual [INM84]*
- *A Tutorial Introduction to OCCAM Programming [PM87]*
- *Programming in Occam [Jon87]*
- *Occam Programming: A Practical Approach [Ker87]*
- *Introduction to occam 2 on the Transputer [BS89]*
- *Occam 2: Including Occam 1 [Gal96]*

The universe is written in the language of mathematics, and its
characters are triangles, circles, and other geometric figures.

> *Galileo Galilei, Florentine astronomer, physicist, and*
> *engineer*

CHAPTER 3

Embracing Array-Centric Programming with APL

When it comes to massively parallel processing of multidimensional arrays—vectors, matrices, datacubes, and so on—nothing seems to beat NumPy, a numerical Python library (hence the name), and Matlab, the Matrix Laboratory (hence the name). However, this wasn't always the case. The first array processing language, APL, was designed much earlier.

The original version of APL dates back to 1962 when Kenneth Iverson, a Canadian computer scientist, introduced it as a form of algebraic and algorithmic notation in his book *A Programming Language [Ive62]*. APL became a powerful interactive problem-solving system, first optimized for legendary IBM OS/360 mainframes (under the name APL\360) and, later, for minis and personal computers. Unless you have a better alternative, you'll work with well-supported and well-documented GNU APL (apl).[1] But first, we must have a serious conversation about the APL character set and the need for a specialized keyboard.

Deciphering APL Character Set

If someone asks you what the only thing that differentiates APL from 99.9 percent of other programming languages is, answer without hesitation: it's APL's character set.

The APL founding fathers were of a solid mathematical background. They intended to create a programming language resembling familiar mathematical notation as much as possible. Ideally, the user could type a formula in an

---

1.   https://www.gnu.org/software/apl/

APL interpreter window and instantly execute it. That's how APL ended up with 65 special characters (in addition to the familiar alphanumerics, spaces, and punctuation), including ⊖, ⎕, ⊞, a "thumbnail" (⍝), and even a grotesque overlay of O, Ø/U, and T (the end of input—see Performing Input and Output, on page 93):

The extended alphabet of the language permitted users to write concise expressions. For example, the following expression calculates the value of e≈2.718281828 through Taylor series expansion with 170 members—1++/1÷(!ι170)—and I don't blame you if you fail to recognize the formula at first glance.

On the bright side, the value of π in APL is at your fingertips: ○1. The function ○ represents multiplication by π and understandably looks like a circle; though it would be even more natural for such a function to look like a half-circle ⌒ or represent multiplication by 2π.

Modern physical computer keyboards don't show the extended APL characters. As an APL coder, you must use a virtual keyboard, buy a pricey specialized APL keyboard—from Dyalog,[2] for example—or install a secondary APL keyboard layout, not unlike a layout for a foreign language (see Activating the APL Keyboard Layout, on page 79). Well, APL *is* a foreign language.

To conclude, the complete APL character set consists of the ASCII alphanumeric characters (A through Z, a through z, and 0 through 9), ASCII punctuation, white spaces, and 65 or more special characters, making APL the black sheep of programming languages, as the sidebar on page 80 explains.

Some special characters went out of use as early as 1970, making the APL reader's life somewhat more manageable.

---

2.   https://www.dyalog.com/

I hope I haven't scared you. You can study J or K instead—they're remote relatives of APL that use only standard ASCII characters—or continue with APL anyway.

J and K

The J programming language[a] is another baby of Kenneth Iverson. It appeared first in 1990. J inherits the compactness and expressiveness of APL but does away with any special characters. Sadly, along with losing the APL special characters, it also lost APL's charm.

The K programming language[b] is from 1993 and out of Morgan Stanley. (To be fully honest, K is a descendant of two more APL-style languages, A and A++.) K's purpose was to facilitate the migration of APL code from IBM mainframes to Sun workstations. K uses heavy operator overloading to make up for the absence of silly special characters. It's not clear to me if 10#{1+1.0%x}\1 in K is more readable than 1++/1÷(!ι170) in APL.

---

a. https://www.jsoftware.com/help/learning/contents.htm
b. https://xpqz.github.io/kbook/Introduction.html

Activating the APL Keyboard Layout

As a Linux or macOS user, you can switch to the secondary APL keyboard layout with the program setxkbmap. The following command makes the combination Right-Alt a layout switch. Note the comma just in front of dyalog. No space is between them (the invisible "empty" variant before the comma refers to the us layout):

```
setxkbmap -layout us,apl -variant ,dyalog -option grp:switch
```

Press the combination to activate the secondary APL layout. Otherwise, the standard U.S. layout is used. The same program with different options removes the Right-Alt binding:

```
setxkbmap -layout us -option grp:switch
```

If you're a Windows user or none of the above worked, visit the Dyalog website[3] for more options.

This introduction to APL programming was longer than expected—blame the APL character set. You're ready to move on to the rest of the language, for it deserves it.

---

3. https://www.dyalog.com/apl-font-keyboard.htm

The Black Sheep of Programming Languages

Aside from APL, special (non-ASCII) characters can be found in PL/I (¬), Fortress (→, ⊂, ⊆, ∞), TI-BASIC (≤, ≠, ≥, √, →), Scala (←, ⇒), Haskell (::, V, ⇒, ↠), Agda (ℕ, V), and perhaps some other exotic languages. It's APL, however, that makes wild and unconstrained use of the special symbols.

In APL's defense, the first version of the American Standard Code for Information Interchange (ASCII) wasn't published until 1963, and before that, no standard character set existed. Any character, technically, was "special."

IBM devised its staple encoding, Extended Binary Coded Decimal Interchange Code (EBCDIC), only in 1963–64. At this point, we can only guess the original encoding of the APL symbols. Fortunately, with the advent of Unicode, the Tower of Babel of the character codes is once again uniting users and programmers instead of dividing them.

Looking at Data Types

Numbers can be integer and real, positive and negative, and here's the catch: APL strongly promotes the one-to-one correspondence between a symbol and its function. In most programming languages, the minus is used as a constituent of a negative literal expression (-5 is a negative 5) or a unary negation function (-X is the negation of X, not necessarily a negative number by itself). In APL, -X is the negation of X, but negative 5 is written as ‾5.

The original APL\360 doesn't support complex numbers.

A one-dimensional numeric array—a vector—is a sequence of scalars separated by one or more spaces. Notice that the APL code traditionally starts in the seventh column. The first six positions are reserved for the output and line numbers within function definitions (see Define and Call Functions, on page 94; Fortran has a similar arrangement). Also, when in the interactive mode, APL displays the value of the most recently entered expression:

```
      1 2.0 3E‾4 ‾5e‾6
1 2 0.0003 ‾0.000005
```

Oddly, you cannot directly define a one-element array (it would be indistinguishable from a scalar), but you can specify a two-element array and truncate it.

APL strings are enclosed in single quotation marks and cannot have line breaks. If a quotation mark is an element of a string, it's represented as two consecutive quotation marks (compare Starset on page 173). A number included in a vector of strings remains a number: string vectors don't have to be homogeneous. By the way, the symbol ⍝, a thumbnail, denotes a comment throughout the line.

```
      'I am a string' ⍝ 13 elements: 'I', ' ', 'a', 'm', ' ', ...
I am a string
      'Me, ''too''' ⍝ 9 elements: 'M', 'e', ' ', '''', ...
Me, 'too'
      'I' 'am' 'a' 'vector' 'of' 'strings' ⍝ 6 elements: 'I', 'am', ...
I am a vector of strings
      'Me,' 2 ⍝ 2 elements: 'Me', 2
Me, 2
```

You can assign variable names to scalars, vectors, and higher-dimensional arrays (the operation known in APL literature as *specification* and *respecification*). A variable name is any combination of letters, underlined letters (obsolete), digits, an underscore, ∆, or ∆ (also obsolete). However, it cannot begin with a digit, S∆, or T∆ (the latter two are reserved for debugging). Variable names are case-sensitive. The assignment function is the left arrow ←.

```
      dataSize←32
      dataSize
32
      DATASIZE
VALUE ERROR
      DATASIZE
      ^
      Data←1 2 3
      Data
1 2 3
```

All APL variables, unless declared local (see Creating User-Defined Functions, on page 94), are global and available to all functions. Once "specified," a global variable becomes a part of a *workspace*—a container for variables, functions, and other objects that the user creates and interacts with during a session (user-defined functions are also stored in workspaces). Workspaces are persistent: they can be saved and later restored. Variables and functions can be listed and erased. Once erased from a workspace, a variable becomes unavailable (compare operator del in Python):

```
      )VARS
Data    dataSize
      )ERASE ata ⍝ Intentional mistake
NOT ERASED: ata
      )ERASE Data
      )VARS
dataSize
      )CLEAR
CLEAR WS
```

Commands whose names begin with a right parenthesis (such as)CLEAR) are system commands. Unlike variable names, they are case-insensitive, but we'll type them in uppercase to emphasize their significance.

Congratulations on your first APL experience! Have some rest, but remember to log off:

```
    )OFF
Goodbye.
Session duration: 59.4107 seconds
```

In the era of the mighty ancient mainframes and remote terminals, a failure to log off might have resulted in a hefty bill!

Executing Scalar Operations

All APL executable units are called functions, even if they're known as operators in other languages (for example, + and *). Many functions have a unary (*monadic*, only with the right argument) and a binary (*dyadic*, with both arguments) form. Function calls can also be nullary (*niladic*, no arguments). All functions are right-associative—executed from right to left, and this is another catch. What do you think is the result of 10-5-3-1? No, it's not 1.

```
    10-5-3-1 ⍝ 10-(5-(3-1))
7
```

If you don't like the default evaluation order, use parentheses.

```
    ((10-5)-3)-1
1
```

The right associativity rule may cause unpleasant surprises that are hard to detect and defuse (here and later, the symbol ⇒ is not a part of APL but shows that one expression follows from the other):

```
    1<5<10 ⍝ 1<(5<10)  ⇒ 1<1 ⇒ 0
0
    0=1=2 ⍝ 0=(1=2)  ⇒ 0=0 ⇒ 1; really?
1
```

Many APL functions behave as intuitively expected, at least partially (for example, +-><=). The table on page 83 gives examples of some unexpectedly behaving functions.

The question mark function needs some further explanation. In its unary form ?N, it produces a random number from 1 to N, inclusive. N can be a scalar or a vector. The example in the table is just an example. You will likely get a different result when you run ?2 3 4 yourself. In the binary form K?N, the function

Unary		Binary	
Signum	×ˉ1 2 4 ⇒ ˉ1 1 1	Multiplication	2×ˉ1 2 4 ⇒ ˉ2 4 6
Reciprocal	÷ˉ1 2 4 ⇒ ˉ1 0.5 0.25	Division	2÷ˉ1 2 4 ⇒ ˉ2 1 0.5
Abs. value	|ˉ1 2 4 ⇒ 1 2 4	Remainder	4|ˉ1 2 4 ⇒ 3 2 0
Exponential	*ˉ1 2 4 ⇒ 0.37 7.39 54.60	Power	4*ˉ1 2 4 ⇒ ˉ4 16 256
Nat. logarithm	⍟1 2 4 ⇒ 0 0.69 1.39	Any logarithm	4⍟1 2 4 ⇒ 0 0.5 1
Ceiling	⌈1 1.5 1 1.5 ⇒ 1 2 2	Maximum	1.5⌈1 1.5 1 1.5 ⇒ 1.5 1.5 1 1.5
Floor	⌊1 1.5 1 1.5 ⇒ 1 1 1	Minimum	1.5⌊1 1.5 1 1.5 ⇒ 1 1.5 1.5
Factorial	!2 3 4 ⇒ 2 6 24	Combination	2!2 3 4 ⇒ 1 3 6
Random	?2 3 4 ⇒ 1 1 3	Deal	2?4 ⇒ 2 4

deals, without replacement, K random numbers from 1 to N. The argument N must be a scalar or one-element vector.

In an expression X op Y, X can be a scalar, and Y can be either a scalar or a vector. In the latter case, APL "automatically" applies the function op to each pair of X and Y_i, as if in a loop, and creates a new vector. Such implicit looping operations are called vectorized. You can also apply binary vectorized operations to pairs of vectors and higher-dimensional arrays as long as their *ranks* (numbers of dimensions) and dimensions are equal:

```
      A←1 2 3
      B←3 2 1
      A+B
4 4 4
      A*B ⍝ Exponentiation, not multiplication!
1 4 3
      A⌈B
3 2 3
      A≠B
1 0 1
```

Vectorized operations dramatically reduce the need for loops to the extent that APL provides limited support for the latter. A hardcore APL programmer uses little or no loops!

A Fuzzy Note

 APL assumes that if two numbers are numerically close, they're equal. The relational functions ≤, <, =, >, ≥, ≠, and ≡ act accordingly. The measure of the smallest distinguishable difference is called *fuzz*. By default, the fuzz is equal to 10^{-13}. You can use the fuzz by setting the workspace indicator)FUZZ (APL\360) or the ⎕CT (comparison tolerance) variable in GNU APL.

A Fuzzy Note

```
        1=1+1E¯13
1
        1=1+9E¯12
0
```

The concept of the fuzzy comparison is often consistent with the users' expectations but is mathematically questionable. If you're concerned about precision, use integer numbers.

The equality and inequality functions = and ≠ work only on the objects of the same rank and dimensions. In particular, you cannot use them to check if two strings or arrays are equal or not equal unless the strings are of the same length. For more flexible comparison, you need functions match ≡ and non-match ("natch") ≠.

```
      1 2 3≠1 2
LENGTH ERROR
      1 2 3≠1 2
      ^       ^
      1 2 3≢1 2
1
```

Both functions are later additions to the language made in 1971. We can only guess how APL programmers compared strings before then.

Compared to other mainstream programming languages, APL supports Boolean operations NOR (⍱) and NAND (⍲) but does not support XOR and XNOR. The operations NOT (~), OR (∨), and AND (∧) work as expected, except that you must carefully watch the order of their execution. Can you automate an entrance gate of an American bar serving alcoholic beverages? (Anyone who enters must be at least 21 years old and have a driver's license as a proof.)

```
      AGES←21 18 20 21 22 17 ⍝ Some are younger, some are older
      HAVE_LICENSE←1 1 0 0 0 1 ⍝ Some do, some don't
      MAY_DRINK←AGES≥21∧HAVE_LICENSE ⍝ Some may, some may not
      MAY_DRINK
1 0 1 1 1 0
```

But what if you want to know if the whole gang is welcome in the bar? Then you need to reduce a Boolean vector to one Boolean value or, in general, reduce any vector to one value.

Mastering Array Operations

Let's first automate vector and other array creating because typing multidimensional structures on the interpreter's command line, even if for testing purposes, is bothersome.

Generate Indexes and Index Arrays

The unary function ⍳N (literally the Greek letter iota) creates a vector of N consecutive integer numbers between 0 and N-1 or 1 and N. The function is called an *index generator*. The first element of the vector is determined by the *index origin* stored in the workspace indicator)ORIGIN (classical APL\360) or system variable ⎕IO (GNU APL; the box before IO is really a box, not a placeholder for a missing character). The variable can be only 0 or 1.

```
      ⍳5 ⍝ The default value of ⎕IO is 1, courtesy of FORTRAN
1 2 3 4 5
      ⎕IO←0 ⍝ or )ORIGIN 0
      ⍳5
0 1 2 3 4
```

The same system variable controls array indexing: FORTRAN-style (starting from 1) vs. C-style (starting from 0). Don't be fooled by the name; the C language appeared when APL was already ten years old! However, regarding the ravel (traversal) order, APL is on the C side: the last (columns) index changes faster than the row index, which changes faster than the plane index, and so forth. In FORTRAN, the first index is the fastest to change.

Index Generator

The index generator ⍳N loosely corresponds to the range(1,N+1) or range(N) function in Python, except that the latter is indeed a generator and produces indexes on demand, not all at once.

Expression ⍳0 produces an empty array of size zero. This array is peculiar: its rank also equals zero, yet it's not a scalar whose rank is undefined.

Empty or not, an array can be assigned to a variable and used in any legal arithmetic, logical, or relational operation. For example, you may want to check membership—learn if a specific element belongs to the array:

```
      IDS←⍳5
      ¯3∊IDS
0
      3∊IDS
1
```

The element is in the array, but where? The friendly *alter ego* of iota, the index-of function HιN, calculates the index of a needle N in the haystack H. The index is reported in accordance with the)ORIGIN. If the needle isn't found, its index is assumed to be just outside the haystack—the largest H index plus one:

```
     IDS←ι5
     IDSι3
3
     IDSι¯3 ⍝ ¯3 not found, index is 5+1
6
     3ιIDS ⍝ 3 is in 3 but 1, 2, 4, and 5 are not
2 2 1 2 2
```

Now, why not replace the element that was found with the one that was not?

```
     IDS←ι5
     IDS[3]
3
     IDS[IDSι3]←¯3
     IDS
1 2 ¯3 4 5
     IDS[3]
¯3
```

The good old 100 percent ASCII-compatible square bracket indexing function [] works in APL like in C, Java, or Python (save for the)ORIGIN thing), both on the left and right sides of an assignment statement.

Reshape

Say you want to beat IBM Deep Blue with its own APL, and for that matter, you need an 8×8 chessboard, also known as a two-dimensional array. APL says, create a 64-element vector and make it square (reshape it, or "restructure" in APL-speak).

The binary function SρA (literally the Greek letter rho) changes the shape of the existing data array A according to the specification of vector S. The size of S equals the rank of the desired reshaped array. Each element of S specifies the size of the new array along the corresponding dimension. For example, S←8 8 specifies a square, 8×8 two-dimensional matrix, just what you need for a chessboard. Likewise, S←2 2 2 2 describes a four-dimensional 2×2×2×2 hypercube with two elements along each dimension (a *tesseract*).

The following code fragment builds an 8×8 chessboard of 1s two ways (not exactly what you want, but close enough). It generates a vector of 64 consecutive

—And He Built a Crooked House—

Robert Heinlein, an American sci-fi writer, wrote his short story —And He Built a Crooked House— in 1941. The story takes place in a fancy experimental three-dimensional building in Los Angeles. As a result of an earthquake, the structure collapses into a four-dimensional tesseract. An APL programmer would explain that unfortunate event as an application of the ρ function.

numbers and compares each number to 0. Since all numbers are strictly positive, all logical conditions are true, and that's how you get the ones.

```
      BOARD←8 8ρ(ι64)>0 ⍝ Either this way
      BOARD←8 8ρ0<ι64   ⍝ Or this way
      BOARD
1 1 1 1 1 1 1 1
1 1 1 1 1 1 1 1
1 1 1 1 1 1 1 1
1 1 1 1 1 1 1 1
1 1 1 1 1 1 1 1
1 1 1 1 1 1 1 1
1 1 1 1 1 1 1 1
1 1 1 1 1 1 1 1
```

Notice how the expression ι64>0, without the parentheses, is wrong: it compares 64 and 0 (the result is 1) and then generates a single-element vector. Right associativity is no joke!

It's time to unleash the full power of APL and create the "checkered" chessboard. Initialize a vector of row markers alternating between 0 and 1 every eight elements. Initialize a vector of column markers alternating between 0 and 1 at every element. Combine the two vectors with an *exclusive or* operation, A^B. APL does not directly support the latter, but you can use the equivalence A^B=(A∧~B)∨(B∧~A) ("either A or B, but not both nor neither"). Note that the first index in a two-dimensional array refers to a row, and the second refers to a column.

```
      LINEAR←ι64
      COLUMNS←2|LINEAR
      ROWS←2|⌈LINEAR÷8
      CHECKERED←(ROWS∧~COLUMNS)∨(COLUMNS∧~ROWS)
      BOARD←8 8ρCHECKERED
0 1 0 1 0 1 0 1
1 0 1 0 1 0 1 0
0 1 0 1 0 1 0 1
1 0 1 0 1 0 1 0
```

```
0 1 0 1 0 1 0 1
1 0 1 0 1 0 1 0
0 1 0 1 0 1 0 1
1 0 1 0 1 0 1 0
      BOARD[1;2] ⍝ 2D index
1
```

As an extension of single-index bracketing, you can list more than one index to be extracted, and as many times as needed, as in the following example:

```
      A←3 3⍴⍳9
      A[1 3;] ⍝ rows #1 and #3, all columns
1 2 3
7 8 9
      A[;1 3 1 3] ⍝ all rows, columns #1, #3, #1 again, #3 again
1 3 1 3
4 6 4 6
7 9 7 9
      A[1 3;1 3 1 3] ⍝ rows #1 and #3, columns #1, #3, #1, #3
1 3 1 3
7 9 7 9
```

Multidimensional Brackets

 APL brackets with more than one index per dimension loosely correspond to *smart indexing* in NumPy. An empty index is a Python equivalent of the slice [:].

When used in a unary way, the function ⍴A calculates the shape of A. Apply it twice to obtain the rank of A.

```
      BOARD←8 8⍴⍳64
      ⍴BOARD
8 8
      ⍴⍴BOARD ⍝ A vector of two elements
2
      ⍴⍴⍴BOARD ⍝ A vector of one element
1
      ⍴1 ⍝ The dimensions of a scalar are an empty vector. Cannot see it.

      ⍴⍴1 ⍝ An empty vector is a zero-dimensional object!
0
```

One of the most helpful features of the binary S⍴A is its ability to go outside the box. The number of elements in A does not have to match the product of elements in S. If the latter is smaller than the former, A is truncated to fit its new shape. Alternatively, if the new shape is bigger than the original, A is repeated to fill it. In particular, if A is a scalar, the scalar is replicated as needed:

```
      3 3⍴⍳64 ⍝ Shrinking: 64 is too many
1 2 3
4 5 6
7 8 9
      3 3⍴7 ⍝ Expansion: one is too few
7 7 7
7 7 7
7 7 7
      3 3⍴⍳6 ⍝ Expansion: ⍳6 is too few, too
1 2 3
4 5 6
1 2 3
```

You'll use this feature in Creating User-Defined Functions, on page 94, to create a better version of the chessboard.

Catenate and Ravel

The binary function X,Y ("comma") catenates arrays X and Y. The arrays must have the same first dimension. (The sidebar below addresses the controversy of catenate vs. concatenate.)

```
      (3⍴¯1),3 3⍴⍳9
¯1 1 2 3
¯1 4 5 6
¯1 7 8 9
```

To Con or Not to Con?

The word *catenate* means "to add pieces (arrays) together." The prefix *con-* introduces a flavor of mutability: "to add pieces (arrays) to self, thus modifying self." Although Google reports 133,000,000 hits for "concatenate" and only 278,000 hits for "catenate," let's stick to the official APL terminology in which arrays are catenated.

Note that a prominent Unix command for combining files is correctly abbreviated as cat, not con or concat. However, the equally prominent standard C library function strcat() should have been called strconcat() because it modifies the first argument.

Use the comma to build strings (character arrays) out of constituents. Speaking of which, here's APL's long overdue "Hello, world!" program:

```
      GREETING←'Hello'
      WHO←'world'
      GREETING,', ',WHO,'!'
Hello, world!
```

Comma

Function "comma" in APL loosely corresponds to the "plus" operator in Python when the latter is applied to strings, lists, and tuples, as in "Hello, "+"world" or [1,2,3]+[4,5,6].

Catenate's sister unary function ,A ravels the array A by flattening it into a vector. In a sense, it undoes the results of restructuring the vector into a multidimensional array.

```
      ,3 3⍴⍳9
1 2 3 4 5 6 7 8 9
      9⍴3 3⍴⍳9 ⍝ Same as above, but with ⍴
1 2 3 4 5 6 7 8 9
      ⍴'Hello' 'World' ⍝ Create a vector of two words
2
      ⍴'Hello','World' ⍝ Create a vector of ten characters
10
```

Compress, Expand, and Reduce

Compression and reduction functions "deflate" an array by eliminating select rows and columns or converting the whole array to a single number. The expansion function, on the contrary, "inflates" it by inserting rows, columns, and hyperplanes.

The compression function IDX/A selects the columns from array A based on the Boolean vector IDX. Vector IDX serves as a mask—a column from A is selected if the corresponding element of IDX is true:

```
      1 0 1/3 3⍴⍳9
1 3
4 6
7 9
      1 0/2 2 2⍴⍳8
1
3

5
7
      0/⍳8 ⍝ You pushed too hard and got an empty vector!
```

Conversely, the expansion function IDX\A inserts new columns filled with zeros or space characters into array A according to the expansion Boolean vector IDX. Vector IDX must be longer than the first dimension of A. A column is inserted into A if the corresponding element of IDX is false:

```
      1 0 1 0 1\3 3ρι9
1 0 2 0 3
4 0 5 0 6
7 0 8 0 9
```

Curiously, the name APL\360 had a hidden meaning—"APL expands IBM OS/360." However, the expression APL\360 is illegal in APL (it causes value error), and so is 'APL'\360 (it causes domain error).

As a side note, the unary transposition function ⍉A transposes the array A (swaps its axes). Combining it with the expansion function creates an exquisite binary N×N frame:

```
      N←3
      BORDER←(N+2)ρ1
      BORDER[1]←0
      BORDER[N+2]←0 ⍝ Prepare a vector 0111...1110
      ~BORDER\⍉BORDER\N Nρ1 ⍝ Expand, transpose, expand, invert
1 1 1 1 1
1 0 0 0 1
1 0 0 0 1
1 0 0 0 1
1 1 1 1 1
```

Compression Function

 The compression function IDX/A corresponds to Boolean-array indexing in NumPy, A[IDX], where IDX is the same Boolean vector.

So compression, expansion, and reshaping partially allow you to restructure arrays. But what about *ultimate restructuring*—converting an array to a single number—say, to the sum of all elements? Enter reduction.

The reduction function op/A is a form of compression function that requires a binary function op as its left argument rather than a value. The function applies op to the last two elements of A, then to the third element from the end and the result of the previous operation, and so on:

```
      +/ι4 ⍝ (1+(2+(3+4)))
10
      ×/ι4 ⍝ (1×(2×(3×4)))
24
      -/ι4 ⍝ (1-(2-(3-4))), not 1-2-3-4!
¯2
      ÷/ι4 ⍝ (1÷(2÷(3÷4))), not 1÷2÷3÷4!
0.375
```

The Starset language that supports similar functionality doesn't allow reduction with asymmetric functions (see Parallel Loops, on page 188). The other functions include maximum ⌈, minimum ⌊, and logical functions ∧∨∀, as in the following examples:

```
      ⌈/⍳4 ⍝ The larges element
4
      ⌊/⍳4 ⍝ The smallest element
1
      ∧/1 1 1 1 0 0 0 0 ⍝ All ones?
0
      ∨/1 1 1 1 0 0 0 0 ⍝ Any ones?
1
```

Take and Drop

The take and drop functions N↑A and N↓A select subvectors, substrings, and subarrays from vectors, strings, and arrays. The take function takes (hence the name) the first N elements of A. The drop function drops (hence the name) the first N elements of A and returns the rest of A. If A isn't long enough, it's padded with 0s or spaces.

```
      4↑3↓⍳100
4 5 6 7
      14↑3↓'programming'
gramming
      ⍴14↑3↓'programming' ⍝ It is longer than you think!
14
```

If A is an array, then N must be a vector of size ⍴A.

```
      4 4↑3 3↓10 10⍴⍳100
34 35 36 37
44 45 46 47
54 55 56 57
64 65 66 67
```

In the latter example, you drop the first three rows and the first three columns and then take the next four rows and the next four columns.

Take and Drop

 A pair of take and drop functions loosely corresponds to Python's slicing operator [x:y]. The functions are not commutative: N↑M↓A is equivalent to A[M:M+N+1], but M↓N↑A is equivalent to A[M:N+1] (unless M>N).

Performing Input and Output

In the spirit of other interpreted languages, APL is based on a REPL loop: read a command, evaluate it, print the results, and loop, making the simplest "Hello, world!" program trivial (the "Hello, world!" code on page 89 is a joke!). However, implicit printing doesn't work when the result is assigned to a variable. To force the printout, assign the result to the system variable □ known as "quad." (The box is really a box, not a placeholder for a missing character; see comment on page 85.) Non-incidentally, the variable looks like a screen or terminal window because it symbolizes your computer's screen.

```
      A←10 ⍝ No printout
      A ⍝ Implicit printout
10
      □←A←10 ⍝ Explicit printout
10
```

The last statement in the preceding code snippet is an example of a multiple assignment. In general, avoid multiple assignments; combined with the right associativity, their results may be pretty cryptic. However, they're fully justified in the case of an assignment to a quad.

Another system variable ⍞ ("quote-quad," a quad with a quotation mark inside) behaves like a quad but doesn't insert unsolicited line breaks. Use it to output several results on the same line in batch mode.

The same two system variables are used for input. A quad pauses the program execution and displays a read prompt □: (not a function). It expects you to type any valid APL command, including numbers, arrays, or quoted strings. The input is evaluated and used at once. You can put □ anywhere where a variable or a literal expression is expected.

```
      □←A←□ ⍝ Read input with echo
□:
      1 2 3
1 2 3
      ⍴A
3
      □+□ ⍝ Read two expressions and add them
□:
      123
□:
      456
579
```

The latter example may confuse the user because the same prompt is shown twice. Display additional instructions before asking for more than one input.

The Quad

The quad function ⎕ corresponds to input() in Python 2.7 or a combination of input() and eval() in Python 3.x. Use it with care. The quote-quad function ⍞ corresponds to raw_input() in Python 2.7 or input() in Python 3.x. It's always safe to use.

A quote-quad behaves like ⎕ but doesn't display the prompt or interpret the input. Anything you type in is treated as a string, even if it's not quoted (and if it is, the quotes become a part of the string).

```
      STR←⍞
Mary had a little lamb
      ρSTR
22
      EMPTY←⍞ ⍝ Simply press Enter

      ρEMPTY
0
```

I hear you saying, but what about file I/O? Sorry, no such thing in APL\360. Use workspaces, explained on page 108.

Creating User-Defined Functions

APL built-in (*primitive*) functions are powerful and priceless but they can do only that much. For everything else, you should write user-defined functions. Technically, they are programmer-defined, but back in the 1960s there was little difference between users and programmers.

Define and Call Functions

An APL function definition consists of the function name, optional result, up to two formal arguments, global and optional local variables, and a body. A definition begins and ends with the symbol ∇ ("nabla" or "del"). Let's create a function that takes no arguments (a niladic function) and returns nothing. Such a function manipulates, and is manipulated through, only the global variables. Our first function, called CHECK_LOGIN, checks the global variables LOGIN and PASSWORD; it sets the global variable LOGIN_OK if they match the internally stored literal constants, which is hardly a useful exercise but a good starting point.

```
      ∇CHECK_LOGIN
[1] LOGIN_OK←(LOGIN≡'admin')∧PASSWORD≡'foobar'
[2] ∇
```

Upon entering a function definition with ∇, APL enumerates each line. Line numbers are used for editing (Edit Functions, on page 96) and flow control (Branching, on page 97). Once created, a user-defined function can be called like any other system function, except its name is usually humane.

```
        LOGIN←'admin'
        PASSWORD←'password' ⍝ Oh, no!
        CHECK_LOGIN
        LOGIN_OK
0
        PASSWORD←'foobar'
        CHECK_LOGIN
        LOGIN_OK
1
```

When asked for, APL happily confirms the function's existence.

```
        )FNS ⍝ Show the list of all defined functions
CHECK_LOGIN
```

Functions with implicit arguments and results have limited applicability because they depend on appropriately named global variables and cannot be called recursively. The following, more flexible function is monadic (takes one argument) and explicitly returns the result. Furthermore, it declares a local variable to protect the global namespace from pollution. It's based on the chessboard code on page 87.

```
        ∇BOARD←CHESSBOARD N;ROW
[1]  ROW←(N⍴⍳2)-1
[2]  BOARD←N N⍴ROW,~ROW
[3]  ∇
        MY64←CHESSBOARD 8
        MY64
0 1 0 1 0 1 0 1
1 0 1 0 1 0 1 0
0 1 0 1 0 1 0 1
1 0 1 0 1 0 1 0
0 1 0 1 0 1 0 1
1 0 1 0 1 0 1 0
0 1 0 1 0 1 0 1
```

The variable N is the right formal argument (a monadic function doesn't have a left argument). The variable ROW, separated by a semicolon, is a local variable. It is deactivated immediately after exiting the function. Any number of semicolon-separated local variables is allowed if they fit on one line. By APL's scoping rules, a local variable in function F is global in function G if F calls G.

The result is in the variable BOARD to the left of the function name, separated by the assignment symbol, which does not constitute an assignment operation here. The function returns the most recent value of BOARD. A similar mechanism is used in Starset, but the result variable name must be the same as the function name (Functions, on page 191).

In the final example, a dyadic function DIVISIBLE_BY returns a subvector of vector V containing the numbers divisible by N:

```
      ∇RESULT←V DIVISIBLE_BY N
[1]   REMAINDERS←N|V
[2]   ZEROREMS←0=REMAINDERS
[3]   RESULT←ZEROREMS/V ⍝ Compression!
[4]   ∇
      STEP_17←(ι100) DIVISIBLE_BY 17
      STEP_17
17 34 51 68 85
```

The argument becomes a global variable if the function fails. It retains its most recently assigned value and cannot be erased with the)ERASE system command.

You can pass more than two arguments to a function but must pack them into an array in the caller and extract them in the function.

Edit Functions

APL\360 doesn't store function definitions in files (see Working with Workspaces, on page 108). An APL terminal has some editing facilities that allow you to edit a function live ("perform open-heart surgery"). Editing is limited to removing or inserting a line and replacing a line with another line.

First, open the function you want to edit by typing ∇ followed by the function name. You can view an open function with a quad [□]. To save a revised function, close it with ∇. To exit the editor without saving, type [→].

Suppose you implemented a trivial dyadic function CAT that catenates its operands:

```
      ∇Z←A CAT B
[1]   AB←A,B
[2]   Z←AB∇
      'hello,' CAT 'world!'
hello,world!
```

You instantly realize that the function isn't perfect. It has an unnecessary assignment (lines 1 and 2 can be combined) and doesn't explain what it does (you're pedantic). These two problems are easy to fix, explained in the code comments here:

```
      ∇CAT ⍝ Open the function
[3] [□] ⍝ Print it out
    ∇
[0]   Z←A CAT B ⍝ Line #0 is the header (can be edited, too)
[1]   AB←A,B
[2]   Z←AB
    ∇
[3] [1] Z←A,B ⍝ Overwrite line #1
[2] [∆2]  ⍝ Delete line #2
[2] [0.5] 'CATENATING...' ⍝ Insert a new line between #0 and #1
[2] ∇ ⍝ Close the function
      'hello,' CAT 'world!'
CATENATING...
hello,world!
```

If you got used to Microsoft VS Code or even vi, you may find the built-in APL editor somewhat inconvenient. But it is better than the ancient command-line editors ed for Unix/Linux and edlin for MS-DOS. Someone should write a book about seven obscure text editors and start with ed and edlin!

When editing a function, be aware that the line numbers in APL are not just numbers. They're mainly used as targets for branches—low-level flow control operations. If line numbers change, branching operations may need to be changed too. The following section outlines the problem and proposes a solution.

Branching

"Branching" is a fancy name for the infamous GOTO statement. To be fair, it became infamous only after Edsger Dijkstra, one of the founding fathers of modern computer science, published his open letter *"Go To Statement Considered Harmful" [Dij68]* in 1968. Before that, GOTO had been considered a preferred way to control program execution flow. One can prove that GOTO suffices for implementing conditional statements, loops, and choices. A powerful tool it is, so don't blame APL for depending on branching.

You can use the branch arrow →L only in a function definition, not in the interaction mode. The function depends on line numbers and labels (neither available in the interaction mode). So, first, a word about labels.

An APL label is a case-sensitive alphanumeric string ending with a colon and optionally followed by an APL statement. A label is an alias for the line number on which it is placed. You don't have to use labels (line numbers are technically as good as labels), but labels add clarity to your code and make it easier to modify. The L in →L is a label or a line number.

When executed, the branch statement transfers control to the designated line. You can start with a ridiculous example: two functions with infinite loops. The functions differ in using line numbers vs. labels for branching. Call these functions at your own risk!

```
      ∇BUSY2
[1]   'HELLO, WORLD'
[2]   →1
[3]   ∇
      ∇BUSY1
[1]   AGAIN: 'HELLO, WORLD'
[2]   →AGAIN ⍝ Go to label AGAIN, currently on line 1
[3]   ∇
```

The preceding code is also an example of unconditional branching: the branching function's destination is defined when writing the program. Unconditional branching has two special cases. If the destination line number does not exist (0 or greater than the largest line number), the function exits and returns to the caller, like this LAZY function:

```
      ∇LAZY
[1]   →0 ⍝ Get out of here!
[2]   'HELLO, WORLD'
[3]   ∇
```

The other special case is branching to an empty array (for example, to ⍳0). Such a branch is ignored, and the function proceeds to the following line. However, if the array isn't empty, the program proceeds to the line whose number is the at the head of the array:

```
      ∇GOODFUN
[1]   →⍳0 ⍝ Branch to an empty array? Oh, just ignore it.
[2]   'HELLO, WORLD'
[3]   ∇
```

Branching through an array head represents a case of a computable branch statement. The content of the array is dynamic and can be controlled by shifting ("rotating," on page 104), compression, or some other mechanism. For example, consider a function that calculates a square root of number A via Newton's method—$x_1=1$; $x_{n+1}=(x_n+A/x_n)/2$:

```
      ∇Y←SQRT A;X;ACC
[1] X←1 ⍝ Initial approximation
[2] Y←(X+A÷X)÷2 ⍝ Iteration
[3] ACC←|Y-X ⍝ Quality control
[4] X←Y
```

```
[5]  →(ACC>1E⁻7)/2  ⍝ Branching
[6]  ∇
     SQRT 81
9
```

On line 5, the achieved accuracy ACC is compared to the target value of 10^{-7}. The Boolean expression is either true (1) or false (0). Therefore, the compression function (which looks like division but isn't) is either 1/2 (the first element "of" scalar 2 is 2 itself) or 0/2 (the zeroth element "of" the same scalar is empty). The function branches, respectively, to line 2 (loop) or the following line (exit).

For your reference, here's the same code in the C language, written and formatted to resemble the APL original as closely as possible:

```
double sqrt(double A) { double Y, X, ACC;
       X = 1;
line2: Y = (X + A / X) / 2;
       ACC = abs(Y - X);
       X = Y;
       if(ACC > 1e-7) goto line2;
       return Y;
}
```

Yes, the C language still supports the goto statement. No, you shouldn't use it: "Go To Statement [still] Considered Harmful."

You're ready to write something not trivial—such as a package to generate the first N prime numbers. The package includes two functions: DIVISORS to obtain a list of divisors and PRIMES to repeat DIVISORS in a loop. The second function is insanely inefficient, but it works.

apl/prime.apl
```
        ∇RET←DIVISORS N;NUMS
[1]  NUMS←⍳N ⍝ All numbers from 1 to N
[2]  RET←(0=NUMS|N)/NUMS ⍝ Select the numbers that divide into N evenly
[3]  ∇
⍝        DIVISORS 111
⍝1 3 37 111

        ∇RET←PRIMES N;K;DIVS
[1]  K←1
[2]  RET←⍳0 ⍝ Initialize an empty list
➤ [3]  DIVS←DIVISORS K
➤ [4]  RET←RET,(2=⍴DIVS)/K ⍝ Save the numbers that have two divisors
➤ [5]  K←K+1
➤ [6]  →(K≤N)/3 ⍝ If not done, repeat from line 3
[7]  ∇
⍝        PRIMES 55
⍝2 3 5 7 11 13 17 19 23 29 31 37 41 43 47 53
```

The loop in the function PRIMES includes lines 3–6 (highlighted). In the language of modern structured programming, it's a do-while loop; it executes the body at least once and only then checks the termination condition.

APL branching is confusing (had APL been "obscure" because of branching?), but some branching-related idioms may strengthen your confidence. Consider the Boolean expression XrY, where r is a dyadic Boolean function and X and Y are its appropriate operands. Then the following three commands branch to the line S if XrY is true and proceed to the following command otherwise:

```
[1] →(XrY)/S ⍝ Select S or empty array through compression
[2] →(XrY)ρS ⍝ Reshape S to a one-element vector or empty array
[3] →S×ι(XrY) ⍝ Multiply S by a 1 or an empty array
```

These commands are equivalent to if(r(X,Y)) goto S; in C. If you want to include an else branch (from a vector of destinations S1 and S2), here are some two-way branching idioms for you, equivalent to if(r(X,Y)) goto S1; else goto S2;.

```
[1] →(S1,S2)[1+XrY] ⍝ Indexing
[2] →((XrY),~(XrY))/S1,S2 ⍝ Compression
```

Finally, if you have many choices based on the integer value N (as in a switch statement in C) arranged in a vector L, look no further than the next three "switching" idioms, even though the rotation and drop functions ⌽ and ↓ will not be known until Adding More Array Operations, on page 101.

```
[1] →L[N] ⍝ Indexing
[2] →(N-1)⌽L ⍝ Rotation
[3] →(N-1)↓L ⍝ Drop
```

The nonrecursive function for calculating the first N Fibonacci numbers illustrates many uses of branching, including error handling (line 1), exiting the function (line 3), and do-while loop organization (highlighted lines 6–9).

```
apl/fibonacci.apl
      ∇L←FIB N;I
[1] →(N≥2)/4 ⍝ Is N large enough? If not, exit
[2] 'VALUE ERROR'
[3] →0 ⍝ Yes, exit
[4] L←1 1 ⍝ The first two numbers
[5] I←2
➤ [6] →(I≥N)/0 ⍝ If done, exit
➤ [7] L←L,L[(ρL)-1]+L[ρL]
➤ [8] I←I+1
➤ [9] →6 ⍝ Rinse and repeat
[10]∇
⍝       FIB 10
⍝ 1 1 2 3 5 8 13 21 34 55
```

Function TABLE displays a table of first, second, and third degrees of the first
N natural numbers and illustrates using labels instead of line numbers. The
loop is also highlighted.

apl/table.apl
```
      ∇TABLE N;I;TAB
[1]  →(N≤0)/BADARG
[2]  TAB←ι0
[3]  I←0
[4]  LOOP: →(N<I←I+1)/DONE
[5]  TAB←TAB,I,(I*2),(I*3)
[6]  →LOOP
[7]  DONE: (N,3)ρTAB
[8]  →0
[9]  BADARG: 'VALUE ERROR'
[10]∇
⍝        TABLE 3
⍝ 1 1  1
⍝ 2 4  8
⍝ 3 9 27
```

Have you noticed an embedded assignment statement on line 4? It's executed
before the comparison and is an equivalent of C's N<++I. Can you write an
equivalent of C's N<I++? The answer is in the footnote.[4]

Now that you know how to build functions yourself, you can look into more
prebuilt array operations, including matrix products, string manipulation,
multidimensional array reduction, and string interpretation.

Adding More Array Operations

Two-dimensional matrices are special in science and technology. Unlike vectors
alone, two-dimensional matrix equations are powerful to describe most processes that surround us (including infection diffusion in social networks).
Unlike three- and higher-dimensional arrays, they're still easy to visualize
and comprehend. Not surprisingly, APL provides special support for two-
dimensional arrays.

Let's revisit the reduction explained on page 91. In the case of a vector, the
reduction function op/A applies the function op to all elements. In the case of
a matrix, there are two ways to reduce: row-wise and column-wise. Unless
the matrix is symmetric, the outcomes will differ, and they will differ even
more in a three-or-more-dimensional case. To choose the direction of reduction, specify the dimension axis as the function modifier in square brackets:

---

4.   N<(I←I+1)-1

```
      A←3 3ρι9
      A
1 2 3
4 5 6
7 8 9
      +/A ⍝ Row sums (default)
6 15 24
      +/[2]A ⍝ Row sums (along the second dimension)
6 15 24
      +/[1]A ⍝ Column sums (along the first dimension)
12 15 18
      +⌿A ⍝ Column sums -- but why?
12 15 18
```

Axis Modifiers

 Axis modifiers are equivalent to the axis=n option in NumPy and Pandas. For example, given a two-dimensional array data, the following expression calculates the row sums: data.sum(axis=1). Naturally, Python axes are numbers starting from 0.

Being a careful reader, you must have noticed a previously unseen function op⌿A in the preceding interaction. The function doesn't have an axis modifier but still calculates column sums. The function is an abbreviated version of op/[1]A in the same spirit as op/A is an abbreviated version of op/[ρρA]A. A matrix has only two dimensions; both are equally important, and each deserves a separate function. That's the APL way.

Another function, scan op\A, also has two versions for the first and the last dimensions. It applies the function op to each element and the result of the previous application, calculating a sequence of partial results. Naturally, an axis modifier is also acceptable.

```
      +\A ⍝ Scan row-wise, same as +⍀[2]A
1  3  6
4  9 15
7 15 24
      +⍀A ⍝ Scan column-wise, same as +⍀[1]A
1  2  3
5  7  9
12 15 18
```

Incidentally, when applied to a vector of natural numbers, a multiplicative scan produces a vector of partial products, also known as factorials! However, the reduction is more efficient if you need just one factorial.

```
    ×\ι10  ⍝ Scan
1 2 6 24 120 720 5040 40320 362880 3628800
    ×/ι10  ⍝ Reduction
3628800
```

What Exclamation Point?

Earlier computer keyboards didn't have the factorial symbol—an exclamation point character. It was entered by typing the quote symbol ' and overtyping a decimal point . over it. I wish I could show you an example, but my keyboard doesn't allow overtyping.

The happy take/drop and reduce/scan pairs are invaluable for string manipulation. Here's how we strip Python-style comments from a line of Python code:

```
TXT←'print(''Hello, World!'') # Comments ## more comments'
CODE←+/0=+\'#'=TXT
CODE↑TXT
print('Hello, World!')
```

In brief, compare each character with a '#'; calculate the partial sums (they switch from 0 to >0 at the first instance of '#'); compare each partial sum to 0; add up; the sum is the number of characters to the left of the first '#'; take them!

In the context of our discovery of axis modifiers, the simple catenation comma function on page 89 shines in a new light. It can put string arrays side by side horizontally (the default behavior—you already know about that):

```
A←'Hello'
B←'world'
A,B
Helloworld
```

It can put them side by side vertically (along the new axis number 1.1):

```
A,[1.1]B
Hw
eo
lr
ll
od
```

And it can put one above the other (along the new axis 0.9):

```
A,[0.9]B
Hello
world
```

You see the same charming concept of fractional line numbers as in the section Edit Functions, on page 96. Perhaps "charming" isn't the word one expects to find in a computer programming book.

Reverse and Rotate

The monadic functions ⌽A and ⊖A reverse array A—flip it horizontally or vertically, respectively:

```
      ⌽⍳5
5 4 3 2 1
      ⌽3 3⍴⍳9
3 2 1
6 5 4
9 8 7
      ⊖3 3⍴⍳9
7 8 9
4 5 6
1 2 3
```

In the dyadic forms N⌽A and N⊖A, the same functions rotate (shift) the array by N positions sideways or vertically. The number of positions may be the same (if N is a scalar) or different for each row or column.

```
      2⌽⍳5
3 4 5 1 2
      (⍳3)⌽3 3⍴⍳9
2 3 1
6 4 5
7 8 9
      (⍳3)⊖3 3⍴⍳9
4 8 3
7 2 6
1 5 9
```

This little and not-so-clever palindrome checker is still smart enough to eliminate white spaces before testing but not intelligent enough to convert the text to lowercase or eliminate punctuation.

```
      TXT←'never odd or even'
      TXT←(TXT≠' ')/TXT
      ∧/TXT=⌽TXT
1
```

Linear Algebra

Linear algebra is a powerful foundation of modern science, technology, and engineering. Remember Matlab, the Matrix Laboratory? APL is a matrix laboratory too; it not only excels in linear algebra—it also expands its applications.

The dyadic function A∘.op B calculates the outer product of A and B. It applies the dyadic function op, either primitive or user-defined, to each pair of elements from A and B. In the following example, APL builds an array of the smallest elements in every combination of natural numbers from 1 to 4 and another array of the sums of such numbers. The sum is calculated in the user-defined dyadic function ADD:

```
      (ι4)∘.⌈ι4
1 2 3 4
2 2 3 4
3 3 3 4
4 4 4 4
      ∇Z←A ADD B
[1] Z←A+B ∇
      (ι4)∘.ADD ι4
2 3 4 5
3 4 5 6
4 5 6 7
5 6 7 8
```

A and B don't have to be vectors, don't have to be of the same rank and dimensions, and don't even have to be of the same data type. Here, one extracts every prefix of lengths 1 through 4 from the you-know-which-words:

```
      (ι4)∘.↑'hello' 'world'
h    w
he   wo
hel  wor
hell worl
```

To make the outer product look more practical, assume you have a highway connecting two major cities 100 kilometers apart. According to the map, there are ten towns on the highway whose coordinates are integer but otherwise look wholly random and even may coincide (don't ask!). What is the maximum distance between two towns?

You can solve the problem with APL in three simple steps. First, you need the "over-each" function A¨B that applies a monadic function A to each element of B—in our case, it draws ten random numbers from 1 to 100. Second, define the function X DIST Y, which calculates the distance between two towns. Finally, use the outer product to generate an array of all distances, flatten it, and reduce it to its maximal element.

```
      TOWNS←?¨10ρ100
      ∇D←X DIST Y
[1] D←|X-Y
[2] ∇
      ⌈/,TOWNS∘.DIST TOWNS ⍝ The result is, naturally, random
80
```

The Double-Dot

The dyadic function op¨A ("diaeresis," "dieresis," or "double-dot") is an equivalent of the map() operation found in Python and other functional languages.

The dyadic function A op1.op2 B calculates the inner product of A and B for the operations op1 and op2. The function op2 is applied to each pair of elements for each row in A and column in B. The function op1 further reduces the results to a single value. In its most familiar form, A+.×B, the inner product is the good old cross product of two vectors or matrix product of two matrices.

```
      VEC1←1 2 3
      VEC2←3 ‾3 1
      VEC1+.×VEC2
0
      B←2 3⍴⍳6
      A←3 2⍴⍳6
      A+.×B
9  12 15
19 26 33
29 40 51
      B+.×VEC1
14 32
```

In a more unorthodox example, the inner product checks if an array of 4-bit patterns A contains a 4-bit pattern P. The function compares P to each row of A bitwise and "and"s the results:

```
      A←4 4⍴1 0 0 1 1 0 1 1 0 0 1 1 1 1 1
      P←1 1 0 1
      +/A∧.=P
1
```

The "domino" function ⌹A (monadic) or B⌹A (dyadic) inverts the matrix A or divides A into the matrix or vector B. The function does not check if the inversion/division is possible. It reports a RANK ERROR if they're not, so you better be prepared.

By the way, you can now use APL to solve systems of linear equations like Ax=B. Naturally, in one line.

```
      A←3 3⍴1 1 6 ‾4 5 5 2 2
      B←2 31 13
      B⌹A ⍝ x
3 ‾2 1
      (⌹A)+.×B ⍝ Same x
3 ‾2 1
```

Sort

Forget bubble sort, insertion sort, selection sort, and even quick sort! APL has two monadic sorting functions, ⍋A ("grade-up") and ⍒A ("grade-down"). They compute an array of indexes of the elements of A in the order of increasing or decreasing values, respectively. You can use the computed arrays later for rearranging the original array.

```
      A←1 3 1 4 6 21
      ⍒A ⍝ The 6th element, 21, is the largest
6 5 4 2 1 3
      A[⍒A]
21 6 4 3 1 1
      A[⍋A]
1 1 3 4 6 21
```

But what about character strings? In APL\360, neither function officially supported character sorting. One needs to know character encoding—the numerical values of the characters—to compare characters. No universal encoding existed in 1962 (actually, not until 1987, when Xerox and Apple joined their effort to produce Unicode), which made sorting unpredictable. The introduction of ASCII and, later, Unicode laid a solid foundation for string ordering. Here's an example of how Galileo could have created his famous anagram *Altissimum planetam tergeminum observavi* ("*I have observed the highest three-form planet*") in APL:

```
      TXT←'ALTISSIMUM PLANETAM TERGEMINUM OBSERVAVI'
      TXT[⍋TXT]
AAAABEEEEGIIIILLMMMMMNNOPRRSSSTTTUUVV
```

No, he could not have—he lived before ASCII and Unicode!

Interpret Strings

Your APL story wouldn't be complete without some acquaintance with the "unquote" function, ⍎E. The function executes the literal APL expression E provided as a string as if typed on the command line.

A cute, though inefficient, example of using unquote is applying the trapezoidal rule for approximating a definite integral of a user-defined function. The function FUN is provided at runtime as the right argument. The left argument is an array containing the integration range endpoints and the number of subdivisions.

```
      ∇Z←RNG INTEGRATE FUN;X;RANGE;DX
[1]   RANGE←RNG[2]-RNG[1]
[2]   DX←RANGE÷RNG[3]
```

```
[3] X←RNG[1]+DX×¯.5+ιRNG[3]
[4] Z←DX×+/⍎FUN
[5] ∇
      0 1 10000 INTEGRATE 'X*2' ⍝ True answer: 1/3
0.3333333325
      0 (○2) 10000 INTEGRATE '1○X' ⍝ True answer: 0
¯2.543364949E¯16
```

Note that in the second test case, 1○X represents a *circular* function number 1 (the sine), and 2○ is 2π, as on page 78.

The Unquote Function

The unquote function ⍎E resembles the notorious Python function eval(), which you are strongly discouraged from using. However, unlike eval(), ⍎E is side-effect-free and is considered harmless.

APL provides a dozen other functions (such as circular functions ○, representation ⊤, base value ⊥, and interaction with the system ⎕). But now it's time to save your work.

Working with Workspaces

APL\360 wasn't just a programming language with an interpreter. It was meant to be a self-sufficient environment, not requiring an operating system and essentially becoming an operating system itself. APL developers could not and did not assume that the host operating system, if any, provided particular abstractions, such as processes and files. That's why APL doesn't support files as we know them today. Instead, it stores data and commands in abstract *workspaces*.

A workspace is a named opaque storage of all your functions and variables. Workspaces in APL loosely correspond to screens in classical Forth. Both are used for filesystem-independent long-term storage of data and commands. In general, you don't need to know its format—let the APL interpreter handle that. For example, GNU APL uses XML, but the original APL\360 relied on something else because XML specification was published only in 2006.

All workspaces together form a workspace library.

Create Workspaces

GNU APL assumes you've created a subdirectory called workspaces in your current working directory. The interpreter uses this subdirectory to store workspaces.

Suppose you defined the function INTEGRATE and the array RANGE that specifies the integration range (code on page 107). You can save the definitions into the workspace 'integrate' for future use with the command)SAVE. The command)LIB will show the workspace's name. Your work is safe; don't hesitate to log off.

```
      RANGE←0 (○2) 10000
      ∇Z←RNG INTEGRATE FUN;X;RANGE;DX
      ...
[5] ∇
      )SAVE 'integrate'
2023-04-14  02:45:49 (GMT-4)
      )LIB
'integrate'
      )OFF
```

When you come back, the workspace will still be in your library. Load it with the command)LOAD. Check the workspace identifier with)WSID to ensure that it's the proper workspace. Check the list of variables (it contains RANGE and INTEGRATE). Both items are ready for immediate use.

```
      )LIB
'integrate'
      )LOAD 'integrate'
SAVED 2023-40-14 20:45:49 (GMT-4)
      )WSID
IS 'integrate'
      )FNS
INTEGRATE
      )VARS
RANGE
      RANGE INTEGRATE '1○X'
¯2.543364949E¯16
      )DROP 'integrate'
2023-04-14  02:51:17 (GMT-4)
```

You can delete a workspace with)DELETE but think twice before you do. Once deleted, a workspace cannot be restored.

Writing Something Big

Now, get serious and write a helpful tool. What could be a better proof of the worth of the language?

Consider a *complex network*—a graph of nodes connected with edges (see *my other book [Zin18]* for a complete story). Say the network has 11 nodes and 12 edges. Note that the network is *bipartite*: a black node is always connected to a white node. Perhaps the black nodes represent people, the white nodes represent organizations, and the edges represent the relationship "works-for," as shown in the following image:

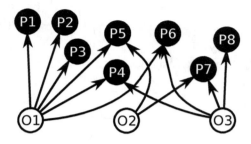

Alternatively, you can describe the network as an *adjacency matrix* EDGES of zeros and ones with three rows and eight columns. The matrix has a 1 if the corresponding nodes are connected.

	P1	P2	P3	P4	P5	P6	P7	P8
O1	1	1	1	1	1	1	0	0
O2	0	0	0	0	1	0	1	0
O3	0	0	0	1	0	1	1	1

You'd like to infer the relationships between the people based on their affiliations with the organizations. For example, P1, P2, and P3 work for O1 and only for O1. They must be similar to themselves but less similar to P4 and P5, which have additional employment. In other words, different people belong to different communities, and you want to unearth the community structure. One way to accomplish such a task is by applying a *generalized similarity algorithm [Kov10]*.

Without going into too much detail, which you can look up in the just-mentioned article, the algorithm iteratively transforms the matrix EDGES and its transposed sister matrix. In the following pseudocode fragment, .T denotes transposition, diag(X) is the diagonal vector of X, and X/[i]Y is the division of matrix X by the vector Y along the axis i:

```
N←Identity
REPEAT
   M ← EDGES×N×EDGES.T; M ← M/[1]√diag(M)/[2]√diag(M)
   N ← EDGES.T×M×EDGES; N ← N/[1]√diag(N)/[2]√diag(N)
UNTIL required accuracy achieved.
```

The APL implementation has 18 lines (excluding the ∇∇ lines), compared to 15 lines in Python with NumPy. It maps nicely to the pseudocode.

```
apl/gensim.apl
       ∇NN←GENSIM MTX;MINEPS;MAXITER;ITER;S;MTX1;MTX2;N;M;NN;MM;NP;EPS;MORE
[1]  MINEPS←1E¯6 ⍝ Initialize precision
[2]  MAXITER←50 ⍝ Initialize max number of iterations
[3]  ITER←0
[4]  S←(⍴MTX)[2] ⍝ Data size
[5]  MTX1←MTX-[1]+/MTX÷S ⍝ Normalize the matrix two ways
[6]  MTX2←⍉MTX-[2](+/[1]MTX)÷(⍴MTX)[1]
[7]  NN←(S,S)⍴1,S⍴0 ⍝ New metric matrix: an "eye"

[8]  LOOP: ⍝ Beginning of the "while" loop
[9]  MM←MTX1+.×NN+.×⍉MTX1 ⍝ Update metric matrix
[10] M←(1 1⍉MM)*.5 ⍝ Normalize it
[11] MM←(MM÷[1]M)÷[2]M
[12] NP←MTX2+.×MM+.×⍉MTX2 ⍝ Update metric matrix
[13] N←(1 1⍉NP)*.5 ⍝ Normalize it
[14] NP←(NP÷[1]N)÷[2]N
[15] EPS←⌈/,|NP-NN ⍝ Calculate accuracy
[16] NN←NP
[17] ITER←ITER+1
[18] MORE←(EPS>MINEPS)∧ITER<MAXITER
[19] →MORE/LOOP ⍝ End of the "while" loop
[20] ∇
```

The algorithm produces the matrix SIMS of similarity measures between the people on the scale -1 (very dissimilar) to +1 (very similar).

```
      EDGES←3 8⍴1 1 1 1 1 0 0 0 0 0 0 1 0 1 0 0 0 0 1 0 1 1 1
      SIMS←GENSIM EDGES
      SIMS>0
1 1 1 1 1 1 0 0
1 1 1 1 1 1 0 0
1 1 1 1 1 1 0 0
1 1 1 1 0 1 0 1
1 1 1 0 1 0 0 0
1 1 1 1 0 1 0 1
0 0 0 0 0 0 1 1
0 0 0 1 0 1 1 1
```

According to SIMS, P1, P2, P3, and P4 are in the same group. P7 and P8 are in another group. P5 and P6 are more similar to the first group than the second. Draw a graph of the similarity network as an exercise. You can even use it for social science simulation—especially if you know some Simula.

Further Reading

- *A Programming Language [Ive62]*

- *APL Programming and Computer Techniques [Kat70]*

- *Handbook of APL Programming [Wie74]*

- *APL: The Language and Its Usage [Pol75]*

- *APL-STAT. A Do-It-Yourself Guide to Computational Statistics Using APL [RM81]*

- *APL: An Interactive Approach [Gil83]*

- *APL Programming Language [Mag83]* (in Russian)

- *Learning and Applying APL [Leg84]*

- *APL with a Mathematical Accent [Rei90]*

- *Mastering Dyalog APL: A Complete Introduction to Dyalog APL [Leg09]*

CHAPTER 4

Unveiling Object-Oriented Programming with Simula

This chapter offers you a gift. Instead of one obscure language, it gives you two: Simula and ALGOL, because Simula is ALGOL in disguise (specifically, Simula-67 is a superset of ALGOL-60). Beyond OOP, Simula's origins in simulation will introduce you to coroutines and discrete event modeling, enabling you to simulate complex systems—a skill increasingly crucial in data-driven decision-making.

But don't get too excited yet; ALGOL had a massive influence on computing in general and specifically on programming languages, but, forgotten for any practical purpose, it's remarkably boring.

ALGOL is the second oldest programming language, designed in 1958 as a direct successor to Fortran. Its antiquated features are a clear reminder of its roots in the early days of computing. ALGOL is characterized by its heavy syntax, reliance on GOTO statements, a clear divide between functions and procedures, lack of dynamic memory allocation, and compatibility with punch cards rather than files.

Such shortcomings, among others, must have prompted the emergence of Simula between 1962 and 1967. Simula stepped in to supplant ALGOL, absorbing its core components while enhancing its capabilities. Developed initially for CDC 3300, it was soon ported to CD 3600, CD 6600, UNIVAC 1108, IBM 360/370, and other computer systems.

Simula rightly prides itself as the pioneer of object-oriented programming. Though the individual components of this paradigm had been present since 1960, Simula was the first to implement the framework fully. Shortly after, in 1972, Smalltalk followed suit, reinforcing the object-oriented programming approach.

"It's ALGOL!"

Boring or not, ALGOL is Simula, and you cannot learn one without learning the other. Let's start with the traditional "Hello, world!" chant to illustrate using comments and compound statements.

```
simula/hello.sim
% A comment
! Another comment ;
BEGIN
    OutText("Hello World!");
    COMMENT One more comment ; OutImage;
END of Program
```

An unterminated comment begins with % and extends to the end of the line. Terminated comments begin with ! or COMMENT and extend to the first semicolon because both are statements, and statements must always conclude with a semicolon. Everything after the END clause to the end of the line is ignored too.

A *compound statement* is a sequence of single or other compound statements wrapped in BEGIN and END clauses. It can be utilized in any situation where a single statement would be expected. A Simula program is typically one compound statement.

Compound Statements

 Simula compound statements correspond to the C/C++/Java compound statements enclosed in curly braces {} or Python blocks indented by the same amount. Compound statements were first introduced in ALGOL.

ALGOL-60 and Simula are case-insensitive languages. As a convention, consider typing keywords in uppercase letters and identifiers in mixed-case letters for better readability and consistency.

Since Simula is a superset of ALGOL-60, treat any reference to Simula as an implicit reference to ALGOL, and the other way around, until you reach the section "It's Simula!", on page 124. The histories of these two languages diverge after that point.

Glancing at Variables, Data Types, and Operators

A variable must be declared at the beginning of the statement in which it's used before any executable statement (such executable statements are called *sentences*). A declaration (or a *qualification*, as it's known in the original Simula documentation) includes the name and the data type.

The set of primitive data types in Simula is almost standard for its time. It has INTEGER numbers (26, -12), REAL numbers (3.14159, 2E-8), BOOLEAN constants (TRUE and FALSE), and EBCDIC CHARACTER ('*'). Explicit type conversion is not supported.

Operators in Simula generally behave as you would expect. Many operators come in two forms: "classical" ALGOL-60 (with non-EBCDIC characters) and "modern" (only with EBCDIC/ASCII characters). The arithmetic operations include addition (+), subtraction (-), multiplication (× or *), division (/), integer division (÷ or //), and exponentiation (↑ or **).

Logical operators encompass the following: greater than (>), less than (<), less than or equal to (≤ or <=), greater than or equal to (≥ or >=), inequality (≠, ¬=, or <>, which compares values), reference inequality (=/=, which compares references), equality (=, compares values), and reference equality (==, compares references).

The language also includes the following relational operators: negation (¬ or NOT), conjunction (∧ or AND), disjunction (∨ or OR), implication (⊃ or IMP, interpreted as "B follows from A" or "NOT A OR B"), and equivalence (≡ or EQV, which is the same as NXOR).

Comparison

Operators = and <> correspond to Python language operators == and !=. Operators == and =/= correspond to Python language operators is and is not.

Characters

Simula characters are enclosed in single quotes. A few procedures are provided to convert them to and from integer character codes and to test their associations with character classes.

- rank(c). Returns the integer character code (compare ord(c) in Python).

- char(n). Returns the character that corresponds to the code n (compare chr(n) in Python).

- digit(c). Returns TRUE if c is a decimal digit.

- letter(c). Returns TRUE if c is a letter (according to the local definition of letters).

Text Objects and Operations

Simula offers two additional data types specific to its structure: REF and TEXT. The REF type is a reference to an object, denoted as NONE if no object is referenced. The TEXT type is used for text strings—for example, "Hello, world!". When not initialized, its value is NOTEXT.

A Simula reference is an alternate identifier for an existing object. An instance of the TEXT type is a reference to a compound object—a *text descriptor*.

Unlike the languages we remember, Simula treats text not as a character array but as a memory file. The text descriptor contains information about the text area (text buffer), including its memory address, size, and current position within the text (it starts at 1). Typically, this position points to the first uninitialized character, but you can reposition it as desired. If T is a text, then Integer T.Pos returns its current position, T.SetPos(n) sets the current position to n, Integer T.Length returns the text area size, and Boolean T.More checks if the position is at the end of the text area.

In Simula, you can create a text object using two methods:

- Allocate a blank space-initialized text area of size n with the procedure Blanks(n) and then initialize by assigning a literal string.

- Copy a literal string s with the procedure Copy(s).

Note that Simula has two assignment operators. := is used for value assignment, and :- is used for reference assignment:

```
TEXT t1, t2;
t1 :- Blanks(10);      ! Reference assignment ;
t1 := "Hello,";        ! Value assignment ;
t2 :- Copy("World!"); ! Reference assignment ;
```

Several procedures can be utilized to manipulate texts in Simula, including the following:

- T.GetChar. Returns the current character and advances the current position.

- T.PutChar(c). Inserts the character c at the current position and advances the current position.

- T.Sub(p,n). Creates a subtext of length n, starting at the position p.

- T.Strip. Eliminates white spaces (blanks) at the end of text area.

- T.GetInt. Interprets the text as an integer number.

- T.GetReal. Interprets the text as a real number.

- T.PutInt(n). Appends an integer number n.

- T.PutFix(n,w). Appends an integer number n of a fixed width w.

- T.PutReal(n,w). Appends a real number n of a fixed width w.

As an example, the following code fragment greets the author. It allocates a 64-character text area, copies the greeting, appends the author's initials, removes unused characters, and displays the results.

```simula
simula/greet.sim
BEGIN
    TEXT txt;
    txt :- Blanks(64);
    txt := "Hello, ";
    txt.SetPos(8); ! Skip over the greeting! ;
    txt.PutChar('D');
    txt.PutChar('Z');
    txt.Strip; ! Remove the trailing blanks ;
    OutText(txt);
    OutText("!");
END;
```

If cim is installed on your system, you can compile and run the program as follows:

```
/home/dzseven> cim greet.sim
Compiling greet.sim:
gcc -g -O2 -c greet.c
gcc -g -O2 -o greet greet.o -L/usr/local/lib -lcim
/home/dzseven> greet
Hello, DZ!
```

Arrays

Simula arrays are static and optionally multidimensional. The type, size, index ranges, and number of dimensions of an array must be declared at compile time. Indices can start from any value, not limited to 0 or 1. Array elements can be accessed and modified using parentheses notation.

```simula
INTEGER ARRAY age, weight(0:16); ! A vector of length 17 ;
CHARACTER ARRAY chess(1:8,1:8); ! A 2D array 8×8 ;
age(0) := 16;
chess(1,1) := 'Q';
```

Simula performs a runtime index check and will terminate your program if an index is out of bounds.

Arrays

 Simula arrays are comparable to statically declared arrays in C and fixed-size arrays in Java.

Investigating Control Structures

Like in most modern programming languages, control structures in Simula have their roots in ALGOL-60/Fortran. As a result, they bear similarities to control statements found in languages such as C, C++, Java, and Pascal.

GOTO and Conditional Statements

As a descendant of ALGOL-60, Simula incorporates the GOTO statement, which wasn't deemed harmful until 1968. In a Simula program, any line can have one or more labels. The GOTO/GO TO can transfer control to any of these labels, paving the way for "spaghetti code" that is notoriously difficult to read and maintain.

However, more than the GOTO is needed to control code execution beyond a linear or infinite-loop format. Another required structure is the conditional statement, which is boringly indistinguishable from its modern counterparts. In the following example, the program reads and displays up to ten characters from the stdin known in Simula as SysIn via procedures InChar and OutChar(c). It uses GOTO and IF to imitate a for loop.

```
simula/goto.sim
BEGIN
    CHARACTER c;
    INTEGER i;
    i := 10;
loop:
    i := i - 1;
    c := InChar;
    OutChar(c);
    IF SysIn.More AND i > 0 THEN ! SysIn = stdin ;
        GOTO loop
    ELSE
        BEGIN END ! Empty block (optional) ;
END;
```

A SWITCH statement, also known as a *computable* or *assigned* GOTO statement, offers a handy mix of GOTO and IF functionalities. It requires a list of target labels and an integer choice expression i. The program flow then jumps to the destination specified by the ith label. Note that the labeling starts from 1.

simula/switch.sim

```
% Switch to the human side!
BEGIN
    INTEGER choice;
    SWITCH heads := L0, L1, L2;

    OutText("How many heads do you have? (0..2)");
    OutImage;
    choice := InInt;

    GOTO heads (choice + 1);
L0: OutText("You are a bot.");   GOTO done;
L1: OutText("You are a human.");  GOTO done;
L2: OutText("You are a mutant."); GOTO done;

done:
    OutImage;
END;
```

The SWITCH Statement

The SWITCH statement in Simula bears a resemblance to the "computed GOTO" in Fortran. For instance, in Fortran, GOTO (10, 20, 30) K proceeds to the label 10, 20, or 30, depending on the value of K.

Loops

Despite only officially supporting a single type of loop, Simula demonstrates a remarkable versatility in creating complex loop structures.

Let's start with the unofficial loop statement WHILE. The WHILE loop isn't a part of the original Simula standard, but it was recommended for implementation and, respectively, was implemented at least in the cim environment. This loop operates similarly to its counterpart in most contemporary procedural and functional programming languages.

simula/copy.sim

```
% Make a copy of a text
BEGIN
    TEXT t1, t2;
    t1 :- Copy("Hello, world!");
    t2 :- Blanks(t1.Length);

    WHILE t1.More DO
        t2.PutChar(t1.GetChar); ! Accumulate characters ;
    OutText(t2);
END;
```

Simula's primary loop structure is the FOR loop. Initiated with the keyword itself, it's followed by what appears to be an assignment statement. However, the right-hand side of the assignment can be a comma-separated combination of individual values, STEP-UNTIL ranges, and WHILE sequences, as illustrated by the next code snippet.

```
simula/loop.sim
% FOR-looping in many ways
BEGIN
   INTEGER v;
   FOR v := 0,1,2,3,4,5,6,7       DO OutInt(v,4); OutImage; ! list ;
   FOR v := 0 STEP 1 UNTIL 7      DO OutInt(v,4); OutImage; ! step ;
   FOR v := 1, v*2 WHILE v <= 128 DO OutInt(v,4); OutImage; ! while ;
   FOR v := 0,1,                  ! list ;
            2 STEP 1 UNTIL 4,     ! step ;
            32, v*2 WHILE v <= 128 ! while ;
                             DO body:
                                OutInt(v,4); OutImage;
END;
```

The loop variable v retains its most recently assigned value after the loop. However, any label defined in the loop (such as body) isn't visible outside.

Functions OutInt() and OutImage collaborate on making the results visible. The former formats an integer number and stores its character representation (digits) in a RAM buffer. The latter forces the content of the buffer to be displayed immediately. If you don't call OutImage, the contents of the buffer will be displayed only when the program terminates.

Introducing Procedures

As a procedural language, Simula incorporates procedures and function procedures. The distinction lies in their return values. Similar to void functions in C and C++, regular procedures don't yield a return value but instead operate through side effects, such as altering global variables and parameters or conducting input/output. On the other hand, function procedures have a specific data type and must return a value of this type. We'll refer to both types as "procedures" for simplicity, with differentiation made only when required.

Unless declared with the EXTERNAL keyword, procedures must be defined prior to their initial usage within the same BEGIN/END block. A procedure's definition includes the return type (for function procedures), its name, a list of parameter names enclosed in parentheses, parameter declarations, and the procedure body enclosed within another BEGIN/END block.

All parameters must have their types declared before the procedure body, akin to declaring variables. By default, parameters of a primitive data type, except for TEXT, are passed by value. Any changes to these parameters within the procedure are confined locally and do not persist upon returning to the caller. Parameters of all other types, by default, are passed by reference, allowing their modification within the procedure. To pass these parameters by value to avoid unintentional modification, denote them with the VALUE keyword.

References

 Simula references resemble C++ references. They're applicable only to non-primitive data types, including TEXT.

The third mode of parameter passing in Simula is by name, applicable to any data type marked with the NAME keyword. In this scenario, the formal parameter's name is replaced with the actual parameter's value within the procedure body, which is subsequently evaluated as part of the procedure execution. This technique bears a resemblance to macro expansion.

To return a value from a function procedure, assign the value to a variable that shares its name with the procedure. This variable should not be declared. A similar return mechanism is used in Starset (refer to Functions, on page 191).

Here's an example of the (in)famous recursive Fibonacci number generation function procedure and another solution based on dynamic programming. (Fibonacci and His Numbers, on page 122, explains the meaning of the *in-* part.)

simula/fibonacci.sim
```
% Two ways to calculate Fibonacci numbers
BEGIN
    ! A silly way ;
    INTEGER PROCEDURE fib1(n); INTEGER n;
    BEGIN
        fib1 := IF n = 1 THEN 0
            ELSE IF n = 2 THEN 1
            ELSE fib1(n-1) + fib1(n-2)
    END;

    ! A smart way ;
    INTEGER PROCEDURE fib2(n); INTEGER n;
    BEGIN
        INTEGER ARRAY F(1:n);
        INTEGER i;

        F(1) := 0;
        IF n > 1 THEN F(2) := 1;
```

```
      FOR i := 3 STEP 1 UNTIL n DO
         F(i) := F(i-1) + F(i-2);

      fib2 := F(n);
   END;

   OutInt(fib1(32), 0); OutImage; ! prints 1346269 ;
   OutInt(fib2(32), 0); OutImage; ! prints 1346269 ;
END;
```

Fibonacci and His Numbers

Fibonacci, also known as Leonardo Bonacci, was an Italian mathematician. He is famous, among other things, for popularizing the Arabic numerals (the Indo-Arabic numeral system) and the Fibonacci sequence of numbers. The first two Fibonacci numbers are zero and one, and each successive number is the sum of the two previous: $F_i = F_{i-1} + F_{i-2}$. The formula screams for a recursive implementation, and the function procedure fib1(n) in the code fragment on page 121 provides it. However, the cost of such implementation is enormous; its computational complexity is $O(2^n)$, where n is the Fibonacci index. A solution based on *dynamic programming* (*memoization*) has an O(n) computational complexity—see the function procedure fib2(n).

Note how the function procedure fib1(n) uses the conditional statement as a conditional expression and returns its value.

The next example illustrates passing parameters by name. The function procedure swap(a,b) is designed to exchange the values of its two parameters. However, if you pass the parameters by value (which is the default method for integers), any changes to these values will only apply within the scope of the procedure's body. In contrast, when you pass parameters by name, the parameters a and b within the procedure are effectively replaced by their corresponding references at the point of the procedure's call. Consequently, the assignments b:=a and a:=c update the actual values of the parameters a and b at the calling location, not just their local copies within the procedure.

simula/swap.sim
```
PROCEDURE swap(a,b); NAME a,b; INTEGER a,b;
BEGIN
   INTEGER c;
   c := b;
   b := a;
   a := c;
END swap;
```

Should you find it intriguing, the presence of the procedure's name swap following the end of the body block is purely informational for the reader. The compiler disregards any text between the END keyword and the subsequent semicolon.

Managing File I/O

From Simula's standpoint, a file, or what it terms a *data set*, is an assembly of data external to the program and organized sequentially or addressably. A file comprises *images*, making it an ImageFile or a text file, or bytes, making it a ByteFile or a binary file. These two types, ImageFile and ByteFile, are subclasses of the File class. (Classes in Simula exist! Refer to Switching to Object-Oriented Programming, on page 125.) You can open files for reading (as InFile and InByteFile), writing (as OutFile and OutByteFile), or both (as DirectFile and DirectByteFile).

With a multitude of operating systems and even computer systems operating without an OS, the definition of *image* within an image file was intended to depend on the specific implementation. An image file, primarily, is a buffered file that necessitates reading an image from the file into the RAM and subsequently extracting characters and numbers from the RAM image. Contemporary implementations of Simula assume that an image refers to a line, which is a series of characters ended by a line break. An image file, therefore, is a text file that performs line-oriented I/O.

The CopyTextFile(in,out) procedure showcases the fundamental operations with image files. This includes declaring references to the future open files (REF(InFile) origin), dynamically creating new file objects (origin :- NEW InFile(inname)—note the reference assignment operator), opening the files (origin.Open(Blanks(100))), performing input/output, and closing the files (origin.Close). The Open(T) procedure requires preallocated image storage, provided by a call to Blanks(n). You're responsible for estimating the maximum string length and supplying enough buffer space. Your program will crash if it encounters a line longer than the buffer.

simula/copytextfile.sim

```
BEGIN
   PROCEDURE CopyTextFile(inname, outname);
   VALUE inname, outname; TEXT inname, outname;
   BEGIN
      REF(InFile) origin;
      REF(OutFile) dest;

      origin :- NEW InFile(inname);
      dest :- NEW OutFile(outname);
      origin.Open(Blanks(100));
      dest.Open(Blanks(100));

      WHILE NOT origin.Endfile DO
        BEGIN
           origin.InImage; ! Read the next image! ;
```

```simula
        WHILE origin.More DO ! Read from the image ;
            dest.OutChar(origin.InChar);
        dest.OutImage;
      END;
    origin.Close;
    dest.Close;
  END;

  ! Testing ;
  CopyTextFile("copytextfile.sim", "copytextfile.bak");
END;
```

A byte (binary) file doesn't have an internal structure visible to Simula. It appears as a contiguous sequence of characters and can be read sequentially, one character at a time (as illustrated in the example that follows), or randomly. For random access, use procedures SetPos(n) and GetPos to control the current position within the file (refer to Text Objects and Operations, on page 116: text objects provide the same interface!).

```simula
simula/copybinfile.sim
BEGIN
    PROCEDURE CopyBinFile(inname, outname);
    VALUE inname, outname; TEXT inname, outname;
    BEGIN
        REF(InByteFile) origin;
        REF(OutByteFile) dest;

        origin :- NEW InByteFile(inname);
        dest :- NEW OutByteFile(outname);
        origin.Open;
        dest.Open;

        WHILE NOT origin.Endfile DO
            dest.OutByte(origin.InByte);
        origin.Close;
        dest.Close;
    END;

    ! Testing ;
    CopyBinFile("copybinfile.sim", "copybinfile.bak");
END;
```

"It's Simula!"

While ALGOL is Simula, Simula is not ALGOL. Simula provides three revolutionary concepts that differentiate it from its ancestor: object-oriented programming, coroutines, and explicit support for computer simulation. We're going to explore these features in the following three sections.

Switching to Object-Oriented Programming

A Simula class consists of a header and a body. The header includes the class name and, if necessary, parameters and their declarations. The body houses local variables, procedures, and the core code (the *lifeline*). This structure is familiar to developers versed in C++, Java, Python, or similar languages. However, when introduced in the late 1960s, the concept of *encapsulation* was revolutionary.

Defining a Simple Class

The code snippet below outlines a simple class representing a two-dimensional point. The point comprises two integer attributes: the coordinates x and y. These attributes must be supplied when creating a new object of the class.

```
simula/point2d.sim
CLASS Point2d(x,y); INTEGER x,y;
BEGIN
    INTEGER seed;

    PROCEDURE bounce;
    BEGIN
        x := RandInt(-10, 10, seed);
        y := RandInt(-10, 10, seed);
    END bounce;

    REF(Point2d) PROCEDURE add(p); REF(Point2d) p;
    BEGIN
        add :- NEW Point2d(x + p.x, y + p.y);
    END add;

    seed := Entier(ClockTime); ! Initialize the seed ;
END Point2d;
```

The class features two methods, bounce and add(p), and a constructor. The constructor may not be readily apparent, because it encompasses the remaining part of the class body after the procedures. It's worth noting that from the perspective of Simula, there's no designated "constructor." Rather, an object is seen as a self-contained program with data and actions.

The first procedure, bounce, randomly adjusts the point's position by generating new coordinates based on a discrete uniform distribution from -10 to 10. The distribution relies on the variable seed, passed by name and updated after each call. The only explicit statement in the object body is the initialization of the seed to the current clock time (in seconds since midnight), truncated to an integer number. Consequently, the point's bounce will be different with each program run.

The second procedure (a function procedure), add(p), adds two points by treating them as vectors and combining them coordinate-wise. It accepts a reference to another existing point as a parameter and returns a reference to a new dynamically allocated point. The original points remain unaltered.

Simula classes don't differentiate between public and private access levels. Any object can access any other object's variables using the familiar *dot notation* ("remote accessing"). You are entrusted with the responsibility of preserving data integrity.

Simula's syntax allows object variable access not just through dot notation but also through a construct called *connections*. Contemporary interpretations equate an object's connection to importing the object's namespace into the namespace of the block that's creating the connection. This connection, established through the INSPECT statement, enables direct access to the procedures and attributes of the connected object. The following code snippet illustrates the use of such a connection, established from the main code to the anonymous object of the highlighted class Informer.

simula/inspect.sim
```
BEGIN
➤    CLASS Informer;
➤    BEGIN
➤       PROCEDURE inform(m); TEXT m;
➤       BEGIN
➤          OutText(m); ! Could be someting else ;
➤          OutImage;
➤       END inform;
➤    END Informer;

     REF(Informer) i;
     i :- NEW informer;
     i.inform("Hello, world!"); ! dot notation ;

     INSPECT NEW Informer DO ! connection ;
        inform("Goodbye, world!")
     OTHERWISE ! "exception" ;
        OutText("Informer not available");
END;
```

While a connection can lessen the burden of repetitive typing, especially if you regularly use procedures like inform(m), it's advisable to use this feature sparingly. Excessive usage of connections can obscure the origin of the procedure and potentially lead to naming conflicts.

The INSPECT Prefix

 The prefix INSPECT X DO is loosely equivalent to the Python language statement from X import * and should be used with equal care.

The OTHERWISE clause functions as an exception handler. If the object being inspected doesn't exist (represented by the reference NONE), or if its creation fails, the code block is prone to crash. The OTHERWISE clause provides a safety mechanism allowing for a graceful exit instead of an abrupt termination. The INSPECT/OTHERWISE statement has one more related use, which you'll master in Class Inheritance, on page 128.

Referencing External Modules

In addition to being overly simplified, the Point2d class mentioned previously faces an even more substantial issue. The class merely exists as a template without any instantiated objects, which hampers its practical applicability. In other words, it needs the "main program."

While placing the test program within the same block as the class definitions may seem acceptable, this method lacks scalability and inhibits the reusability of classes and procedures. Simula offers a solution to this issue by facilitating separate compilation and presenting the keyword EXTERNAL to denote procedures and classes formulated in distinct compilation units (source code files). A compilation unit that exclusively comprises definitions—without any directly executable code—is treated as a library module. Meanwhile, a unit incorporating executable code alongside external references is automatically combined with the precompiled modules to construct a unified program.

The subsequent code fragment refers to an external class, Point2d, defined elsewhere. As you'll see in the upcoming section, it's possible to employ the same class definition in multiple projects, either directly or via subclassing.

simula/point2d-test.sim
```
EXTERNAL CLASS Point2d;
BEGIN
   REF(Point2d) p1, p2, p3;
   p1 :- NEW Point2d(3, 4);
   p2 :- NEW Point2d(4, 3);
   p2.bounce;
   p3 :- p1.add(p2);
   OutFix(p3.x, 2, 6);
   OutFix(p3.y, 2, 6);
END
```

Compile the code in the correct order and enjoy your first compound Simula project.

```
/home/dzseven> cim point2d-test.sim
Compiling point2d-test.sim:
gcc -g -O2 -c point2d-test.c
/home/dzseven> cim point2d.sim
Compiling point2d-test.sim:
gcc -g -O2 -o point2d-test point2d-test.o point2d.o -L/usr/local/lib -lcim
/home/dzseven> point2d-test
 9.00  7.00
```

Class Inheritance

Class inheritance and hierarchy are vital concepts that Simula developers innovatively introduced. They referred to the process of creating subclasses as "concatenation," entailing the fusion of the parent class with additional blocks.

Multiple Inheritance Is Bad

 Multiple inheritance can lead to several problems and should be used sparingly and with caution, if at all. A common issue with multiple inheritance is the *diamond problem*, arising when a class inherits from two or more classes with a common superclass. If a method is overridden in one or both parent classes, it can be ambiguous which version of the method the subclass should inherit. Multiple inheritance can lead to high coupling between classes, making the design more rigid and less modular.

To incorporate a radius into your point class, thereby transforming it into a circle class, there's no need to recreate the procedures for adding and bouncing. The notation X CLASS Y extends (or "subclasses") the class X into Y. Separating code into distinct compilation units makes subclassing efficient and straightforward. The following program demonstrates the subclass, including an external reference to the superclass, and showcases the subclass's application.

```
simula/circle.sim
BEGIN
   EXTERNAL CLASS Point2d;
   Point2d CLASS Circle(radius); REAL radius;
   BEGIN
      REAL PROCEDURE area;
      BEGIN
         area := 3.141538 * radius ** 2;
      END;
   END Circle;
```

```
   REF(Circle) c;
   c :- NEW Circle(1, 2, 10);
   OutFix(c.area, 3, 7);
END;
```

The object constructor for the Circle class requires three parameters: two for the superclass Point2d and one for the subclass itself. The Circle class could then serve as a superclass for various subclasses (for example, annulus, sector, and a circular segment). Likewise, the Point2d class could be a subclass of a broader GeometricFigure class, which might be derived from a fundamental Object class. Simula imposes no restrictions on the depth of the class hierarchy.

Class inheritance paves the way to overriding and virtual procedures.

Imagine a class and its subclass have procedures with the same name. Which one of them will be called? According to Simula, the procedure that is lexically closest to the object that calls it—that is, the procedure in the deepest subclass. If a method is invoked on an object, Simula will first look for that method in the object's class. If the method isn't found there, Simula will look for it in the parent class and up the inheritance chain. This behavior is called *overriding*.

Procedure Overriding

Procedure overriding in Simula corresponds to method overriding in C++, Java, and Python.

A virtual procedure is a procedure with *dynamic dispatch*. Suppose you create a superclass Animal and several subclasses: Dog, Cat, and Fish. Some animals can make specific sounds, such as meowing or barking, but some (Fish) cannot. Respectively, some subclasses implement the method sound, and some don't.

```
simula/animal.sim
CLASS Animal;
➤ % VIRTUAL: PROCEDURE sound; -- According to the standard
➤ VIRTUAL:
➤ PROCEDURE sound IS
➤    PROCEDURE sound; ! Empty body; ;
   BEGIN
   END Animal;

Animal CLASS Cat;
BEGIN
   PROCEDURE sound;
   BEGIN
      OutText("Meow");
   END sound;
END Cat;
```

```
Animal CLASS Fish; ! Empty body; ;
Animal CLASS Dog;
BEGIN
   PROCEDURE sound;
   BEGIN
      OutText("Bark");
   END sound;
END Dog;
```

You can now create an array of Animal objects. Traverse the array in a FOR loop, query the most specific class of each object, and call the sound-making procedure, if available. You've got the right sounds, but the implementation is awkward and doesn't scale well. A better, *polymorphic* solution is to declare that an Animal generally has a callable sound-making procedure; Simula will determine the specifics of the procedure and select the most suitable, subclass-specific implementation at runtime. This process of selection is called dynamic dispatch. The declared general procedure is called virtual (highlighted in the previous code snippet).

Simula standard introduces virtual procedures with the keyword VIRTUAL. However, cim follows its own quirky syntax. CLASS Animal demonstrates both variants.

Virtual procedures significantly streamline the "pets" code. Once the sound procedure is declared virtual, you can invoke it without manually selecting the appropriate variant. If a choice exists, Simula will take care of the selection for you. (That's why the loop skips the fish: the fish makes no sound.)

simula/pets-1.sim
```
BEGIN
   EXTERNAL CLASS Animal, Cat, Fish, Dog;

   INTEGER v;
   REF(Animal) ARRAY pets(1:3);
   pets(1) :- NEW Dog;
   pets(2) :- NEW Cat;
   pets(3) :- NEW Fish;

   FOR v := 1 STEP 1 UNTIL 2 ! No fish! ; DO
      BEGIN
         pets(v).sound;
         OutImage;
      END;
END
```

But how do you manage the case of the silent fish? You've got two potential strategies. The first involves implementing a generic instance of the sound procedure within the superclass. This procedure is invoked if no local instance has been defined. This method is costly, as it requires reengineering the superclass.

The second option is to utilize the full power of the INSPECT statement (refer to the example on page 126). On the one hand, the statement allows "local" access to the "remote" object variables. On the other hand, though via a different syntax, it can inspect the class of an object and select an appropriate treatment method, as in the following code fragment. Using the INSPECT statement doesn't affect the superclass.

```
simula/pets-2.sim
BEGIN
    EXTERNAL CLASS Animal, Cat, Fish, Dog;

    INTEGER v;
    REF(Animal) ARRAY pets(1:3);
    pets(1) :- NEW Dog;
    pets(2) :- NEW Cat;
    pets(3) :- NEW Fish;

    FOR v := 1 STEP 1 UNTIL 3 DO
        BEGIN
            INSPECT pets(v) ! What kind of Animal? ;
            WHEN Cat DO sound
            WHEN Dog DO sound
            OTHERWISE OutText("Fish are silent");
            OutImage;
        END;
END
```

The Inspect Statement

 The INSPECT statement loosely corresponds to a combination of the type() or isinstance() functions in Python and a conditional statement.

An object Y can access another object X via a reference. However, you may ask how X could reference itself, for example, for inclusion in a linked list. (More information about linked lists is available in Class SIMSET, on page 136). This scenario might prompt Java/C++ programmers to instinctively employ the this keyword, unaware of its Simula origins and consistent naming. In Simula, the expression THIS C provides a reference to the current object, cast as a reference of class C. Class C could be the object's class or any of its superclasses or subclasses.

The following blatantly synthetic example is intended to reconcile Python programmers (*selfies*) and C++/Java programmers (*thisies*). It does so by assigning a self-reference to a variable named self:

```
CLASS Point2d(x,y); INTEGER x, y;
BEGIN
    REF(point2d) self;
    self :- THIS Point2d;
    self.x := x;
    self.y := y;
END Point2d;
```

In practice, the code between BEGIN and END is redundant.

The remaining two statements related to class hierarchies are IN and IS. Boolean x IS C checks if object X is an instance of class C. Boolean x IN C checks if object X is an instance of class C or its subclasses.

The In Expression

 The expression x IN C corresponds to a call to the Python function isninstance(x,C).

Prefixed Blocks

You can convert a Simula block of code (a sequence of statements between BEGIN and END) into a *prefixed block* by placing an anonymous object before it. A prefixed block is identical in purpose to the DO form of the INSPECT statement (see the code on page 126): it allows the enclosed statements unrestricted access to the object's variables and procedures, as illustrated in the following example:

```
simula/prefixed.sim
BEGIN
    CLASS SillyClass(v); INTEGER v; ! Empty body; ;
    REF(SillyClass) sc;

    sc :- NEW SillyClass(123);
    INSPECT sc DO ! INSPECT ;
        BEGIN
            OutInt(v, 0); OutImage;
        END;

    SillyClass(123) ! Prefixed block ;
    BEGIN
        OutInt(v, 0); OutImage;
    END;
END;
```

Beware of Friends!

Both prefixed blocks and the DO form of the INSPECT statement breach the principles of code and data encapsulation. They share similarities with the concept of friend functions and methods in C++.

Unfortunately, existing Simula documentation doesn't clarify whether either of these "friendly" statements should be preferred or the reasoning behind such a preference.

Designing Coroutines

Simula's concept of coroutines was genuinely revolutionary in the era of single-CPU computers (see the list on page 113) with limited or no multitasking.

A coroutine is a dynamic instance of a block of executable code, such as the body of a class, with its local variables and the program counter. A coroutine can be in one of four states: attached, detached, resumed, or terminated, as illustrated by the following UML diagram. (Not familiar with UML? No problem! You'll find numerous UML resources in both printed—*UML Distilled: A Brief Guide to the Standard Object Modeling Language [Fow03]*—and electronic form.)[1]

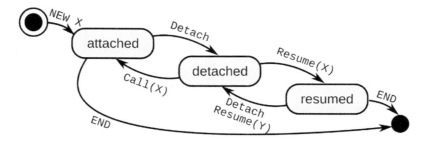

Your program may comprise several coroutines, but at most one can be attached. For example, a new class object is created (via NEW) as an attached block. The attached coroutine, if present, is executed by the CPU until it terminates by passing through the terminating object END or explicitly detaches itself from the program's main block. The procedures in a terminated coroutine remain available to external callers, but the coroutine's lifeline ends.

---

1. www.visual-paradigm.com/guide/uml-unified-modeling-language/what-is-uml/

If an attached block detaches itself by calling the procedure Detach, it becomes dormant. The state of the block (including the local variables and the program counter) is saved so that the execution can be resumed later. The control is passed to the main program to which the subroutine was attached. The latter may call the subroutine again with the Call(X) procedure. However, unlike a "traditional" subroutine call, the execution won't start from the beginning of the block but resumes from the most recently saved state.

You can also resume the execution of a detached coroutine by calling the Resume(X) procedure without reattaching it to the main program. Such a coroutine is called *resumed*. A resumed coroutine can terminate, detach itself (the control reverts to the main program), or resume the execution of another detached block. This way, two coroutines can collaborate by resuming each other after completing the assigned tasks. Such activity is called *non-preemptive* or *cooperative multitasking*. It assumes that all involved coroutines are cooperative and always eventually yield control to their gangmates.

Pthreads vs. Coroutines

 As recently as 2011, POSIX Pthreads was a non-preemptive threads library resembling Simula coroutines. Likewise, *goroutines* in Go language and the Python's asyncio-based coroutines loosely correspond to Simula coroutines.

To understand coroutines better, let's consider a program simulating the iconic game of Nim.[2] Two players take turns removing at least one match from a pile of matches. The player who takes the last match loses.

The main program that starts on line 28 of the code fragment on page 135 creates two players ("Alice" and "Bob") as instances of the class NimPlayer and initializes the seed of the random number generator and the pile. Upon initialization, each player calls Detach (line 23) and becomes detached. This concludes the first *active phase* of the coroutines.

The main program resumes the execution of p1 "Alice" (line 37). The second active phase begins, during which the coroutines execute the WHILE loop until one of the players cannot move (loses). After making its turn, a player awakens its opponent (line 25), and the game continues.

---

2.   https://en.wikipedia.org/wiki/Nim

simula/nim.sim

```
Line 1  BEGIN
            INTEGER matches, seed;

            CLASS NimPlayer(id); TEXT id;
     5      BEGIN
                REF(NimPlayer) opponent;

                BOOLEAN PROCEDURE move;
                BEGIN
    10              INTEGER taken;
                    taken := RandInt(1, matches, seed);
                    matches := matches - taken;
                    OutText(id); OutInt(taken, 3); OutInt(matches, 3); OutImage;
                    IF matches = 0 THEN
    15                  BEGIN
                            OutText(id); OutText(" lost"); OutImage;
                            move := FALSE;
                        END
                    ELSE
    20                  move := TRUE;
                END move;

                Detach; ! ;
                WHILE move DO
    25              Resume(opponent) ! ;
            END NimPlayer;

            REF(NimPlayer) p1, p2; ! ;
            p1 :- NEW NimPlayer("Alice");
    30      p2 :- NEW NimPlayer("Bob  ");
            p1.opponent :- p2;
            p2.opponent :- p1;

            seed := Entier(ClockTime);
    35      matches := 100;

            Resume(p1); ! ;
        END
```

You can implement a similar behavior by having the main block dispatch both players. Each player will Detach at the end of the turn, and the main block will Call(X) the players as needed. The benefit of this solution is that there's no need for the players to know their opponents: the main program is in charge of turns, allowing more intricate scheduling patterns.

You might have recognized that the recent code example is essentially a computer simulation. Simula is the programming language that owns its existence to ALGOL-60, duly noted, and the need to simulate real-world systems using computer software. It's time for the simulation story.

Introducing Computer Simulation

By prefixing code with top-level system classes, Simula can be transformed into application-specific languages. For instance, class Animal lays the foundation for a zoo, SIMSET (class for manipulating two-way lists, called *sets*) turns your code into a list processor, and class Simulation makes it a discrete-event simulator.

Drawing Random Numbers

The first order of business in any simulation environment is (pseudo-)random number generation. Random numbers are the soul of computer simulation. They introduce variance and uncertainty, making otherwise deterministic algorithms lifelike. Genuine random numbers are cryptographically safe (impossible to predict) but also are hard to generate and cannot be reproduced if necessary. Since cryptographic safety is typically not a property expected of a computer simulation system, random numbers are often substituted with pseudo-random numbers. Simula includes various pseudo-random number generators for different use cases, with each generator accepting the seed as a parameter:

- BOOLEAN Draw(p,seed). Generates TRUE with the probability p and FALSE otherwise.

- INTEGER RandInt(a,b,seed). Generates a uniformly distributed integer number from a to b, inclusive.

- REAL Uniform(a,b,seed). Generates a uniformly distributed real number from a to b, inclusive.

- REAL NegExp(a,seed). Generates an exponentially distributed real number with the exponent a.

- INTEGER Poisson(a,seed). Generates an integer number with Poisson distribution.

- REAL Erlang(a,b,seed). Generates a real number with Erlang distribution.

The selection of a generator depends on the characteristics of the simulated random process. For instance, an exponential distribution can accurately model the intervals between customer arrivals at a service counter. The specifics of choosing the appropriate distribution, however, fall beyond the scope of this book.

Class SIMSET

The system class SIMSET, short for simulation set, implements a circular two-way linked list, primarily designed to represent a SQS, or a *sequence set*, more commonly known as the event queue. This event queue acts as a future predictor for simulations, holding the events that will transpire in the simulated future along with their respective timestamps.

SIMSET provides subclasses LINKAGE, LINK (a list element), and HEAD. The latter supplies procedures CLEAR (empty the list), INTEGER CARDINAL (calculate the list size), BOOLEAN EMPTY (check if the size is zero), and REF(LINK) FIRST and REF(LINK) LAST (get references to the first and last list elements). The classes are implemented in Simula (the cim implementation has only 120 lines of code with comments). This system class provides convenience to application programmers who may not be very familiar with complex data structures, such as linked lists.

Class Simulation

The class Simulation, a subclass of class SIMSET, contains an inner class, Process.

Process Abstraction

A *process* is an abstraction denoting an ongoing simulated activity. Take, for instance, a service counter—perhaps the most frequently simulated system. It's a process of serving customers sequentially, one at a time. Where do these customers originate? From the perspective of the simulated system, they're generated by a "customer generator"—another process. Computer modeling is essentially the art of recognizing processes, including those that don't exist in the physical world.

Simula maps processes to coroutines. A process can be in one of four states: passive, active, suspended, or terminated.

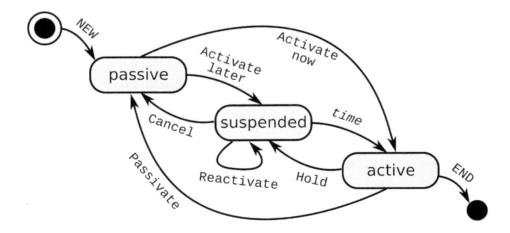

A process in its initial state is considered passive, representing a subsystem ready to operate but yet to be initiated ("activated"). The statement ACTIVATE triggers a process, scheduling it for immediate or future execution, causing the process to transition to an active or suspended state, respectively. Only one active process is active at any given moment; you can reference it using the method Current.

A suspended process shifts to an active state at its prearranged activation time. If a suspended process no longer needs activation (for instance, if the prerequisites for its activation no longer exist), you can abort it using the Cancel(P) method or adjust the activation time with the REACTIVATE statement.

Finally, an active process can place itself on hold (suspend its execution until later) with the Hold(time) method, make itself passive with Passivate, or terminate. If needed, a passivated process can be reactivated. For example, a service counter that closes at 17:00 and reopens at 9:00 doesn't need to remain active overnight.

Other useful methods include Simulation.Wait(q), which inserts a process into a waiting queue denoted by q and passivates it; Simulation.Time, which provides the current simulation time; Process.Idle, which verifies whether the process is inactive, and Process.Terminated, which checks if the process has been terminated.

Process Activation

The (RE)ACTIVATE statement in the class is highly versatile, offering a variety of ways to schedule the execution of process p.

- (RE)ACTIVATE p. Activate the process immediately.

- (RE)ACTIVATE p AT t. Activate the process at time t. Naturally, the time t is simulation time, not physical time.

- (RE)ACTIVATE p DELAY dt. Activate the process after delay dt.

- (RE)ACTIVATE p AT t PRIOR or (RE)ACTIVATE p DELAY dt PRIOR. Activate the process at time t before all other processes scheduled at that time or after that delay. This statement essentially assigns p the highest priority.

- (RE)ACTIVATE p BEFORE p1 or (RE)ACTIVATE p AFTER p1. Activate the process immediately before or after another process p1. In the case of the AFTER command, p1 could be the CURRENT process.

Simulating a Service Counter

Let's move again into the familiar territory of simulating a simple service counter system. This model comprises a hypothetical customer generator, a queue, and several counters. The total number of counters is represented by NCounters and the currently occupied counters by NBusyCounters. The average time between customer arrivals and the average service duration are denoted as AMean and SMean, respectively. Both of these times are determined using an exponential random number distribution.

It's Not Normal

 It's a frequently observed misstep to model service duration and customer interarrival times using a normal (*Gaussian*) distribution. The first issue is that a normal distribution can yield negative values, which are nonsensical in the context of time. Secondly, these times often display a skewed distribution rather than a symmetrical one. The most appropriate distribution for these scenarios is typically the *exponential* distribution.

The model requires two new classes: the Generator and the Counter. A customer queue is an instance of the system class Head. The queue is passive; its sole function is to orderly store the waiting customers.

Don't confuse this queue with SQS, the event queue that we can think of as our "future predictor."

The generator runs a seemingly infinite loop that creates and activates a new arriving customer and waits ("holds") for as long as the random number generator prescribes.

```
simula/counter.sim
Process CLASS Generator;
BEGIN
    WHILE TRUE DO BEGIN
        ACTIVATE NEW Customer(Time);
        Hold(NegExp(1 / AMean, seed)); ! Wait for the next "arrival";
    END;
END Generator;
```

The experience of a customer is elucidated within the Customer class. A customer represents a single-use object without any loops. Upon arrival, a customer checks for the availability of a counter. If all counters are occupied, the customer joins the queue. If not, the customer claims a counter (irrespective of which one), receives service, and departs. As it leaves, the customer reactivates the next customer in the queue (provided the queue isn't empty) and updates the statistics. Simula includes a basic procedure, histo(), for the iterative construction of histograms, although it doesn't seem particularly helpful in this context.

```
simula/counter.sim
Process CLASS Customer(Arrival); REAL Arrival;
BEGIN
   IF NBusyCounters = NCounters THEN
      Wait(Queue);                       ! Enqueue the customer;

   NBusyCounters := NBusyCounters + 1;  ! Seize a counter;
   Hold(NegExp(1 / SMean, seed));       ! Service;
   NBusyCounters := NBusyCounters - 1;  ! Release the counter;

   IF NOT Queue.Empty THEN
      BEGIN
         REF(Customer) Next;
         Next :- Queue.First;
         Next.Out;                       ! Dequeue;
         REACTIVATE Next AFTER Current;
      END;

   ! Collect statistic ;
   CustomersOut := CustomersOut + 1;
   TotalTime := TotalTime + (Time - Arrival);
END Customer;
```

The main program is straightforward. A single experimental run is integrated into the namesake procedure run. This procedure returns the average turnaround time (TAT)—the total time a customer spends in the system, from entry to exit. The procedure resets the counters, establishes a new event queue and customer generator (which introduces the first customer), and waits for eight simulated hours before reporting the result and closing down.

```
simula/counter.sim
Simulation BEGIN
   INTEGER seed;
   INTEGER NCounters, NBusyCounters;      ! Numbers of service counters;
   INTEGER CustomersOut; ! Number of served customers;
   LONG REAL TotalTime, TimeSpent;        ! Variables for statistics;
   REAL AMean, SMean;     ! Mean arrival/service duration;
   REF(Head) Queue;       ! The customer queue;
```

«Class definitions are here.»

```
   REAL PROCEDURE run;
   BEGIN
      TotalTime := TimeSpent := 0;
      CustomersOut := NBusyCounters := 0;

      Queue :- NEW Head;                     ! Create an empty queue;
      ACTIVATE NEW Generator;                ! Start the generator;
      Hold((17 - 9) * 60);                   ! Work day: 9:00-17:00 ;

      TimeSpent := TotalTime / CustomersOut;
```

```
      OutInt(NCounters, 2);
      OutFix(TimeSpent, 3, 10); OutImage;
   END;

   AMean := SMean := 1;
   seed := Entier(ClockTime);
   FOR NCounters := 1 STEP 1 UNTIL 10 DO
      run;
END program;
```

The said procedure runs ten times in a loop for different numbers of counters. Technically, this part is not a true simulation anymore—it's the first step toward system optimization. You might be asked, "How many counters should we install so that adding another one would not make a significant difference?" Based on our simulation, the answer would be, "Three counters are sufficient (given the current arrival frequency and mean service time)."

```
/home/dzseven> ./counter
  1    10.160
  2     8.711
  3     1.118
  4     1.016
  5     1.089
  6     0.998
  7     0.999
  8     0.998
  9     1.000
 10     0.992
21 garbage collection(s) in 0.0 seconds.
```

Lastly, the Simula runtime environment provides a message at the end of the program output, stating "21 garbage collection(s) in 0.0 seconds." Like Java, Go, APL, and Python, Simula utilizes a *garbage collector*—a tool that reclaims the memory that has been allocated but is no longer referenced. In contrast, languages like C, Forth, and Occam don't have garbage collectors, requiring you to manage memory cleanup yourself.

Writing Something Big

An emergency room isn't a happy place to be. Patients, germs, pain, blood, nurses, doctors, and the smell of medication obsessively remind you of the imminent end of your bodily journey. An emergency room is an even worse place to experiment, with human health and lives at stake. That's why nobody experiments with an actual emergency room but with its computer model. Simula is a great language to simulate such a model.

This book isn't about modeling and simulation, so we'll use a simplified model. Adhering to the principle of "garbage in, garbage out," it's essential to note that our simulation results, while insightful, won't necessarily reflect a reliable representation of a real-life emergency room.

An emergency room operation typically commences with a reception and waiting area where incoming patients queue for medical attention. In reality, life-threatening situations are promptly escalated, allowing critical patients to bypass the waiting queue and proceed directly to an examination room. In our simulation, we remove the element of mortality—all simulated patients will wait their turn, irrespective of their condition. However, each patient will be assigned a Boolean urgency level upon arrival, influencing their subsequent examination and treatment duration.

Further simplifications include, most notably, these:

- No differentiation is made between nurses and doctors. Every healthcare professional is considered equal in their capacity to provide treatment.

- No preemption. Newly arriving patients with urgent conditions must wait their turn, even if their need is greater than those being currently treated.

- No interaction with the broader hospital system. Patients who require hospitalization are immediately admitted, disregarding any real-life constraints like bed availability.

You can remove these and other restrictions by progressively improving the model and adding more features.

So far, the model has three classes: Arrivals, Doctor, and Patient.

The class Arrivals serves as patients' generator. It draws patients' interarrival times from an exponential distribution. It further uses the uniform distribution to model the urgency of the visit, assuming 67 percent of visits are typically not urgent.

```
simula/hospital.sim
Process CLASS Arrivals;
BEGIN
   id := 1;
   WHILE TRUE DO BEGIN
         BOOLEAN urgency;
         urgency := Draw(1 - 0.67, seed);
         ACTIVATE NEW Patient(id, urgency);
         Hold(NegExp(1 / arrival_mean, seed));
         id := id + 1;
      END;
END Arrivals;
```

The Doctor class emulates a healthcare practitioner. The life cycle of a "doctor" consists of an infinite loop (bounded only by the duration of the simulation experiment). A Doctor is activated by the arrival of the first patient (see code that follows). The doctor then assesses the patient for the urgency of the visit, estimates the duration of the examination, and pauses execution with the Hold(exam_t) function. After the pause, the doctor reactivates the patient (who also was in the passive state) and inspects the waiting queue. If the queue is empty (no patients waiting), the Doctor gets passivated. Otherwise, it selects the next patient from the queue and reactivates it.

```
simula/hospital.sim
Process CLASS Doctor(id); INTEGER id;
BEGIN
   REF(Patient) pat;

   WHILE TRUE DO BEGIN
         REAL exam_t, exam_mean;
         doctors_availabe := doctors_availabe - 1;

         exam_mean := IF pat.urgent
            THEN exam_mean_urgent
            ELSE exam_mean_normal;
         exam_t := NegExp(1 / exam_mean, seed);

         Hold(exam_t);
         REACTIVATE pat BEFORE current;

         IF NOT queue.Empty THEN BEGIN
               pat :- queue.First;
               pat.Out;                    ! Dequeue;
               pat.doc :- THIS Doctor;
               doctors_availabe := doctors_availabe + 1;
               REACTIVATE pat;
            END
```

```
        ELSE BEGIN
            pat :- NONE;
            doctors_availabe := doctors_availabe + 1;
            Passivate; ! Have some sleep ;
        END;
    END;
END Doctor;
```

Unlike a doctor's life cycle, the timeline of a patient, represented by the Patient class, is linear and finite. Upon arrival, a patient checks for the availability of doctors. If no doctors are available, the patient settles in the waiting room and awaits their turn to be called by the next available medical professional. Alternatively, if a doctor is available (an "idle doctor," in Simula's derogatory parlance), the patient approaches them. In both cases, the patient reactivates the chosen doctor and enters a passive state for the duration of the examination.

simula/hospital.sim

```
Process CLASS Patient(id, urgent); BOOLEAN urgent; INTEGER id;
BEGIN
    INTEGER v, arrived;
    REF(Doctor) doc;

    PROCEDURE stats;
    BEGIN
        wait_t := wait_t + (Time - arrived);
        queue_len := queue_len + queue.Cardinal;
        n_discharged := n_discharged + 1;
    END;

    arrived := Time;

    IF doctors_availabe = 0 THEN
        Wait(queue)
    ELSE BEGIN
            ! Find a doctor ;
            FOR v:=1 STEP 1 UNTIL n_doctors DO
                IF docs(v).idle THEN BEGIN
                    doc :- docs(v);
                    doc.pat :- THIS Patient;
                    GOTO found;
                END;
            ! This should never happen ;
            Error("No doctors available!");
        END;
found:
    ! Start exam ;
    stats;
    REACTIVATE(doc);
    Passivate;
END Patient;
```

The remaining portion of the code initializes the variables and constructs the necessary data structures. The simulation commences with the activation of the Arrivals generator.

simula/hospital.sim

```
Simulation BEGIN
    INTEGER seed, id, n_doctors, doctors_availabe, n_discharged;
    INTEGER wait_t, queue_len;
    REAL arrival_mean, exam_mean_normal, exam_mean_urgent;
    REF(Head) queue;
    REF(Doctor) ARRAY docs(1:3);
```

«Class definitions are here.»

```
    INTEGER v;

    arrival_mean := 15; exam_mean_normal := 20; exam_mean_urgent := 40;

    n_doctors := UpperBound(docs, 1) - LowerBound(docs, 1) + 1;
    doctors_availabe := n_doctors;

    queue :- NEW Head; ! Waiting room ;
    FOR v := 1 STEP 1 UNTIL n_doctors DO BEGIN
        docs(v) :- NEW Doctor(v);
    END;

    seed := Entier(ClockTime);
    ACTIVATE NEW Arrivals;

    Hold(24 * 60); ! One complete day ;

    OutText("Patients arrived: "); OutInt(id, 0); OutImage;
    OutText("Patients discharged: "); OutInt(n_discharged, 0); OutImage;
    OutText("Waiting time: "); OutFix(Wait_t / n_discharged, 2, 0); OutImage;
    OutText("Queue length: "); OutFix(queue_len / n_discharged, 2, 0); OutImage;
END Simulation;
```

The program displays the number of arrived and discharged patients, the average waiting time in the queue, and the average queue length:

```
/home/dzseven> ./hospital
Patients arrived: 92
Patients discharged: 90
Waiting time: 19.49
Queue length: 1.28
```

You can add visualization and optimization if necessary, but that's a topic for another book (for example, *Discrete-Event Simulation: A First Course [LP06]*). Or you may swing far to the other side and dive into what is now called *digital humanities*, using SNOBOL.

Further Reading

- *SIMULA Information. Common Base Language [DMN70]*
- *Introduction to SIMULA 67 [Lam83]*
- *Introduction to Programming with Simula [Poo87]*
- *Object-oriented Programming with SIMULA [Kir89]*
- *Discrete-Event Simulation. A First Course [LP06]*

Patterns are not just diagrams that describe the way the world works, they are the world.

> *Alan Watts, English writer and speaker*

CHAPTER 5

Streamlining Text Processing with SNOBOL

How old would you estimate the field of digital humanities to be? The origins of digital humanities can be traced back to the late 1940s and 1950s. However, the term *digital humanities* first emerged in printed materials around 1982, as indicated by the Google Ngram Viewer,[1] and it only gained widespread popularity after 2002. Alongside the development of this field was the advent of SNOBOL (string-oriented and symbolic language), a programming language specifically designed for text manipulation and pattern matching. Developed between 1962 and 1967, SNOBOL was a significant tool for early computational approaches in the humanities, as highlighted in *SNOBOL Programming for the Humanities [Hoc86]*. SNOBOL gradually went out of use by the early 1990s, but we'll bring back our memories of it.

SNOBOL was implemented for a broad variety of mainframes and minicomputers, such as CDC 3600, UNIVAC 1108, IBM S/360, CDC 6600, RCA Spectra70, GE 635, PDP-10, Sigma 5/6/7, and Atlas 2. It's still supported by enthusiasts and available for all major operating systems.

In keeping with tradition, let's begin with a look at how comments are made in SNOBOL. A comment in SNOBOL starts at the beginning of a line, marked by either an asterisk * or a vertical bar |, and extends to the end of that line. If any character other than these comment markers appears in the first position, the line doesn't qualify as a comment, but it's not necessarily a syntax error either.

```
|   This line is a comment.
*   And this line is a comment too.
 *  But this line is a mistake.
C   This line is not a mistake and not a comment.
```

---

1. https://books.google.com/ngrams/graph?content=digital+humanities%2Csnobol&year_start=1960&year_end=2008&corpus=en-2019&smoothing=0

```
1  This line is not a mistake and not a comment.
+  This line is a continuation of the previous line.
.  And this line is a continuation of the previous line too.
```

Also, keeping tradition, you must welcome the world in your new language of study:

```
   OUTPUT = "Hello, world!"
END
| Hello, world!
```

Beware that all operators, including the assignment operator =, must be surrounded by spaces. Also, depending on the implementation, SNOBOL identifiers may be case-sensitive or case-insensitive and have a period in their names (but not at the first position). Throughout this chapter, let's assume that the case of identifiers is irrelevant.

Processing Lines

SNOBOL is a line-oriented pattern-based text processing language.

- Its object of analysis is text: an ordered collection of human-readable symbols (letters, digits, spaces, and punctuation).

- Its unit of analysis is an individual line of text: a segment of text without any line breaks, typically constrained in length. For instance, a Python program line is up to 80 characters, and a typewriter line ranges from 45 to 75 characters. The concept of a line is defined in a subtly recursive manner: it's characterized by the absence of line breaks—characters that terminate a line. Fortunately, line breaks (also known as newlines) are independently clearly defined by their ASCII/Unicode codes: 10 (LF, "line feed," \n), 13 (CR, "carriage return," \r), or 30 (RS, "record separator" in QNX environments, \036) along with an EBCDIC code of 15 (NL, "newline," \025), and others.

- Its text-processing mechanism is pattern matching and replacement.

SNOBOL isn't the only programming language that relies on pattern matching: it's in excellent company with *AWK [AKW23]*, *Perl [chr15]*, *Erlang [Arm13]/Elixir [Alm18]*, *Haskell [Ski23]*, *Rust [Wol21]*, and *Prolog [Tat22a]*. However, it was the first language designed specifically for pattern matching. Unlike many later languages where pattern matching is facilitated through specific syntax or libraries (with a notable exception of Prolog), SNOBOL integrates pattern matching into the core of its language design, making it a fundamental aspect of programming in SNOBOL without the need for any special notation.

The SNOBOL virtual machine works by the following algorithm:

1. The subject is evaluated.
2. The pattern is evaluated.
3. The pattern match is performed.
4. The conditional assignments are made.
5. The object is evaluated.
6. The object is assigned.
7. The goto (conditional destination) is evaluated, determining the next statement in the execution flow.

Note how SNOBOL uses the words *subjects* and *objects*. A subject is the input string to which a pattern is applied during pattern matching operations. An object is the replacement string in a pattern-matching and substitution operation. A pattern acts like a "verb," though this name is not officially recognized.

Objects ≠ Objects

 SNOBOL objects don't have the same meaning as those in contemporary object-oriented programming languages.

Exploring Statements

SNOBOL statements can be informally categorized into one of four classes based on their function and purpose within the language: assignment, pattern matching, replacement, and end. The distinctions between these classes are merely semantic. They relate to the meaning and purpose of the statements rather than their syntax.

Any SNOBOL statement consists of at least one of the following—a label, a subject group, and a goto:

- Optional label
- Optional subject group:
    - Subject
    - Optional pattern
    - Optional object group:
        - " = " (don't forget the spaces!)
        - Optional object
- Optional goto

The simplest statement, and by extension, the simplest SNOBOL program, consists solely of the END label. The label has a special meaning: it represents the end of the program. Any label, including the END label, must start at the first position of a line; otherwise, it's interpreted as the beginning of a subject group. Here's the program:

```
The Macro Implementation of SNOBOL4 in C (CSNOBOL4B) Version 2.3.2
    by Philip L. Budne, Janurary 1, 2024
SNOBOL4 (Version 3.11, May 19, 1975)
BLOCKS (Version 1.10, April 1, 1973)
    Bell Telephone Laboratories, Incorporated

snobol4> END
No errors detected in source program

Normal termination at level 0
-:0: Last statement executed was 0
```

You can see the complete output of a SNOBOL interpreter in the preceding program, but only the program code will be shown in the future. Note that this shortest statement was a part of the "Hello, world!" program on page 148.

Labels and Gotos

Labels and the infamous goto commands, which you've already seen in the section on GOTO and Conditional Statements, on page 118, are key to controlling the execution flow in SNOBOL. This approach differs from languages like Simula and Fortran, where GOTO statements are mainly used within the context of conditional IF and SWITCH statements. In SNOBOL, goto commands (gotos) integrate both decision-making and the program's execution path control.

To illustrate labels and gotos, consider creating a program that copies the standard input to the standard output, acting as a "do-nothing" filter. The first step is to copy the first line (*"A journey of a thousand miles begins with a single step."*):

```
    OUTPUT = INPUT
END
```

Here, OUTPUT is a predefined subject variable whose value is the standard output stream of the program. Remember, SNOBOL was developed for mainframes and minicomputers in the pre-C, pre-Unix, and pre-stdout times. The value of OUTPUT could be a teletypewriter (TTY), line printer, magnetic tape, or visual display unit (VDU). Another predefined SNOBOL subject, PUNCH, would represent a keypunch punching holes in paper cards or tapes. The variable still exists but has no actionable behavior unless your computer has a keypunch attached.

INPUT, conversely, is a predefined object variable for the standard input stream. It would be associated with a teletypewriter (yes, it was a half-duplex device), a punched card/paper tape/magnetic tape reader, or even a light pen.

The purpose of the preceding program, therefore, is to copy *a single line of text* from the standard input to the standard output. To extend this to copying an entire file, you would incorporate the command into a while loop.

However, SNOBOL doesn't have a special syntax for loops. Looping is accomplished through a combination of a beginning-of-a-loop label and a goto command that either conditionally or unconditionally redirects control back to that label, as demonstrated here:

```
LOOP OUTPUT = INPUT :(LOOP)
END
```

LOOP is a label (and so is END). Unlike the END label, the label LOOP is not predefined and does not presuppose any condition or action. It acts as a target of the unconditional goto command :(LOOP) consisting of the :(...) syntax and the destination name. The modified program runs forever—but practically until an exceptional condition occurs, such as the end of the input file.

A minor modification of the goto fixes the problem: introducing the "goto-on-success" command, :S(...). It's a form of a conditional goto taken if and only if the rest of the statement was executed without failure (to be defined). Its counterpart, :F(...), activates upon statement failure. You can use :S(...) and :F(...) together to specify different destinations, but you cannot combine them with :(...).

snobol/copy.sno
```
* Copy stdin to stdout
AGAIN OUTPUT = INPUT :S(AGAIN)
* Alternative solution:
* AGAIN OUTPUT = INPUT :S(AGAIN)F(END)
END
```

This completes the overview of labels and gotos in SNOBOL. While you may see the concept as straightforward, the intricacies lie in its practical application.

A Note on Arithmetics

 In arithmetic expressions, SNOBOL treats number-like string literals as numbers and converts them to a numeric data type before evaluating the expression. The division operator, when applied to integer numbers, performs integer division.

Concatenation

Several programming languages, such as Python and C/C++, offer a feature where adjacent string literals are automatically concatenated without an explicit operator. SNOBOL furthers this concept by allowing implicit concatenation of all adjacent space-separated strings and variables:

```
    OUTPUT = 'Enter your name:'
    name = INPUT
    OUTPUT = 'Welcome, ' name "!"
* Just a line break
    OUTPUT =
    END
```

This example demonstrates various aspects of handling strings: strings can be enclosed in either single or double quotes; an empty string is implicit and invisible; and a string literal can be concatenated with a variable and vice versa. Note that parentheses are required when concatenation occurs on the subject (left-hand) side, due to its low precedence.

Pattern Matching

To match a pattern to a string, write the string (the "subject") followed by spaces and the pattern (the "verb"). The simplest pattern type is a string literal, which only matches a string that exactly matches its value. The statement fails if the strings are not equal. The following example imitates a simple login procedure by displaying a prompt, reading the user's password, and checking it against a hardcoded password:

```
snobol/password.sno
* One BAD password
      hardcoded.password = "qwerty"
      OUTPUT = "Enter your password:"
      password = INPUT
      password hardcoded.password      :F(BAD.P)
      OUTPUT = "Welcome to SNOBOL!"    :(END)
BAD.P OUTPUT = "Bad password!"
END
```

Replacement

The replacement operation clarifies the role of objects. An object is an expression on the right-hand side of the evaluated assignment operator. It replaces the first found match within the subject string. The subject is modified in place. If no modification occurs, the statement fails, potentially triggering an :F(...) goto if specified.

The next example illustrates replacing all occurrences of the placeholder {NAME} in the template template with the actual name provided by the user. The operation repeats in a loop until there are no more placeholders left to replace:

snobol/template.sno

```
        template = "Dear {NAME}! Welcome to SNOBOL! Thank you, {NAME}!"
        OUTPUT = "Enter your name:"
        name = INPUT

LOOP template "{NAME}" = name :S(LOOP)
        OUTPUT = template
END
```

```
* Enter your name:
* DZ
* Dear DZ! Welcome to SNOBOL! Thank you, DZ!
```

A Note on Line Breaks

 SNOBOL doesn't support the inclusion of explicit newline characters within strings for formatting. This limitation stems from the language's design, which is line-oriented; inherently, lines don't contain line breaks.

Text deletion is a special case of text replacement, where the target text is replaced with an empty string. An empty string can be denoted by "" or the absence of text:

snobol/nospaces.sno

```
* Remove all spaces
OUTER line = INPUT    :F(END)
INNER line " " =      :S(INNER)
        OUTPUT = line :(OUTER)
END
```

The preceding program is an example of a nested loop. The outer loop reads the text line by line to the end of the file. The inner loop removes spaces from the current line, one space at a time. The program doesn't handle tabs yet, but you'll fix this deficiency later.

Constructing Patterns

A general SNOBOL pattern is more complex than a mere string of characters. It's defined recursively: it can be a simple string, the joining (concatenation) of two patterns, or a choice (alternation) between them, with the alternation operation taking precedence over concatenation.

Similar to regular expressions, SNOBOL uses a vertical bar | to denote alternation between two options. A pattern like P1 | P2 is considered a match if the subject string matches P1 or P2. The following example demonstrates how to use alternation to detect either "Alice" or "Bob" within a line of text:

```
LOOP line = INPUT                    :F(END)
     line "Alice" | "Bob"            :F(LOOP)
     OUTPUT = "Found a match!" :(LOOP)
END
```

Conditional Assignment

This snippet successfully identifies a line containing "Alice" or "Bob" but doesn't specify which one was found. To determine the exact match, you can use a conditional assignment to capture the matched string into a variable immediately following the pattern (separated by a period). This variable is only set if the pattern matches:

```
LOOP line = INPUT                         :F(END)
➤    line ("Alice" | "Bob") . match      :F(LOOP)
     OUTPUT = "Found a match «" match "»" :(LOOP)
     END
```

The conditional assignment operator is the most tightly bound and attaches to the nearest pattern to the left. Without enclosing the alternation on the highlighted line in parentheses, the match variable would only ever capture "Bob" due to the precedence rules.

The conditional assignment operator is executed once after the first found match. To find and report every instance of "Alice" or "Bob" in a line, your pattern should loop through the line, replacing each found instance with an empty string, allowing for multiple occurrences.

```
LOOP line = INPUT                          :F(END)
NEXT line ("Alice" | "Bob") . match =      :F(LOOP)
     OUTPUT = "Found a match «" match "»" :(NEXT)
END
```

⇒ **Alice likes Bob**
❮ Found a match «Alice»
  Found a match «Bob»
⇒ **Chuck hates Bob**
❮ Found a match «Bob»
⇒ **Chuck means Chuck**
⇒ **Alice --[Chuck]-- Bob**
❮ Found a match «Alice»
  Found a match «Bob»

You can also use OUTPUT in a conditional assignment to simplify your code, although this approach limits your ability to format the output text:

```
LOOP line = INPUT                           :F(END)
NEXT line ("Alice" | "Bob") . OUTPUT = :F(LOOP)S(NEXT)
END
```

⇒ **Alice likes Bob**
⟨ Alice
  Bob
⇒ **Chuck hates Bob**
⟨ Bob
⇒ **Chuck means Chuck**
⇒ **Alice --[Chuck]-- Bob**
⟨ Alice
  Bob

This modification reduces the code's length but at the cost of custom output formatting flexibility.

Immediate Assignment

SNOBOL executes a conditional assignment operator . (period) only if the entire pattern matches. If you want to store the results of a partial match, you can use immediate assignment with the operator $ (dollar sign). The immediate assignment is useful in a large pattern to learn how much of it has been matched and extract specific subpattern matches. The following code snippet attempts to parse a URL by extracting and stripping off the protocol name. Once you learn about primitive functions on page 157, you'll be able to parse URLs in full.

```
    address = ("http" | "https" | "ftp" | "telnet") $ protocol "://"
    site = "http://networksciencelab.com/"
    site address = ""
    output = protocol "://" site
END
```

You can nest the operators . and $, as in PAT = P1 $ V1 . V2 or PAT = P1 . V1 $ V2.

Cursor Position

Sometimes you may want to know the current pattern-matching cursor position (the distance from the beginning of the current string to the currently matched position)—for example, to replace or eliminate the subpattern match. Operator @ stores the position into the argument variable as an integer number. Here's how to redact censored words from a predefined list by replacing them with an equal number of asterisks:

snobol/censor.sno
```
* Replace censored words with asterisks
     &TRIM = 1
     censored = ('foo' | 'bar')
     pattern = @x censored @y

LOOP text = INPUT                      :F(END)
MORE text pattern = DUPL("*", y - x) :S(MORE)
     OUTPUT = text                     :(LOOP)
END

* Danger zone! Do not foobar!
| Danger zone! Do not ******!
```

Function DUPL(s, n) replicates string s n times and is described on page 157.

Using Indirect References

The indirect reference operator $ (dollar sign) turns a string str into a namesake variable or label. The str might be a direct string literal, an outcome of a string concatenation, or a string produced by a string function (refer to the section Understanding Functions and Predicates, on page 157). In the following program, the operator concatenates the label prefix "L" and the numerical user input, directing the program flow to the designated label.

snobol/menu.sno
```
* Display the menu
    OUTPUT = "Menu:"
    OUTPUT = "Press 1 for action, 2 for help, 3 for panic" :($("L" INPUT))
* Invoke a menu item
L1  OUTPUT = "Thank you for using Snobol!"  :(END)
L2  OUTPUT = "Help is on the way!"          :(END)
L3  OUTPUT = "Do not panic!"                :(END)
END
```

Computed GO TO

SNOBOL indirect reference resembles Fortran's computed GO TO statement, which determines the control flow path based on the evaluation of an integer or a real expression.

When employed as a subject, the indirect reference serves as a dynamic code injection tool, effectively inserting the referenced variable's value into the program as if it were an existing variable name. This technique opens up various possibilities for code manipulation and dynamic variable usage.

```
    day = "Monday"
    $day = " is a hard day"
    OUTPUT = day Monday
END
* Output: Monday is a hard day
```

A more practical implication of this mechanism is its ability to bypass prescribed naming constraints, enabling the creation and reference of variables with names that would otherwise be prohibited, such as dates ($"2024-02-23").

Understanding Functions and Predicates

SNOBOL provides a rich set of functions, including primitive and predicate, and a mechanism for creating user-defined functions.

Primitive Functions

Primitive functions in SNOBOL are similar to those in languages like Python or C, returning a value for subsequent use. Key examples include the following:

ANY(str). Generates a pattern that matches any one character from str. This function is complementary to NOTANY(str).

ARBNO(pattern). Generates a pattern that matches any number of repetitions of the pattern.

APPLY(func,p1,…,pn). Applies function named func with at least n parameters to the parameters p1, …, pn.

BREAK(str). Generates a pattern that matches strings *not* containing any character from str. This function is complementary to SPAN(str).

COPY(a). Returns a new array, which is a copy of array a (see the section Arrays, on page 162).

DATE(). Returns the current date as a string in the format "MM/DD/YY HH:MM:SS".

DUPL(str, times). Creates a string by repeating str a specified number of times.

ITEM(a,i1,…in). References an element of the array a without using the bracket form of reference (see the section Arrays, on page 162).

LEN(n). Generates a pattern that matches strings of length n.

NOTANY(str). Generates a pattern that matches any one character *not* in str. This function is complementary to ANY(str).

POS(n). Generates a pattern that matches if the current cursor position is n.

REMDR(x, y). Calculates x modulo y.

REPLACE(text, str1, str2). Produces a version of text where each character from str1 is replaced with the corresponding character in str2. The strings must be of equal length.

RPOS(n). Generates a pattern that matches if the current cursor position is n from the end of the line.

POS and RPOS

 SNOBOL patterns POS(0) and RPOS(0) correspond to the regular expression operators ^ (beginning of line) and $ (end of line), respectively.

RTAB(n). Generates a pattern that matches a string from the current cursor position to the nth position from the end of the line.

SIZE(str). Determines the length of a string.

SPAN(str). Generates a pattern that matches strings containing any character from str and nothing else. This function is complementary to BREAK(str).

TAB(n). Generates a pattern that matches a string from the current cursor position to the nth position.

TIME(). Returns the program execution time in milliseconds.

To demonstrate some of these functions, consider a simple game that prompts the user to input words of matching lengths, utilizing the SIZE() and LEN() functions for its logic. The game stops when the player succeeds.

snobol/matchgame.sno
```
* A silly matching game
      OUTPUT = "Enter a word: "
      pattern = LEN(SIZE(INPUT))
LOOP OUTPUT = "Enter a word of the same length: "
      text = INPUT
      text pattern :F(LOOP)
      OUTPUT = "It's a match!"
END
```

Primitive Patterns

In addition to pattern-generating functions, SNOBOL provides several pre-generated primitive patterns, some shown on the following list:

ABORT. Causes an immediate failure.

ARB. Matches any arbitrary sequence of characters.

BAL. Matches any substring surrounded by balanced parentheses.

FAIL. Forces to back up and search for another alternative:

```
        "MISSISSIPPI" ("IS" | "SI" | "IP" | "PI") $ OUTPUT FAIL
END
```

⇒ **IS**
⇒ **SI**
⇒ **IS**
⇒ **SI**
⇒ **IP**
⇒ **PI**

REM. Matches a string from the current cursor position to the end of the line. Essentially, it stands for RTAB(0) .

Predicate Functions and Predicates

Unlike the primitive functions, SNOBOL predicate functions fail or return a null string. You can use them for flow control.

LE(n1, n2). Fails if the numbers are not equal. Other functions in the same family are GT(n1, n2), NE(n1, n2), EQ(n1, n2), and the like.

LGT(str1, str2). Fails if string str1 is not alphabetically (lexicographically) greater than str2. Other functions in the same family are LNE(str1, str2), LEQ(str1, str2), and the like.

DIFFER(p1, p2). Fails if the parameters are identical.

IDENT(p1, p2). Fails if the parameters differ.

INTEGER(n). Fails if the parameter is not an integer number.

~x. Negation unary operator/predicate fails and returns an empty string if the operand x succeeds. If x fails, then ~x succeeds. In the original SNOBOL, this operator was known as ¬x.

?x. Interrogation unary operator/predicate fails if the operand x fails. If x fails, then ?x succeeds and returns an empty string.

Suppose you want to report very long strings (with more than 80 characters) in a text file. The following program calculates the length of the current string and compares it to the column width (80). If the predicate function GT() doesn't fail, it returns an empty string, which is concatenated to the current line and printed. Otherwise, the function fails and the program returns to the beginning of the loop without producing any output.

```
snobol/showlong.sno
* Report long lines
    column.width = 80
LOOP line = INPUT                                      :F(END)
    OUTPUT = GT(SIZE(line), column.width) line :(LOOP)
END
```

User-Defined Functions

Creating custom functions in SNOBOL involves defining a function header and body. The header includes a prototype, which has the function's name and parameters and may also feature an optional entry label.

A function's prototype is a string that specifies the function name and a list of parameters, optionally followed by local variables. This string is the first argument in a call to the built-in DEFINE(proto[, entry]) function. The function's name is the default entry label if another entry label isn't provided. For example, the zip(str1, str2) function combines two strings character by character, akin to Python's zip(seq1, seq2) function:

```
* Default entry label
    DEFINE("zip(str1,str2)")
* Default entry label, some local variables
    DEFINE("zip(str1,str2)c1,c2")
* Explicit entry label
    DEFINE("zip(str1,str2)", "ZIP.LABEL")
```

Functions receive parameters by value, allowing for fewer actual parameters compared to the formal ones listed. Unspecified parameters and local variables are initialized as empty strings. Any function can be called recursively.

With a grasp of function structure, you can implement the function body. Let's proceed with the zip(seq1, seq2) function example:

```
snobol/zip.sno
➤ * The function zips two strings, discards extra symbols
➤       DEFINE("zip(str1,str2)") :(SKP)
➤ LOOP str1 LEN(1) . c1 =          :F(RETURN)
➤       str2 LEN(1) . c2 =          :F(RETURN)
➤       zip = zip c1 c2             :(LOOP)

  SKP  var1 = INPUT
       var2 = INPUT
       OUTPUT = zip(var1, var2)
  END

⇒ Hello
⇒ World
❮ HWeolrllod
```

The function (highlighted) operates by successively removing the first character from each input string and appending these characters to a result variable zip (being a local variable, it was implicitly initialized with an empty string). The loop concludes when it exhausts one of the strings, utilizing pattern matching to detect this condition.

The result variable, named after the function, is crucial in returning the output. The predefined RETURN label corresponds to the function's call site, facilitating the return process alongside the result variable. The goto :F(RETURN) and the variable zip act as the return zip statement in the less obscure languages.

The last three lines comprise the test case: read two strings, zip them, and display the result.

One more predefined label, FRETURN, marks failure in predicate functions, as illustrated by a function that checks for a character's presence in a string. Should the sought-after character be found, the function succeeds; otherwise, it exits upon depleting the input string by returning via :F(FRETURN).

```
     DEFINE("contains(text,char)", "LOOP")  :(SKP)
LOOP text char                              :S(RETURN)
     text LEN(1) =                          :S(LOOP)F(FRETURN)
```

Between :F(RETURN) and :F(FRETURN), the former indicates a successful return despite internal failures, while the latter signifies the function's failure.

Lastly, an unconditional goto (such as :(SKP)) at the function's start instructs SNOBOL to bypass the function body initially, executing it only upon an actual function call.

Keywords

Though not directly related to functions, SNOBOL so-called keywords serve as runtime language configuration mechanisms and, in that sense, are functional. A keyword starts with an ampersand, &, and controls a specific aspect of SNOBOL's behavior. SNOBOL provides more than thirty keywords. Here are the most useful of them:

&ALPHABET. Contains a string of the 256 characters in the ASCII collating sequence. Read-only.

&ANCHOR. Requires that a pattern matches at the beginning of a line.

&DUMP. "Dumps" (prints) the values of all variables (if 1) or variables and arrays (if 2) on exit.

&INFINITY. Contains the floating point value of infinity. Read-only. Available on some implementations.

&NAN. Contains the floating point value of NaN ("not a number"). Read-only. Available on some implementations.

&STNO. Contains the current statement number. Read-only.

&TRIM. Ignores trailing blanks when reading a line.

To illustrate how keywords affect SNOBOL's behavior, consider the &ANCHOR keyword. In the first example, attempting to find "lice" in "Alice" fails with &ANCHOR set to 1, as it requires the pattern to match from the beginning of the line:

```
    &ANCHOR = 1
    "Alice" "lice"                :S(END)
    OUTPUT = "Alice has lice!"
END
```

Conversely, with &ANCHOR at its default value (zero), the pattern can match anywhere within the string, allowing the search for "lice" in "Alice" to succeed:

```
    "Alice" "lice"                :S(END)
    OUTPUT = "Alice has lice!"
END
| Alice has lice!
```

Comprehending Data Structures

SNOBOL offers two built-in compound data types: arrays and tables. It also provides you the ability to define your data structures.

Arrays

In SNOBOL, an array is a heterogeneous ("mix-and-match"), dynamically created multidimensional structure. The dimensions cannot be altered once an array is defined through an array prototype.

To instantiate an array, use the ARRAY(proto[, init]) primitive function. The first parameter is a prototype: a string containing a comma-separated list of dimensions or dimension slices, such as "2,2:8". This prototype can be a direct string literal or derived from a string expression through operations like concatenation or other function calls. An optional second parameter allows for setting an initial value for all elements within the array.

Accessing array elements is done with an indexing operator that lists integer indices within angle brackets, starting at 1. Thus, in a 2×4 array, the highest index is <2,4> and the corresponding element is array<2,4>. An alternative way to reference the same array element is by calling the function ITEM(array,2,4). An attempt to access outside the array's defined bounds fails.

To sort a one- or two-dimensional array by the nth column, call functions SORT(array[, n]) or RSORT(array[, n]) (for sorting in descending order).

The following program prompts the user for the array size, creates the array accordingly, and populates it through a loop. Note that this program doesn't validate the user-provided array size to ensure it's a positive integer, which may lead to a runtime error.

snobol/array.sno
```
* Create and initialize an array
    OUTPUT = "Enter vector size:"
    size = INPUT
    data = ARRAY(size)
    i = 1

MORE OUTPUT = "Enter item #" i ":"
    data<i> = INPUT                    :F(DONE)
    i = i + 1                          :S(MORE)
DONE OUTPUT = "Done!"
END
```

SNOBOL lacks a built-in loop structure common in many programming languages. Instead, iteration over an array requires managing the flow of execution manually through the use of gotos. The highlighted block of the preceding code demonstrates a pseudo-loop technique by initializing a loop variable i, implicitly checking its validity in the array access expression data<i>, and incrementing it.

Tables

Tables in SNOBOL function similarly to dictionaries in Python or maps in Java, acting as collections that map heterogeneous unique keys to values. To start using a table, create it with the TABLE([size]) primitive function. The optional size parameter allows you to specify an initial capacity, although the table can automatically expand to accommodate more entries as needed.

Tables vs. Dictionaries

Tables in SNOBOL loosely correspond to dictionaries in Python and maps in Java.

You can convert a table into a two-dimensional array of two columns—keys and values—and back with the function CONVERT(object, type). The type designator is a string "ARRAY" or "TABLE" describing the target data type. As a note, CONVERT(object, type) can convert anything to a "STRING". It can also convert some other data types (for example, "REAL") to other data types (for example, "INTEGER"). When conversion isn't possible, the function fails.

To illustrate the practical application of tables, arrays, and data conversion, consider calculating the frequency of characters in a string. This process involves splitting the input into constituent characters, counting their occurrences, and displaying the results, as shown here:

```
snobol/count.sno
* Calculate characters' use frequencies
* Read the text:
      text = INPUT

* Create and populate the table, one character at a time
      counts = TABLE()
MORE text LEN(1) . char = :F(DONE)
      counts<char> = counts<char> + 1              :(MORE)

* Display the counts
DONE counts = RSORT(CONVERT(counts, "ARRAY"), 2)
      i = 1
LOOP OUTPUT = counts<i, 1> " appears " counts<i, 2> :F(END)
      i = i + 1                                    :(LOOP)
END
```

User-Defined Data Types

Primitive function DATA(template) defines a new data type matching the string template. Think of a new data type as a C/C++ structure or Java class without methods or visibility attributes. The template looks like a function prototype where the new data type name is the function name, and the data type fields are the formal parameters.

Data Types vs. Structures

 SNOBOL user-defined data types loosely correspond to structures (struct) in C and C++.

For example, the following statement defines a new data type called STACK.FRAME (presumably a stack frame) with two fields: value (the payload) and prev (a reference to the previous frame).

```
DATA("STACK.FRAME(value,prev)")
```

You can create a stack, an instance of a STACK.FRAME, by calling the namesake function (essentially, a constructor) with the initializing parameters. After that, the functions value(stack) and prev(stack) serve as accessors to the respective fields.

With some justifiable effort, you can create an abstract data type by encapsulating the accessors into higher-level functions. Following is an attempt to create a general-purpose stack, a quintessential element of text parsers. The implementation provides functions stack() (a constructor), push(stack, item), pop(stack), and peek(stack). You can test the class without knowing the underlying implementation.

snobol/stack.sno

```
Line 1  * Abstract stack implementation
            DATA("STACK.FRAME(value,prev)")

        * New stack: constructor
     5      DEFINE("stack()")               :(STACK.END)
        STACK stack =                       :(RETURN)
        STACK.END

        * Push
    10      DEFINE("push(s,item)")          :(PUSH.END)
        PUSH push = STACK.FRAME(item, s)  :(RETURN)
        PUSH.END

        * Pop
    15      DEFINE("pop(s)")                :(POP.END)
        POP DATATYPE(s) "STACK.FRAME"     :F(FRETURN)
            pop = prev(s)                  :(RETURN)
        POP.END

    20  * Peek
            DEFINE("peek(s)")              :(PEEK.END)
        PEEK peek = value(s)               :(RETURN)
        PEEK.END

    25  * Testing
            my.stack = stack()
            my.stack = push(my.stack, "Alice")
            my.stack = push(my.stack, "Bob")
            OUTPUT = peek(my.stack)
    30      my.stack = pop(my.stack)
            OUTPUT = peek(my.stack)
            my.stack = pop(my.stack)
        ||| stack underflow! |||
            my.stack = pop(my.stack)
    35  END
```

Note how the function pop(stack) defined on line 14 validates the parameter by calling another primitive function, DATATYPE(object), before attempting to pop. If the stack is empty (degenerated into an empty string), the function fails via :F(FRETURN), preventing the program from an uncontrollable crash.

Evaluating Unevaluated Expressions

A SNOBOL pattern may not include subpatterns that haven't been defined yet. But what if a pattern depends on a dynamically updated variable whose value changes, for example, in a loop? Shouldn't you redefine it after every change to the variable? You can, but you don't have to. An alternative solution is to use an unevaluated expression prefixed with an asterisk *.

An unevaluated expression is a reference to an actual expression that's evaluated at the time of pattern matching. By that time, the values of all variables are expected to be already known.

The program that follows extracts and displays the common words in two strings. A word is defined as a substring that doesn't contain any punctuation. The list of punctuation punct is user-defined. Note that SNOBOL has no escape notation; you have to enter the tab symbol and all sorts of quotation marks literally.

The program defines two patterns: needle.1 for the first string and needle.2 for the second string. The first pattern finds a sequence of non-punctuation symbols via BREAK(punct), stores it in the variable word, and proceeds to match as many punctuation symbols as possible via SPAN(punct). The extracted word is used to construct the second pattern by enclosing it in a combination of any punctuation character or line extents. Since the word isn't known before the loop starts, the second pattern treats it as an unevaluated expression (which it is). Any word in the first string and all matching words in the second are replaced with empty strings. The shared words are collected into a string and eventually displayed.

snobol/sharedwords.sno
```
* Find shared words in two strings

    &ANCHOR = 0; &TRIM = 1
    punct = " .,;:!?|@()$%{}[]'          " '"'

    needle.1 = BREAK(punct) . word SPAN(punct)
    needle.2 = (ANY(punct) | POS(0)) *word (ANY(punct) | RPOS(0))

    s1 = INPUT              :F(ERROR)
    s2 = INPUT              :F(ERROR)
```

```
MORE s1 needle.1 =               :F(DONE)
     s2 needle.2 =               :F(MORE)
     list = list word "|"    :(MORE)
DONE OUTPUT = list
END
```

As a side note, storing the words in an array or a table would be more efficient and appropriate for further processing.

The most powerful application of the unevaluated expression operator is recursive patterns—patterns that refer to themselves as their subpatterns. You can use this feature to implement a simple arithmetic expression checker (supports integer numbers, identifiers with lowercase letters and digits, parentheses, and the four principal arithmetic operators).

snobol/expression.sno

```
    &TRIM = 1
    &ANCHOR = 1

    letter = "abcdefghijklmnopqrstuvwxyz_"
    digit = "0123456789"
    var = ANY(letter) ARBNO(ANY(letter digit))
    num = ARBNO(ANY(digit))
    add.op = ANY("+-")
    mult.op = ANY("*/")
    factor = var | num | "(" *expr ")"
    term = factor | *term mult.op factor
    expr = add.op term | term | *expr add.op term
MORE text = INPUT                      :F(ERROR)
     text expr RPOS(0)                 :F(BAD)
     OUTPUT = "An expression"       :(MORE)
BAD  OUTPUT = "Not an expression"   :(MORE)
END
```

The complex patterns expr and term refer to themselves, directly and indirectly, using the asterisk operator. Bear in mind that recursive pattern definitions cannot use conditional or immediate assignments, because they don't own local variables. Only recursive functions are allowed to have them.

You can evaluate an unevaluated expression by pattern matching and calling the primitive function EVAL(e):

```
    expression = *(x * x * x)
    x = 3
    OUTPUT = EVAL(expression)
END
| 27
```

Direct String Evaluation

Function EVAL(e) loosely corresponds to the namesake Python and JavaScript functions. The latter functions are considered unsafe because they execute the string passed to them as code, which can lead to serious security risks if the string contains malicious code.

Managing Input and Output

Designed for mainframes and minicomputers, SNOBOL has a cumbersome and not very user-friendly (rather, it's more user-unfriendly) input/output subsystem built around the concept of an external input/output unit—essentially, a file, using modern-day terminology. The I/O system is also dependent on Fortran-style formatting. Fortunately, it's easy to turn this dependency off.

Function INPUT(sname,unit,buffer,fname) (not to be confused with the namesake predefined variable) opens the existing disk file fname for reading and associates it with the stream name sname and I/O unit—an integer number related to the C language file handle. The number must be 1 through 32, but doesn't seem to affect any further operation. The maximum buffer length buffer is another tribute to the days of mainframes.

Function OUTPUT(sname,unit,format,fname) (also not to be confused with the namesake predefined variable) opens the disk file fname for writing and associates it with the stream name sname and I/O unit. Set the format to an empty string unless you're eager to learn Fortran-style formatting.

Function DETACH(sname) closes a previously opened file/stream as close() would do in C or Python.

Detaching a File

Function DETACH(sname) loosely corresponds to the functions close(f) and fclose(f) in other modern programming languages.

Once the streams are open, you can use them for reading and writing lines like INPUT and OUTPUT. Here, the program copies the content of the file "input.dat" to the file "output.dat" one line at a time, overwriting its previous contents, if any.

```
     INPUT("infile", 3, 80, "input.dat")
     OUTPUT("outfile", 4, "", "output.dat")
MORE outfile = infile                        :S(MORE)
     DETACH("outfile")
     DETACH("infile")
END
```

Writing Something Big

What better way to honor a programming language created to facilitate studies in digital humanities (application of computing or digital technologies to the disciplines of the humanities) than to run a study in digital humanities, namely, in text analysis. One of the fundamental tasks in text analysis is word frequency calculation, the process of identifying the most frequently used words. Later, you can use those words and their frequencies for text summarization and comparison.

Developing a solid word-counting program in SNOBOL isn't so hard. The first step is to read the text from a file and normalize it—that is, convert it to the standard character case (lower or upper) to recognize and adequately count the same word written in different cases. Function freqs(fname), highlighted in the code listing, creates a table for counting, opens the file fname for reading, reads the next line, converts it to lowercase, and eliminates non-alphabetic characters at the beginning of the line.

SNOBOL doesn't have the convenient case-conversion functions such as str.upper() available in Java and Python. You must do case conversion via character replacement (primitive function REPLACE(text, from.str, to.str)).

The function then extracts the next word, a continuous sequence of alphabetic characters, by matching the line to the pattern wordpat, stores the word through conditional assignment, and deletes the matching part from the line. Each successful match makes the line shorter. When the line becomes empty, the function reads the next line.

snobol/freq.sno

```
* Find the most frequently used words
        &ANCHOR = 1
        &TRIM = 1

        punct = " ;:.,'~!@#$%^&*()=+[]{}\|/?0123456789   " '"'
        lc = 'abcdefghijklmnopqrstuvwxyz'
        uc = 'ABCDEFGHIJKLMNOPQRSTUVWXYZ'
        wordpat = SPAN(lc) . word SPAN(punct)

* Function definition
        DEFINE("freqs(fname)counter,line")          :(END.FREQS)
* The main reading and counting loop
FREQS   counter = TABLE()
        INPUT("infile", 3, 80, fname)
MORE    line = infile                               :F(DONE)
        line = REPLACE(line, uc, lc)
        line BREAK(lc) =
```

```
➤  WORD.L  line wordpat =                                :F(MORE)
➤         EQ(stops<word>, 1)                             :S(WORD.L)
➤         counter<word> = counter<word> + 1             :(WORD.L)
➤
➤  * Sort and trim the counts
➤  DONE counts = RSORT(CONVERT(counter, "ARRAY"), 2)
➤         i = 1
➤         DETACH("infile")
➤         freqs = counts :(RETURN)
➤  END.FREQS
```

Each extracted word is checked against the list of stopwords: words like *the*, *a*, and *when*, which are so commonly used that they don't contribute to the structure of the text or its story. The list of stopwords is often application-specific. The one below is taken from the NLTK Python library and augmented with very Shakespearean words like *thy*, *thou*, *hath*, and *thee*. The stopwords are prestored in the table stops as keys, and their values are 1. To test whether a word is a stopword, function freqs(fname) tests if the corresponding value in the table is 1 (a stopword) or 0 (the default value of a freshly created table item, indicating not a stopword).

The function concludes by converting the table to an array, reverse-sorting the array by frequency of occurrences, closing the file, and returning the counts.

```
* Prepare the table of stopwords
        stops = TABLE()
        stopwords = "i me my myself we our ours ourselves you "
+       "your yours yourself yourselves he him his himself she "
+       "her hers herself it its itself they them their theirs "
+       "themselves what which who whom this that these those am is "
+       "are was were be been being have has had having do does did doing "
+       "a an the and but if or because as until while of at by for with "
+       "about against between into through during before after above below "
+       "to from up down in out on off over under again further then once "
+       "here there when where why how all any both each few more most other "
+       "some such no nor not only own same so than too very s t can will "
+       "just don should now d ll m o re ve y ain aren couldn didn doesn "
+       "hadn hasn haven isn mightn mustn needn shan shouldn  wasn weren "
+       "won wouldn tis thy thou shall thee th would mine must hath st "
+       "may enter exit doth exits till upon "
SW.LOOP stopwords wordpat =                              :F(TEST)
        stops<word> = 1                                  :(SW.LOOP)
```

In the testing phase—the most intriguing part of the exercise—you apply the function to three datasets. The program displays the first 50 most frequently used words for each input file, and the file name. Consequently, you can use the program's output in other processing tools (such as statistical or Venn diagram visualization software). Alternatively, you can challenge yourself and implement the next steps of the text processing pipeline in SNOBOL.

```
* Test the program
TEST     files = ARRAY(3)
         files<1> = "macbeth.txt"
         files<2> = "antony-and-cleopatra.txt"
         files<3> = "a-midsummer-nights-dream.txt"

         j = 1
TEST.LOOP result = freqs(files<j>)              :F(END)
         i = 1
         results = files<j> ":"
CONCAT   results = results " " counts<i, 1>     :F(PRINT)
         GT(i, 50)                              :S(PRINT)
         i = i + 1                              :(CONCAT)
PRINT    OUTPUT = results
         j = j + 1                              :(TEST.LOOP)
END
```

The data for the experiment—Shakespeare's *Macbeth, Antony and Cleopatra,* and *A Midsummer Night's Dream*—comes from Folger Shakespeare Library,[2] which offers a free collection of Shakespeare's works in plain text format.

Even the raw-eye inspection of the output reveals an intricate pattern of words (not to be confused with SNOBOL patterns!). Some words are common to all three pieces (*good, lord, man, speak, say, come*), some occur in the plays pairwise (for example, *love* in *Antony and Cleopatra* and *A Midsummer Night's Dream*), and some are unique to the plays (mostly proper names).

---

2.   https://www.folger.edu/explore/shakespeares-works/download/

macbeth.txt: macbeth lady macduff banquo yet us come first good malcolm let make lord like time king say ross done man well speak great sir duncan scene see fear murderer know second one thane doctor lennox go look siward third give sleep night hand things son witch death knock blood cannot heart.

antony-and-cleopatra.txt: antony caesar cleopatra enobarbus let charmian good come well sir make pompey us messenger go say like give madam lord soldier lepidus take menas eros great egypt scene man one octavia yet queen world first agrippa speak iras see love hear done know dolabella heart made noble hand death tell gods.

a-midsummer-nights-dream.txt: love bottom lysander demetrius hermia come quince pyramus thisbe sweet theseus man one robin let helena see night go good eyes never lion fair make wall flute well play moon titania look lord say yet speak like oberon true fairy away take us know lovers heart give day eye thus hippolyta.

Further analysis of the results could lead to more intriguing observations, but now you should continue your journey. Your next destination is Starset, the language so similar to SNOBOL and so different from it.

Further Reading

- *The Snobol4 Programming Language [GPP71]*
- *SNOBOL Programming for the Humanities [Hoc86]*

Set theory is a disease from which mathematics will one day recover.

> *Henri Poincaré, French mathematician, theoretical physicist, engineer, and philosopher of science*

CHAPTER 6

Harnessing Set Data with Starset

The five obscure programming languages you've encountered—Forth, Occam, APL, Simula, and SNOBOL—have been obscured by time. All of them, except Occam, were designed in the late 1960s to early 1970s, in the early age of modern computing, when the language developers' dreams and expectations didn't match the available hardware and didn't have adequate community support, commercial backing, and suitability for the tasks at hand. They failed to displace Fortran, COBOL, PL/I, and ALGOL 60, the back-then workhorses of the computing industry.

The Starset language, on the other hand, was obscured by space. It was designed in the last years of the Soviet Union behind the crumbling Iron Curtain to produce a homegrown alternative to Fortran, Pascal, and C. The language description was *published as a book in Russian [GS91]*, later *partially translated into English [Gil94]*. The only known Starset compiler worked under the MS-DOS operating system. Its source code hasn't been preserved, so my team and I had to reimplement it from scratch.

"Hello, Sets!"

Starset is one of the few set-oriented languages. Actually, to the best of our knowledge, it's one of two set-oriented programming languages, the other being SETL (*Programming with Sets: An Introduction to SETL [SDDS86]*). While many languages, such as Prolog, Oz, Coq, Haskell, Erlang, Datalog, and Python, support sets, only Starset and SETL consider them their primary data types.

Set-oriented languages offer some advantages over other classes of languages. Set operations are naturally parallelizable, which makes them well-suited for modern multicore and distributed computing environments. They are better aligned with mathematical foundations, which can provide a solid theoretical basis for reasoning about data and operation. Finally, they offer an alternative view on data persistence, replacing relations between data columns with set relations.

Starset's set-orientedness does not preclude it from greeting you in a no-nonsense way:

```
/* The obligatory first program */
PROC helloworld()
  WRITE 'Hello, world!'
ENDPROC
```

The code in the example declares a procedure called helloworld() that takes no parameters. The procedure doesn't return a value. It executes the operator WRITE (Starset is case-insensitive, but let's agree to use all uppercase letters for keywords and built-in, or primitive, subroutines), which prints a string enclosed in single quotation marks. The comment notation in the first line of the excerpt is the same as in C or C++.

A Starset program consists of one or more subroutines—procedures operating via side effects and functions returning values. In the Suffolk StarSet (s3) implementation, the first procedure (not a function!) in a file is the main one, regardless of its name, and acts as the program's entry point. The main procedure calls all other subroutines if necessary.

Getting to Know Starset Data Types

Starset is a set-oriented language, but what is a set exactly?

A Starset *set* is a possibly empty collection of distinct words, similar to a Python set(), Java Set, or C++ std::set—but what exactly is a word? Let's dive deeper.

Words

A Starset *word* is the most fundamental data type, similar to a character string in languages that support them. In a program, words are enclosed in single quotation marks. For instance, 'Hello, world!' and 'Starset' are both valid words, but "Hello, world!" is not (it uses double quotation marks).

If a word resembles a valid integer or floating-point number (possibly in scientific notation), it can be written without quotation marks for convenience. Thus, -216.000, 3.14159, and .67E+3 are words; from Starset's point of view, they are indistinguishable from '-216.000', '3.14159', and '.67E+3'.

A word is the only atomic data type in Starset. You can use it to represent strings, numbers, and logical (Boolean) conditions.

Everything Is a String

 Starset's ubiquitous words—capable of being strings, numbers, or Boolean conditions—resemble values in the early implementations of Tcl (Tool Command Language, 1988) and various Unix shells. Those were stored as character strings, too, and were converted to numbers or Booleans and back as needed.

Depending on the operation (an operator, primitive subroutine, or user-defined subroutine), a word can behave as a number, string, or condition. For string operations like concatenation A^B, a word written in numeric notation is converted to the *canonical numeric notation*, either in fixed-point without trailing zeros or integer notation, whichever is shorter. For instance, .67E+3 becomes '670', -216.000 becomes '-216', and 3.14159 remains '3.14159'.

```
n1 := .67E+3;
n2 := -216.000;
WRITE n1 ^ ' is larger than ' ^ n2 ^ '.'
/* Output: 670 is larger than -216. */
```

Conversely, a word used in a numerical operation (for example, multiplication A*B) is implicitly converted to a number. The numeric value of a word is the longest initial subword that represents a valid number, with the remainder of the word (the invalid part) ignored. An empty string (') has a numeric value of 0.

```
width := '2 meters';
height := '3.7 centimeters';
area := width * height;
WRITE area
/* Output: 5.4 */
```

This allows you to include units with values but doesn't offer unit conversion or validation. The numeric values of logical expressions are 0 for false and 1 for true. For example, (10>5)+(10<5) is 1 because 10>5 is true and, therefore, has the numeric value of 1, and for a similar reason (10<5) is 0.

For Boolean operations like logical disjunction A|B, a word is false if its numeric value is 0 (including empty strings), and true otherwise. In the following example, both operands are malformed numbers. Their longest initial numeric subwords are empty strings interpreted as false Boolean values.

```
truth := 'to be' | 'not to be' ;
WRITE truth
/* Output: 0 */
```

Word Operators and Functions

Starset provides various word operators for arithmetic, logical, relational, pattern matching, and membership operations. For instance, the string multiplication operator S^^N concatenates N copies of string S. So 'ho'^^'3 times' evaluates to 'hohoho', akin to Python string multiplication.

The numeric/string duality of Starset words requires separate relational operations for numbers and strings. For example, words word_A and word_B can be compared numerically (arithmetically) or lexicographically (based on the alphabetic positions of the constituent characters). Starset offers different operators for each ambiguous operation, such as word_A = word_B, word_A != word_B, and word_A <= word_B for lexicographical comparison vs. word_A == word_B, word_A <> word_B, and word_A <<= word_B for numerical comparisons.

Both comparison modes can be legally used in most cases, as illustrated in the following code. The word 'null' is lexicographically (alphabetically) smaller than the word 'zero' because the character n is closer to the beginning of the alphabet than the character z. However, the numerical interpretation of both words is 0, which makes the second relationship false.

```
WRITE 'null' << 'zero';
/* Output: 1 */
WRITE 'null' < 'zero'
/* Output: 0 */
```

Only you can decide which mode is suitable.

Starset offers some support for first-order logic quantifiers: "exists" (∃) and "for all" (∀). Operator (EXIST var IN $set)(ex) checks if a value exists in the set $set, which, if assigned to the variable var, makes expression ex true. Operator (ALL var IN $set)(ex) checks if each value in S makes ex true. Both operators loop through the set $set, evaluate the expression, and stop when it becomes true (for EXIST) or false (for ALL).

Quantifiers as List Comprehensions

Operators EXIST and ALL can be explained as list comprehension expressions using Python-like pseudocode:

```
∃ ::= min(bool(exp(var)) for var in $set); # True if any is true
∀ ::= max(bool(exp(var)) for var in $set); # True if all are true
```

The difference lies in the choice of the aggregator function (min vs. max).

In the following example (aligned for clarity), the expressions check if a set contains at least one long word or only long words, respectively. The primitive function LEN(w) returns the number of characters in the word w or its canonical numeric representation.

```
has_long_word  := (EXIST w IN $set)(LEN(w) >= 10);
all_long_words :=   (ALL w IN $set)(LEN(w) >= 10)
```

Another notable primitive function is CUT(w,pos,len). It extracts a subword from the word w, starting at position pos (beginning at 1) and containing up to len characters. If either pos or len is too large, the result is an empty string.

Now, let's return to sets.

Sets

A set is an unordered collection of literal words or word expressions. In a program, they are comma-separated and enclosed in curly braces. The name of a set variable (a variable referring to a set) always begins with a dollar sign, as if implying that a set holds more value than a single word. An empty set is denoted as $0, where the metaphor falters because zero dollars is just as valuable as zero of anything else.

```
/* Ten decimal digits */
$decimal_digits := {0, 1, 2, 3, 4, 5, 6, 7, 8, 9};
/* The same set: The order does not matter */
$decimal_digits := {4, 1, 5, 3, 0, 2, 9, 7, 6, 8};
/* The same set: Duplicates are eliminated */
$decimal_digits := {0, 1, 2, 3, 4, 5, 6, 7, 9, 0, 2, 3, 4, 1, 2, 4, 9, 4};
/* Two binary digits */
$binary_digits := {0, 1};
/* One unary digit */
$unary_digits := {0};
/* No nullary digits */
$nullary_digits := $0
```

A significant difference between Starset sets and those in other languages is that Starset sets cannot be recursive and contain other sets or, as you'll see, classes. This limitation results in a strict tree-like data hierarchy that simplifies implementation but restricts the expressive power of the language.

Sets can be naturally tested for equality ($set_A = $set_B, $set_A != $set_B), membership (word IN $set, $set_A SUBSET $set_B), and pattern matching (Set IS Pattern). They also support common set operations like intersection ($set_A # $set_B), union ($set_A + $set_B), and difference ($set_A \ $set_B, $set_B \ $set_A).

Primitive functions MINL($set), MAXL($set), MIN($set), and MAX($set) return the smallest and the largest words in $set, either lexicographically or numerically.

The function WORD($set,sep) converts a set into a word by concatenating its members in lexicographical order and using the word sep as a separator. The function CARD($set) returns the cardinality of $set—the total number of items in the set.

Finally, set comprehension {Word IN $set : expr} builds a subset of all words Word in the set $set that make the expression expr true. If you're familiar with mathematical set theory, you may recognize the colon as the "such that" symbol. For example, $a_words is a set of words from $word_set such that each word starts with the letter 'a':

```
$a_words := {a_word IN $word_set : /* such that! */ CUT(a_word,1,1)='a'}
```

Classes

Classes are the third Starset data type. Just as sets group words, classes group sets. For most purposes, think of them as sets of sets. Class variable names start with two dollar signs. The special constant $$0 signifies an empty class. Note that while $0 is equivalent to {}, $$0 differs from {{}}. The latter denotes a class containing one element, which is an empty set. Following is an example of a three-element class where two elements are duplicates.

```
$$data := {{1, 2, 3}, {'a', 'b', 'c', 'd'}, {}, $0};
WRITE CARD($$data)
/* Output: 3 */
```

As you can see in the preceding example, the CARD($$class) function also works for classes. Since a class is a "glorified set," it supports intersection ($$class_A # $$class_b), union ($$class_A + $$class_B), difference ($$class_A \ $$class_B), and class comprehension:

```
$$large_sets := {$s IN $$data : CARD($s) >= 3};
WRITE $$large_sets
/* Output: {{1, 2, 3}, {'a', 'b', 'c', 'd'}} */
```

Mapping Your Data to Words, Sets, and Classes

One way to map your data to Starset words, sets, and classes is by considering Starset data types as relational database components: words correspond to individual items, sets represent rows or columns, and classes resemble tables. However, this analogy is imperfect because a database table (or a spreadsheet at a smaller scale) is rectangular and addressable:

- All rows have the same number of items.
- All columns have the same number of items.
- Any item is addressable by its row and column indices.

Sets in a class are not required to be the same size, and a class, being a set of sets, cannot be directly addressed (as sets are unordered).

Another approach is to treat sets as key-value pairs, like so, for example:

```
$$names := {{'_0', 'Mary'}, {'_1', 'John'}, {'_2', 'Ann'}};
$$ages := {{'_0', 24}, {'_1', 27}, {'_2', 18}}
```

The somewhat odd notation for the keys arises due to the unordered nature of sets; you cannot determine which word is a key or a value based on their position for the lack of positions. Keys should possess a unique characteristic (for example, the prefix '_' followed by a number) that can be identified through pattern matching.

You can combine an attribute and its value into one word, separated by a predefined symbol or combination of symbols (for example, '='). This approach allows you to treat a set like a dictionary, but pattern matching incurs additional overhead:

```
$$club := {{'name=Mary', 'age=24'}, {'name=John', 'age=27'},
           {'name=Ann', 'age=18'}}
```

What if the club in the example has two members with the same name and age? To handle this situation, consider adding a unique user identifier to each set:

```
$$club := {{'id=00001', 'name=Mary', 'age=24'},
           {'id=00002', 'name=John', 'age=27'},
           {'id=00003', 'name=Ann', 'age=18'}, /* an Ann */
           {'id=00004', 'name=Ann', 'age=18'}} /* another Ann */
```

To summarize, you can represent your data in Starset in a "natural" way. Let your understanding of language statements and procedures, particularly pattern matching, guide your choice.

Patterns

A *pattern* is how Starset describes the structure of an object—another word or a set. Starset provides operations for checking if an object matches the pattern, and if so, for extracting its components. Patterns are of two types: word patterns and set patterns.

Word Patterns

Word patterns resemble regular expressions. They consist of one or more atomic or assigning patterns joined by the word concatenation operator ^. Atomic patterns identify structures, while assigning patterns extract matching subwords.

Patterns as Regular Expressions

 Word patterns in Starset resemble regular expressions in languages like C++, Java, Perl, and Python.

An atomic pattern can be the following:

- A word literal or expression that matches a subword in the object. For example, in 'id=00001' subwords match 'id=' (literally 'id=') and '0'^^'4 times'^'1' ('00001').

- A primitive (built-in) pattern, as shown in the following table.

Pattern	Interpretation	Regex Equivalent
[X]	Any symbol	.
[..]	Any subword	.*
[l]	A lowercase letter	[a-z]
[L]	An uppercase letter	[A-Z]
[Ll]	A letter	[a-zA-Z]
[lw]	One or more lowercase letters	[a-z]+
[LW]	One or more uppercase letters	[A-Z]+
[Lw]	One or more letters	[a-zA-Z]+
[N]	A decimal digit	[0-9]
[Num]	A decimal number	[0-9]+

- A primitive (built-in) function, as shown in this next table.

Function	Interpretation
[aA(w)]	The word w in the opposite character case
[Any(w)]	Any character in w
[Notany(w)]	Any character not in w
[Span(w)]	The longest subword made of characters in w
[Break(w)]	The longest subword made of characters not in w
[Pos(k)]	The kth position from the start
[Rpos(k)]	The kth position from the end
[Tab(k)]	Any subword ending at the kth position from the start
[Rtab(k)]	Any subword ending at the kth position from the end

Note that [Tab(k)] and [Rtab(k)] are shortcuts for [..]^[Pos(k)] and [..]^[Rpos(k)].

Primitive patterns and functions are not strings (they're enclosed in square brackets rather than quotation marks) and must be concatenated properly.

Unlike regular expressions in other languages, Starset patterns lack the operators *, ?, and + for optional fragments and repetitions.

Last but not least, patterns are not considered word expressions and cannot be assigned to variables.

You can now write patterns to match a person's identifier, name, and age in the club membership example on page 179. These patterns are no longer atomic:

```
/* id_pat   */ 'id='   ^ [Num];
/* name_pat */ 'name=' ^ [Lw];
/* age_pat  */ 'age='  ^ [Num]
```

Atomic patterns identify matches but cannot extract the matching parts (like identifiers, names, and ages). Assigning patterns serve this purpose. An assigning pattern is an atomic pattern enclosed in parentheses and suffixed with a period and a word variable name (a *free variable*).

```
/* id_pat   */ 'id='   ^ ([Num]).id;
/* name_pat */ 'name=' ^ ([Lw]).name;
/* age_pat  */ 'age='  ^ ([Num]).age
```

The free variable must be declared previously. If the atomic pattern within the parentheses matches a subword, that subword is assigned to the free variable, a process known as *localization* in Starset. You can use a localized variable within the pattern after its assignment. The following pattern verifies that the left side of a comparison operator equals the right:

```
/* same_pat */ ([..]).var ^ '=' ^ var
```

The subword before the equal sign localizes the variable x, which is then reused to match the subword on the right.

Set Patterns

Set patterns match sets. A set pattern is represented as a collection of templates (which may be empty) enclosed in curly braces. A *template* can be one of the following:

- A word pattern P, which can be either atomic or assigning.
- A word pattern P enclosed in angle brackets, <P>.
- A word pattern P enclosed in angle brackets and parentheses, followed by a period and a free set variable name, (<P>).$var. The variable is localized if the pattern matches.

As you can see, set patterns are defined in terms of word patterns.

A set pattern effectively partitions a set into disjoint subsets. The splitting rules are as follows:

Word pattern. If a template is a word pattern, the corresponding subset is a single-element set (a singleton) containing the word that matches the pattern.

Angle-bracketed word pattern. If a template is a word pattern enclosed in angle brackets, the subset contains all words matching that pattern. Once matched, words are "temporarily removed" from the original set, preventing them from being matched again. Starset processes templates from left to right sequentially, meaning template order can impact how sets are partitioned.

Assigning pattern. If a template is an assigning pattern, the free variable gets localized as a result of the match.

The following examples illustrate set patterns.

- The pattern {([..]).abc, [Span(abc)]} matches a two-word set: one item is an alphabet (stored in the localized variable abc), and the other item is a word in that alphabet.

- The pattern {<[Num]>} matches a set of decimal integer numbers. Its extended version, {<[Num]>, <[Num] ^ '.' ^ [Num]>}, also accommodates floating-point numbers.

- The pattern {(<[lw]>).$text, Card($text)} matches a set containing lowercase strings and their count, for example, {'alice', 3, 'in', 'wonderland'}.

Pattern matching is Starset's primary mechanism for data retrieval. Instead of using positions or keys to access a value, Starset programmers use patterns that capture its "look and feel."

The pattern matching operator in Starset is x IS y. In this expression, x is a word or set, and y is a word or set pattern. The expression is true (1) if a match exists and false (0) otherwise. If there's a match, all free variables are initialized as a side effect and can be used within the subroutine.

Curiously, Starset distinguishes between conditional statements that use relational operators (such as equality, inequality, and membership) and those that use pattern matching operator IS. In the former case, the statement is called IF; in the latter case, it's ON. Apart from this difference, their syntax is identical. Compare the following examples:

```
$member := {'name=Alice', 'age=23', 'id=12345'};
IF CARD($member) = 3
    DO
    do_something_with($member)
END ELSE DO
    WRITE 'Invalid record'
END
```

vs.

```
$member := {'name=Alice', 'age=23', 'id=12345'};
ON $member IS {'name=' ^ [Lw], 'id=' ^ [Num], 'age=' ^ [Num]}
DO
    do_something_with($member)
END ELSE DO
    WRITE 'Invalid record'
END
```

Incidentally, you've just learned something about the structure of Starset control statements. Like in other modern languages (such as Ruby, Lua, Elixir, and, to some extent, Erlang, Julia, and MATLAB), they use DO-END syntax to denote compound statements in the body, and the ELSE block is always optional.

In addition to direct pattern matching, you can use patterns to create class indexes, as explained in the following section. They can also organize index-free sequential loops for sets and classes. The section Exploring Loops, on page 186, explains how.

Indexing Classes

Adding an *index* to a class is one way to manage the absence of a natural order within it. An index is a sequence of keys that prescribes the order in which the sets within the class are processed. A class can support multiple indexes, each uniquely named and precomputed before its first use.

Indexes are created using the CREATE INDEX statement:

```
CREATE INDEX name FOR $set IN $$class;
CREATE INDEX name FOR $set IN $$class BY key;
CREATE INDEX name FOR $set IN $$class ON pat BY key
```

The statement creates a new index named name for the class $$class, replacing any existing index with the same name.

As part of index creation, the word expression key is evaluated for each set in the class (temporarily assigned to the $set loop variable) that matches the set pattern pat, or {<[..]>} if pat isn't specified. Any free variable in key must be localized in the pattern pat.

If the BY key option is absent, the set key is a lexicographically ordered list of all words in the set. This list is created solely for executing this statement and isn't accessible to the program or you.

Each variant of the CREATE INDEX statement may have optional keywords DESC (descending), NUM (numerical), or both at the end. Without these options, the index consists of the calculated keys in increasing lexicographical order. The options change the order accordingly.

The following examples illustrate index-building operations. They create indexes for traversing the class $$club in decreasing order of the number of member attributes, in alphabetic order by name, and numerical order of identifiers.

```
CREATE INDEX size_idx FOR $member IN $$club BY CARD($member) DESC NUM;
CREATE INDEX name_idx FOR $member IN $$club
    ON {'name=' ^ ([Lw]).name, <[..]>} BY name;
CREATE INDEX id_idx FOR $member IN $$club
    ON {'id=' ^ ([Num]).id, <[..]>} BY id NUM
```

You can use class indexes for accessing and modifying classes (see the next section) or in sequential loops (see the section Sequential Loops, on page 187). When your program no longer needs an index, remove it by executing the DROP INDEX statement:

```
DROP INDEX name CLASS $$class
```

The statement is silently ignored if the requested index doesn't exist.

Accessing and Modifying Classes

With indexes in place, your program can manipulate classes by finding, modifying, deleting, and inserting sets. The respective statements are nonde-structive FIND and EXTRACT, and destructive MODIFY and INSERT. All of them, except INSERT, have a STATUS error clause. If the statement succeeds, the word variable error becomes 0. Otherwise, it becomes 1 or 2, depending on the reason for the failure.

The FIND statement locates a set in the class $$class whose key in the index name starts with key. If key is an empty string, the statement finds the first set in the index. The set is assigned to the variable $set and, as a side effect, becomes the *current element* of the $$class in the index. When executed with the options NEXT or PREV, the statement finds the next or the previous set in the index and updates the current element. (You must first execute the BY key form of FIND to establish the current element.)

```
/* Synopsis */
FIND $set IN $$class BY key IN INDEX name STATUS error;
FIND $set IN $$class NEXT IN INDEX name STATUS error;
FIND $set IN $$class PREV IN INDEX name STATUS error;
/* Example */
FIND $member IN $$club BY 23 IN INDEX age STATUS error;
IF !error /* Logical negation */
DO
    WRITE $member
END
```

You can modify the current element with the MODIFY statement or look it up again with the EXTRACT statement:

```
EXTRACT $set FROM $$class IN INDEX name STATUS error
```

The latter statement has two forms (both assume that the index has the current element). The BY $set form replaces the current element with $set. The DROP form removes the current element from the class.

```
MODIFY $$class IN INDEX name BY $set STATUS error;
MODIFY $$class IN INDEX name DROP STATUS error
```

After the modification, all existing indexes in the $$class are updated. If the modification didn't affect the current element, it remains the current element. Otherwise, the current element becomes undefined.

Finally, the INSERT statement inserts a new set into a class and automatically updates all the class indexes.

```
INSERT $set IN $$class
```

Data Persistency

Starset imitates some aspects of database management systems, particularly its built-in persistent storage concept. You can save any word, set, or class to external memory (a file) under a user-defined name. When you save a class, all its indexes are saved too.

```
SAVE val AS w
```

Conversely, a saved variable can be loaded from external memory. The file "knows" the data type of the variable. The type of the variable var must be consistent with the recorded type. You cannot save a set and later load it as a class.

```
LOAD var FROM w
```

External Storage

Starset documentation doesn't specify the external storage format. In the Suffolk Starset (s3) implementation, we assume each variable is stored in a separate file in a Starset-specific format.

The DELWORD w, DELSET $s, and DELCLASS $$c statements remove words, sets, or classes from external memory. If the target doesn't exit, the program crashes.

In the following section, you'll learn more about Starset loops.

Exploring Loops

Starset has an elaborated system of loop statements, including simple, sequential, and parallel loops.

Simple Loop

A simple loop is a familiar WHILE loop that executes its body—a compound DO-END statement—as long as the loop condition is true. Consider a code fragment that implements a procedure for calculating the first count prime numbers. This example illustrates not only simple loops but also other important concepts:

1. The procedure is defined with the keywords PROC and ENDPROC. If it's the first procedure in the program, it'll be considered the main procedure and executed (see the example on page 174).

2. The procedure begins with variable declarations. You must declare every variable in a subroutine according to its type, which might seem redundant because variable names are type-specific.

3. The READ statement reads a value of any type according to the variable name from the standard input.

4. The simple loop repeats the body as long as the set of discovered prime numbers is smaller than requested. The body contains a conditional statement that's in charge of discovery.

starset/primes.ss
```
PROC get_primes()
    WORD: x, current, count;
    SET: $primes;

    $primes := {2};
    current := 3;
    WRITE 'How many?';
    READ count;
    WRITE 'Prime number=' ^ 2;
```

```
    WHILE CARD($primes) < count
    DO
        IF (ALL n IN $primes)((current - (current % n) * n) <> 0)
        DO
            WRITE 'Prime number=' ^ current;
            $primes := $primes + {current};
        END;
        current := current + 1
    END;
    WRITE $primes
ENDPROC
```

The header of the conditional statement checks if the current number is prime by verifying it's not divisible by any prime number discovered so far. The expression (current - (current % n) * n) <> 0 effectively calculates the remainder of dividing n into current and compares it to zero. The "for all" quantifier repeats the test for each prime number found so far. If all tests pass, the current number is declared prime and added to the result set. The procedure contains a nested loop, though it's not immediately apparent.

Sequential Loops

A sequential loop processes a set or class elements in a sequence determined by a class index or calculated on the fly as needed. You may want to look at sequential class loops first for reasons that will soon become clear. Here's a synopsis of the sequential class loop statement:

```
FORORD $set IN $$class ...
FORORD $set IN $$class BY ex ...
FORORD $set IN $$class ON pat BY ex ...
FORORD $set IN $$class BY INDEX name ...
```

Additionally, each variant of the loop may include optional keywords DESC and NUM before the loop body.

The syntax in the first three lines mirrors the CREATE INDEX statement (see the section Indexing Classes, on page 183). This resemblance isn't coincidental; you can use a previously created index to guide the loop (as in the fourth line of the synopsis) or create an index implicitly while running the loop. In the latter case, an index is ad hoc and discarded after the loop termination. In the former case (CREATE INDEX), the index becomes a part of the class and is even saved into persistent storage. If you plan to use the same index more than once in your program, consider investing in building and saving it! On the other hand, if you loop through a class only once, using a throwaway index might be more efficient.

Sequential set loops follow the same rules as sequential class loops, except that you cannot replace them with indexed access. Note that if pat is omitted, it's implied to be [..] (the whole word).

```
FORORD var IN $set ...
FORORD var IN $set BY ex ...
FORORD var IN $set ON pat BY ex ...
```

With that in mind, display the prime numbers in reverse order:

```
FORORD p IN $primes NUM DESC
DO
    WRITE p
END
```

You can achieve the same effect using negated numbers as the sorting keys:

```
FORORD p IN $primes BY -p NUM
DO
    WRITE p
END
```

Parallel Loops

With proper precautions, you can process elements of sets or classes in parallel. If you're familiar with programming languages like Java or Python, a parallel loop's syntax will also look familiar:

```
FOR var IN $set /* accumulating variables here */ ...
FOR $var IN $$class /* accumulating variables here */ ...
```

Parallel Loops

 Parallel loops in Starset resemble *foreach* loops found in PHP, Perl, Ruby, Swift, Kotlin, Python, Java, and other similar languages with the addition of parallel processing.

In each loop iteration, the loop variable var or $var takes the value of the current set or class item. The order of iterations is determined by the compiler. You must design the loop body such that the outcome is not affected by the order of execution. The following constraints must be enforced:

- The loop body may not access the $set or $$class variables to prevent concurrent modifications.

- The following statements with side effects are not allowed in the loop body: DELWORD, DELSET, DELCLASS, SAVE, LOAD, CREATE INDEX, DROP INDEX, FIND, INSERT, MODIFY, READ, WRITE, USE, DRIVE. (The last two statements are implementation-specific and not covered in this book.)

- The loop body cannot invoke any subroutine that uses any of the afore-mentioned statements, either directly or recursively.

- The QUIT and LEAVE statements are not allowed within a parallel loop body.

These and the previous limitations essentially transform Starset into a nearly pure functional language.

Accumulating variables and their accompanying operators provide mechanisms for gathering set/class data. The variables are of word type for set loops and set type for class loops. Word variables support operators + (arithmetic addition), * (multiplication), & (logical "and"), and | (logical "or"). Set variables support operators + (set union) and # (set intersection). An accumulating variable A with an operator $\otimes$ can only be used in the loop in a reassignment statement in the forms A := A $\otimes$ var or A := A $\otimes$ $var.

Any non-accumulating variable altered during a loop iteration doesn't retain its value for the next iteration. Effectively, a non-accumulating variable in a loop is replaced with a temporary shadow copy discarded after each iteration. This restriction isolates iterations from one another, facilitating parallel execution.

The name "parallel" in the language documentation is misleading. A loop would be genuinely parallel if your computer had enough computing cores to run each iteration at the same time. In practice, only some iterations may run simulta-neously, or perhaps only one. The term implies that the loop is potentially parallelizable, but the compiler isn't obligated to generate parallel code.

The following example calculates the standard deviation of a numerical set:

```
WORD: sum, sum2, n, std;
sum := 0; sum2 := 0; n := 0

FOR w in $data ACCUM sum+, sum1+, n+
DO
    sum := sum + w;
    sum2 := sum2 + w * w;
    n := n + 1
END;
sum := sum / n;
std := (sum2 / n - sum * sum) ** 0.5
```

Other Loop Elements

Like most procedural languages, an iteration of any loop in Starset can be terminated by executing the ITERATE statement. Likewise, executing a LEAVE statement can terminate any simple or sequential loop (but not a parallel loop).

Designing Subroutines

Starset provides two types of subroutines (callable code fragments): procedures and function procedures, also known as simply functions.

The difference between procedures and functions dates back to the early days of computing and concerns parameter passing and return values. A procedure is a subroutine that does not return a value (it's void, as in C/C++) but receives its parameters by reference and can modify them. A function is just the opposite: it always returns a value but receives the parameters by value. The copies of the original parameters essentially become the function's local variables.

Procedures and Functions

 Procedures and functions in Starset loosely correspond to procedures and functions in Occam. Procedures in both languages don't return values and, by default, pass parameters by reference. Functions in both languages return values and pass parameters by value.

Both procedures and functions consist of three parts: the header (the subroutine name and the list of formal parameters), local variables' declarations, and the body. The body consists of one or more statements separated by semicolons and executed sequentially, unless a conditional statement (IF, ON, or CHOICE) directs the control flow around them or a loop statement makes them repeat. The QUIT statement, found anywhere in the body, leads to immediate termination of the subroutine, *passivation* (that is, deletion) of all local variables, and return to the caller.

Note that all variables in Starset belong to a subroutine. Global variables are not possible, further supporting parallel loops and recursive subroutine calls.

Any subroutine can be called recursively, either directly or indirectly. Tail recursion elimination isn't supported. Make sure that any subroutine meant to be recursive has the base case.

Procedures

Starset procedures are more versatile than functions.

- They can have an empty body (consisting of a null statement).

- They take any number of formal parameters of any type.

- The formal parameters are passed by reference and can be altered in place. Unfortunately, this feature does not allow to pass expressions as parameters. Any expression to be used in a procedure must be evaluated, its value stored in a variable, and that value passed to the procedure.

- Procedures don't return values directly but can manipulate their parameters, including those responsible for passing operation status out of the procedure.

A procedure is invoked by executing the CALL statement that takes the procedure's name and a comma-separated (or empty) list of actual parameters.

You've already seen some examples of procedures in this chapter, but here's one more. This procedure recursively counts down from n (an integer word) to 0. Its execution can cause stack overflow for large values of n.

```
PROC count_down(n)
WORD: n; /* Declaration */
IF n > 0 DO
    n := n - 1;
    CALL count_down(n)
END
ELSE DO /* This clause is illustrational and can be removed */
    QUIT
END
ENDPROC
```

Functions

Unlike procedures, a function can return a computed value. However, only words can be passed as parameters (no sets or classes), and they are passed by value. It means any modifications to the copy of a parameter in the function body are discarded after the function quits.

To return a value from a function, assign the value to a variable with the same name as the function. Unlike in Simula (consult Introducing Procedures, on page 120), this variable must be declared like any other variable. You can then assign the returned value to a variable in the caller subroutine.

The "simple" (inefficient) implementation of the function calculating the nth Fibonacci number is shown here:

starset/fibonacci.ss
```
FUNC fib(n)
WORD: fib, n;
    CHOICE
        CASE n==1 DO fib := 0 END
        CASE n==2 DO fib := 1 END
        OTHERWISE DO fib := fib(n-1) + fib(n-2) END
ENDFUNC
```

```
PROC test_fib()
    WRITE fib(22) /* Output: 10946 */
ENDPROC
```

Since a function cannot be a program entry point, you must provide a testing procedure known as a *driver*.

Writing Something Big

This example aims to show how you can use Starset, a set-based programming language, to solve a problem that seems utterly unrelated to sets: the eight queens problem.

The problem and its solution reportedly date back to 1848 when chess composer Max Bezzel published them. If you play chess or at least know the rules, the problem is about placing eight queens on an eight-by-eight chessboard such that no queen attacks any other queen. If you don't play chess, the problem is about selecting eight locations in an eight-by-eight square grid such that no two chosen locations share the same row, column, or diagonal.

You can generalize the problem to N queens on an N×N square board. The problem is trivial for N=1, has no solutions for N=2 or N=3, and has asymptotically $(0.143 \times N)^N$ solutions in general.

The following problem-solving algorithm is adapted with modifications from *Iazyk Programmirovaniia Starset (in Russian) [GS91]*, where it's attributed to S. Vorobyov.

The main procedure, queens(), declares and initializes the variables, obtains the board size, and creates a set of the first N natural numbers. If the board size is known at the time of writing the program, the highlighted lines may be replaced with a set literal. At the end, the procedure calls another procedure, put_queen(size, col, $solutions, $free_rows, $free_main_d, $free_anti_d, solution_id), which recursively calculates the solutions.

```
starset/queens.ss
PROC queens()
    WORD: column, solution_id, size, k;
    SET: $solutions, $free_rows, $free_main_d, $free_anti_d;

    $solutions := $0;
    $free_rows := $0; /* free rows */
    $free_main_d := $0; /* free main diagonals */
    $free_anti_d := $0; /* free anti-diagonals */
    column := 1; /* number of queens so far */
    solution_id := 0;

    WRITE 'Enter chessbord size: ';
    READ size;

➤   k := 1;
➤   WHILE k <= size DO /* Initialize free rows */
➤       $free_rows := $free_rows + { k };
➤       k := k + 1
➤   END;

    CALL put_queen(size, column, $solutions, $free_rows,
                    $free_main_d, $free_anti_d, solution_id)
ENDPROC
```

The recursive procedure takes the following: the size of the board, the current column being processed, a set storing the positions of the queens placed so far, a set of rows that are still available for placing a queen ($free_rows), a set of main diagonals that are still free ($free_main_d), a set of anti-diagonals that are still free ($free_anti_d), and a counter for the number of solutions found (solution_id). The large number of parameters is due to the lack of global variables.

The procedure iterates over each row in $free_rows in numerical order and calculates the main diagonal and anti-diagonal for the current position. The current position is valid for placing a queen if neither the main diagonal nor the anti-diagonal is occupied.

```
starset/queens.ss
/* -------- Recursive part --------------- */
PROC put_queen(size, column, $solutions, $free_rows,
                $free_main_d, $free_anti_d, solution_id)
    WORD: size, column, column_, row, solution_id, main_d, anti_d;
    SET: $solutions, $free_rows, $free_main_d, $free_anti_d;
    SET: $solutions_, $free_rows_, $free_main_d_, $free_anti_d_;
    SET: $free_rows_copy;
```

```
/* No access to $free_rows in the FORORD loop */
$free_rows_copy := $free_rows;
FORORD row IN $free_rows NUM DO
    main_d := column - row;
    anti_d := column + row;
    IF !(main_d IN $free_main_d) & !(anti_d IN $free_anti_d) DO
        $solutions_ := $solutions + {'(' ^ column ^ ',' ^ row ^ ')'};
        IF column < size DO
            $free_rows_ := $free_rows_copy \ {row};
            $free_main_d_ := $free_main_d + {main_d};
            $free_anti_d_ := $free_anti_d + {anti_d};
            column_ := column + 1;
            CALL put_queen(size, column_, $solutions_,
                $free_rows_, $free_main_d_, $free_anti_d_, solution_id)
        END ELSE DO
            solution_id := solution_id + 1;
            WRITE 'Solution #' ^ solution_id ^ ':' ^ WORD($solutions_)
        END
    END
END
ENDPROC
```

If there are more columns to process, the procedure updates the sets to exclude the current row and include the current diagonals, increments the column counter, and recursively calls itself with the updated parameters to place a queen in the next column. When all columns are processed, the procedure increments the solution counter and prints the current solution.

```
❮ Enter chessbord size:
⇒ 5
❮ Solution #1:(1,1)(2,3)(3,5)(4,2)(5,4)
  Solution #2:(1,1)(2,4)(3,2)(4,5)(5,3)
  Solution #3:(1,2)(2,4)(3,1)(4,3)(5,5)
  Solution #4:(1,2)(2,5)(3,3)(4,1)(5,4)
  Solution #5:(1,3)(2,1)(3,4)(4,2)(5,5)
  Solution #6:(1,3)(2,5)(3,2)(4,4)(5,1)
  Solution #7:(1,4)(2,1)(3,3)(4,5)(5,2)
  Solution #8:(1,4)(2,2)(3,5)(4,3)(5,1)
  Solution #9:(1,5)(2,2)(3,4)(4,1)(5,3)
  Solution #10:(1,5)(2,3)(3,1)(4,4)(5,2)
```

As an exercise, consider using a class to represent the solutions and a set of queens' coordinates to represent an individual solution.

Some Starset deficiencies, such as the large number of passed parameters and the need to create local copies of variables for procedure calls, are annoying. You can automate such repetitive and tedious tasks in Starset and other languages by using m4—an obscenely underestimated language for text manipulation and code generation, which you'll explore in the next chapter.

Further Reading

- *Starset Programming Language [GS91].* This book is in Russian, but it's much better than the translated English edition.

- *The Set Model for Database and Information Systems [Gil94]*

Machines take me by surprise with great frequency.

Alan Turing, English mathematician, computer scientist,
logician, cryptanalyst, philosopher, and theoretical biologist

CHAPTER 7

Automating Text Generation with m4

APL, Forth, Occam, Simula, and SNOBOL have been obscured by time. Starset was obscured by space. m4, the last protagonist of this book, is obscured in plain sight. It's used in systems like GNU Autoconf (a tool for producing shell scripts that automatically configure software source code packages), GNU Automake (a tool for automatically generating Makefiles), and Sendmail (a popular mail transfer agent)—and yet few programmers know about its existence.

What makes m4 (that's right, spelled with a lowercase *m*) different from the other six obscure languages is its role in the programming ecosystem. m4 is a *preprocessor*.

Understanding Preprocessors

A preprocessor is a program that converts one text into another by following specific rules written in a specific language. Unlike compilers that convert texts in human-readable (but not necessarily human-spoken) languages into machine code or any other inhumane representation, preprocessors stay at the same level of abstraction. If you feed a natural-language text into a preprocessor, the output is expected to be in a natural language. If you feed a program written in a programming language into a specialized source-to-source preprocessor (a *transpiler*), the output is another program. Preprocessors act as language translators, which makes them uniquely suitable for automated program code generation, a crucial aspect of modern programming.

All preprocessors may be roughly assigned to one of the following classes: lexical, syntactic, and general-purpose preprocessors.

- Lexical preprocessors operate on the lexical level, processing text and performing substitutions based on predefined rules. They work with tokens or sequences of characters without understanding the syntax or structure of the text. An example of a lexical preprocessor is the C preprocessor (cpp), which handles directives like #include, #define, and #if to manage code inclusion, macro expansion, and conditional compilation.

- Syntactic preprocessors go a step further by understanding the syntactic structure of the input text. They can manipulate code based on its syntax, making more complex transformations possible. A syntactic preprocessor can analyze the grammatical structure of the text and make changes that respect this structure. An example of a syntactic preprocessor is XSLT (extensible stylesheet language transformations), which transforms XML documents into other formats like HTML, text, or more XML documents based on the document's tree structure.

  Another example is LaTeX, a powerful typesetting system that fundamentally operates as a preprocessor for TeX (another powerful typesetting system) by abstracting, simplifying, and extending its functionalities.

- General-purpose preprocessors are versatile tools that can handle a broad range of preprocessing tasks. They're not limited to specific types of input or transformations and can be used in various contexts. GNU m4 is a prime example of a general-purpose preprocessor. It can perform macro substitution, file inclusion, text manipulation, and more. Essentially, m4 is a full-scale, Turing-complete programming language, which is why it's the subject of this chapter.

  Some argue that SNOBOL (see Chapter 5, Streamlining Text Processing with SNOBOL, on page 147) is a general-purpose preprocessing language too, but it has already had its moment of glory in this book.

Turing-Completeness

A programming language is Turing-complete if any program that can be written for a Turing machine can also be written in this language. To meet this requirement, a language must be able to manipulate an arbitrary amount of data storage, support conditional and repeated execution, and be able to read (input) and write (output) data. XSLT, LaTeX, and m4 are Turing-complete, but the C preprocessor is not.

The required "Hello, world!" program in m4 looks suspiciously non-programmatic. In fact, it doesn't look like a program at all.

m4/hello.m4
```
Hello, world!
```

That's one of the core features of m4: anything that's not explicitly a command is data. Data is output verbatim. The language has no output statement because there's no need for one. In the same spirit, there's no input statement in m4: data is read as it comes through the standard input.

No Read, No Write

 m4's pass-through approach to data processing, which requires no explicit input or output statements, resembles the AWK language approach, except that AWK reads the input one line at a time.

A program that takes data and instructions from the standard input and outputs the transformed data to the standard output is called a *filter*. m4 is a filter.

Last but not least, there's more than one m4. The original m4 was developed by UNIX pioneers Brian Kernighan and Dennis Ritchie (K&R) in 1977 as an extension to m3. The version discussed in this book is GNU m4, designed in 1990. GNU m4 offers many enhancements but remains mostly compatible with the original m4.

Defining and Using Macros

Macro substitution, also known as macro expansion, is the workhorse of m4.

Simple Macros

Simple macros are names replaced at runtime with their definitions. The following classical example greets the book author by using the function define(name, definition) to define a macro named AUTHOR. The value (definition) is Dmitry Z.. No quotation marks are needed, and spaces are allowed in the definition. By the way, define() is a macro too.

```
m4/greet.m4
define(AUTHOR, Dmitry Z.)
Hello, AUTHOR!
```

Let's execute the code:

```
/home/dzseven> m4 code/m4/greet.m4

Hello, Dmitry Z.!
```

The substitution worked, but where does this bothersome blank line come from? m4 isn't trying to be too clever; quoting myself, "anything that is not explicitly a command is data." "Anything" includes the line break after the macro definition on the first line. This line break breaks the line in the output. m4 may be the only programming language in which you need to comment a line break!

Fortunately, comments aren't hard. The dnl ("delete to newline") macro does what it says: deletes everything to the end of the line, including the end of the line. The following code works as expected:

m4/greet-w-comment.m4

```
define(AUTHOR, Dmitry Z.)dnl
Hello, AUTHOR!
```

```
/home/dzseven> m4 code/m4/greet-w-comment.m4
Hello, Dmitry Z.!
```

Sometimes, AUTHOR is just a string literal. To prevent m4 from expanding it, enclose it in a combination of a backtick ` and a single quote '. m4 removes both but doesn't treat AUTHOR as a macro name. But what if you want to preserve the quotes too? No problem—double them!

```
Hello, `AUTHOR'!
Hello, ``AUTHOR''!
dnl Output:
dnl Hello, AUTHOR!
dnl Hello, `AUTHOR'!
```

You should quote macro names within the define command to avoid quirky, unexpected expansions. Also, avoid Python-style line comments starting with a pound sign #. They don't do what you expect them to do.

---

define() vs. #define vs. DEFMACRO

 The define() macro in m4 corresponds to the #define directive in the C preprocessor and (remotely) the DEFMACRO function in Lisp. Unlike m4 and cpp, Lisp supports both macros and functions. Function arguments are evaluated before a function call, but macro arguments are not evaluated before a macro expansion.

You're ready for the first practical application of m4: combining a response template with specific details.

m4/detail.m4

```
define(`AUTHOR', Alice)dnl
define(`MANUSCRIPT', My Friend Bob)dnl
define(`MOOD', sorry)dnl
define(`STATUS', rejected)dnl
```

m4/template.m4

```
Dear AUTHOR,

We are MOOD to inform you that your manuscript "MANUSCRIPT" has
been STATUS.

Editors
```

You can save the output to a file or, if you're a command-line geek, pipe it to a mail-handling program for delivery.

```
/home/dzseven> m4 code/m4/detail.m4 code/m4/template.m4
Dear Alice,

We are sorry to inform you that your manuscript "My Friend Bob" has
been rejected.

Editors
```

Nested Macros

Two macros used in the manuscript acceptance/rejection template, MOOD and STATUS, are not independent. Misusing these macros, such as pairing "happy" with "rejected," might perplex the intended reader.

Fortunately, m4 macros can be nested: a body of a macro can be another macro. In this example, the macros ACCEPT and REJECT each define MOOD and STATUS; the definitions are internally consistent. For instance, "happy" can be paired with "accepted" but not with "rejected."

```
m4/detail-nested.m4
define(`AUTHOR', Alice)dnl
define(`MANUSCRIPT', My Friend Bob)dnl
define(`REJECT', define(`MOOD', sorry)define(`STATUS', rejected))dnl
define(`ACCEPT', define(`MOOD', happy)define(`STATUS', accepted))dnl
ACCEPT`'dnl
```

The last line of the file (which could be the first line of the template or a part of another file, decision.m4) selects the decision. The syntax in m4 is delicate; an empty string between the macro name and a comment is required to prevent the two from being read as a single token ACCEPTdnl, which is incorrect.

Ratfor

Ratfor [Ker75] (Rational Fortran), the brainchild of Brian Kernighan and Dennis Ritchie, was the first programming language dependent on m4. It introduced C-style structural features such as code blocks and modern conditional and loop statements to the traditional Fortran 66. Rather than altering the language directly, Ratfor translated C-style code into core Fortran using m4 macros. As such, m4 was a crucial component of any standard Ratfor distribution.

In a more advanced scenario, the ACCEPT macro changes its definition after its first use to indicate that the action has been completed, transforming from `Accepted' to `Already accepted'. A self-modifying macro is a sophisticated form of nested macro that can change its definition or even delete itself, acting as a one-time-use macro.

```
define(`ACCEPT', `define(`ACCEPT',`Already accepted')Accepted')dnl
```

⇒ **ACCEPT**
❮ Accepted
⇒ **ACCEPT**
❮ Already accepted

Another macro, potentially more useful for programmers like you but still needing more work to become practical, ensures that the header file, foo.h, is included exactly once in your C/C++ program. This macro deletes its definition after a single use.

```
define(`ensure_foo',`undefine(`ensure_foo')`#'include <foo.h>')dnl
```

⇒ **ensure_foo**
❮ #include <foo.h>
⇒ **ensure_foo**
❮ ensure_foo

---

undefine() vs. #undef

 The undefine() macro in m4 is equivalent to the #undef directive in the C preprocessor and the del statement in Python.

Remember to quote the # in the macro definition because, otherwise, m4 treats it as a comment.

Macros with Arguments

You can "call" (more accurately, "expand") any macro with any number of arguments. The macro body has full access to the argument list and decides how to handle it. Compare the behavior of the user-defined macro foo and built-in macro len().

```
define(`foo', `bar')dnl
```

⇒ **define(`foo', `bar')dnl**
⇒ **foo**
❮ bar
⇒ **foo()**
❮ bar
⇒ **foo(`hello')**
❮ bar
⇒ **foo(`hello', `world')**
❮ bar

```
⇒  len
‹  len
⇒  len()
‹  0
⇒  len(`hello')
‹  5
⇒  len(`hello', `world')
‹  m4:stdin:1: Warning: excess arguments to builtin `len' ignored
   5
```

The foo behaves the same regardless of the number of arguments: one, two, or none, or even when expanded without the parentheses. On the contrary, len() calculates the length of a string when given a string, becomes a 0 if the string is absent, expands to its name when used without parentheses, or reports a warning if you provide too many arguments.

A macro body refers to the argument list using the $ notation shown as follows:

- $# expands to the number of arguments. Since # is a comment character, remember to quote $# as `$#'.

- $0 expands to the macro name.

- $* expands to the list of arguments.

- $@ expands to the list of arguments but does not expand quoted arguments.

- $n, where n is a positive integer, expands to the nth argument; if no such argument is provided, it defaults to an empty string.

False Friends in Makefiles

 Some $ notations in m4 look similar to the *automatic variables* in the language of the make utility ($@ and $*), but they serve a different purpose. The make utility has other automatic variables not used in m4: $<, $^, $?, $%, and $|.

You can now write a macro that explores and reports its argument list:

```
define(`my_args', ``$0' // format(`%05d', `$#') // $@ // $*')dnl
my_args(1, Hello, `eval(`1+2')')
dnl Output:
dnl my_args // 00003 // 1,Hello,eval(`1+2') // 1,Hello,3
```

The macro outputs its name (which must be quoted—otherwise, the macro spirals into infinite recursion), the number of arguments, and the argument list in two forms: original and expanded. Note that the code fragment uses two new built-in macros: eval() and format().

The eval() macro takes a well-formed string representing an arithmetic expression and produces the value of the expression. Just like Starset on page 173, m4 treats numbers as strings but doesn't support floating-point numbers.

The supported operations are parentheses (); arithmetic, bitwise, and logical negation -~!; exponentiation **; multiplication, division, modulo, addition, and subtraction */%+-; relational operations > >= == != < <=; shifts << >>; binary bitwise operations &^|; and logical operations || &&. The macro follows the "traditional" POSIX/C evaluation rules.

```
eval(`1')
dnl Output: 1
eval(`2**4-7')
dnl Output: 9
eval(`2^4!=2**4')
dnl Output: 3
eval(`(2^4)!=(2**4)')
dnl Output: 1
eval(`(2^4)==(2**4)')
dnl Output: 0
```

For some reason, m4 creators added two overly specialized macros, incr(n) and decr(n), that expand to an incremented or decremented n, respectively.

```
incr(100)
dnl Output: 101
decr(101)
dnl Output: 100
incr(eval(`100/'decr(3)))
dnl Output: 51
```

Note that neither macro can be embedded into the string passed as an argument to eval(), because the quotes protect it from expanding.

The format(format_string, ...) macro is another homage to the C language—specifically, the printf() function. The first argument is the format string with % specifications. The macro supports most ANSI C specifiers with widths, precisions, and other flags. It expands to a formatted string.

More ANSI C Legacy

Macros format() and eval() correspond to the C language printf() function and general ANSI C integer arithmetic expressions.

Returning to the my_args() macro in the code on page 203, the eval() macro in the $@ output is not expanded and still looks like a function call: eval(`1+2'). However, in the $* output, the macro is expanded and replaced by the result of the expression evaluation, which is the sum of 1 and 2.

More examples of accessing the argument list await you in the following sections.

Controlling Execution Flow

m4 macros can function as global variables when expanded without arguments or as functions when arguments are provided. In both cases, m4 can use the existence of a macro to control program execution flow.

Conditional Expansion

The built-in macro ifdef(name,true_string,false_string) tests if the macro name is defined and expands to true_string or false_string, depending on the outcome.

With this macro, you can reorganize the code fragment on page 201 to focus on the decision (ACCEPT vs. REJECT) and define the MOOD and STATUS appropriately.

```
m4/detail-ifdef.m4
divert(-1)
define(`AUTHOR', Alice)
define(`MANUSCRIPT', My Friend Bob)

# The status of the manuscript
define(`ACCEPT')
define(`MOOD', ifdef(`ACCEPT',happy,sorry))
define(`STATUS', ifdef(`ACCEPT',accepted,rejected))
divert
```

In this example, the divert() macro is used twice to avoid the need for multiple dnl commands. You'll read more about its full power in the section Diverting Output and Including Files, on page 212.

The ifelse() macro, or *multibranch* macro, is a powerful extension of ifdef(). It's essentially a condensed switch statement, as known in C, C++, or Java.

The macro takes 3N+1 arguments, with the last one defaulting to an empty string. Each triplet of arguments has the form s1,s2,equal_string and is evaluated as follows:

1. The first two arguments, s1 and s2, are strings compared, character by character.

2. If the strings are equal, the macro expands to equal_string.

3. Otherwise, the first three arguments are discarded, and the macro is evaluated with the remaining arguments.

4. If no two strings in the argument list match, the macro expands to its last argument (which, remember, may be an empty string).

---

ifdef() vs. #ifdef

 The ifdef() macro in m4 is equivalent to the #ifdef/#if defined and #ifndef directives in the C preprocessor. There's no direct cpp equivalent of ifelse().

As a special case, when called with just one argument, the ifelse(comment) macro is treated as a comment and is discarded.

In the following example, the macro takes ten arguments. The first nine are arranged in three triplets. The value N is sequentially compared with 1, 2, and 3 until the match (3) is found. If N were not on the list, the macro would expand to the tenth argument, more than three.

```
define(N,3)
ifelse(N,1,one,N,2,two,N,3,three,more than three)
dnl Output:
dnl three
```

To reinforce your understanding of ifelse() and refresh your knowledge of recursion, let's reimplement the ifelse() macro. Imagine that, because of the negligence of the language developers, it can be called only with four arguments: ifelse(s1,s2,equal_string,nonequal_string). You want to extend its functionality and define a new macro recur_ifelse() that behaves like the real built-in ifelse() without restrictions.

The unrestricted macro definition will rely on recursion and, most importantly, on another built-in macro, shift(args). The shift() macro takes an argument list args and discards its first element.

The argument list in m4 is a string of comma-separated arguments. It can be defined as a "variable" (a macro without arguments) or supplied via $ notation as $@ or $*.

```
⇒ define(`alist',`Mary,had,a,little lamb')
⇒ shift(alist)
❰ had,a,little lamb
⇒ shift(shift(alist))
❰ a,little lamb
⇒ shift(shift(shift(alist)))
❰ little lamb
```

Shifts in Shells

 The shift() macro in m4 is equivalent to the shift command in many POSIX-compatible shell scripting languages (for example, in Bourne shell, bash, ksh, and zsh).

After shifting, the new argument list can be further used to call another macro. As shown in the code that follows, the recursive macro recur_ifelse() first uses the "broken" ifelse() to check the number of arguments $#. If only one argument is left (presumably, the last one), it becomes the result. Otherwise, ifelse($1,$2,$3,args') attempts to equate $1 and $2 and returns $3 on success. If the first two arguments don't match, the macro expands itself recursively with the thrice-shifted original argument list.

m4/recur_ifelse.m4
```
divert(-1)
define(`recur_ifelse', `ifelse(`$#',`1',`$1',
                              `ifelse($1,$2,$3,
                 recur_ifelse(shift(shift(shift($@)))))')')
# Testing
define(`DEFAULT',`unknown')
define(`name1',`Bob')
define(`name2',`Alice')
define(`name3',`Foobar')
divert`'dnl
name1 is recur_ifelse(name1,`Alice',girl,name1,`Bob',boy,DEFAULT)
name2 is recur_ifelse(name2,`Alice',girl,name2,`Bob',boy,DEFAULT)
name3 is recur_ifelse(name3,`Alice',girl,name3,`Bob',boy,DEFAULT)
dnl Output: Bob is boy
dnl Output: Alice is girl
dnl Output: Chuck is unknown
```

Each recursive call shortens the argument list. The macro expects that, eventually, its length becomes one (the base case). The base case is unreachable if the number of original arguments isn't 3N+1, leading to infinite recursion. Properly implementing a recursive macro must ensure that it doesn't happen—for example, by checking the original argument list length and reporting an error via errprint(), yet another built-in macro. The latter is often followed by a call to m4exit(retval) that instantly exits m4 and returns an integer number retval to the caller. The m4exit(retval) macro corresponds to the exit(retval) function in the C language and similar functions in other languages.

Indirect Calls

In addition to calling a macro directly by providing its name with an argument list in parentheses, m4 allows you to call a macro indirectly by passing its name as part of the argument list to the built-in macro indir(name,a1,a2,...). Essentially, the macro name becomes the zeroth argument, which explains why you access it as $0. (Compare this to how C and C++ refer to the program name as the zeroth command-line argument.)

```
define(`raise',`incr($1)')dnl
define(`lower',`decr($1)')dnl
define(`operation',``raise'')dnl
indir(operation,10)dnl
dnl Output:
dnl 11
define(`operation',``lower'')dnl
indir(operation,10)dnl
dnl Output:
dnl 9
```

---

indir() and FUNCALL

The indir(args) macro corresponds to the (FUNCALL func arg1 ...) function in the Lisp language, which is equivalent to (func arg1 ...) but treats the function name as a regular argument, allowing dynamic function calls.

A similar macro, builtin(name,a1,a2,...), exists for accessing built-ins. Curiously, indir() also works for built-ins, but builtin() doesn't work for user-defined macros.

With indirect macro calls, you can invoke macros whose names don't meet m4's expectations—for example, if they contain illegal characters:

```
define(`foo-bar',foo`$1'bar)dnl
foo-bar(10) # Not recognized as a macro!
dnl Output: foo-bar(10)
indir(`foo-bar',10)
dnl Output: foo10bar
```

Naturally, you should avoid giving your macros such convoluted names, but you may find this feature helpful if dealing with third-party macro packages and computed macro names.

From Recursive Macros to Loops

Since any problem that can be addressed with a loop can also be transformed into a tail-recursive format, m4 indirectly supports loops through recursive macro definitions.

As you've already noticed, the macro ifelse() is at the core of any other recursive macro. Looping is accomplished by shortening the argument list and treating a macro as a *variadic function* (a function that accepts a variable number of

No Loops? No Problem!

m4 isn't the only programming language that trades loop statements for tail recursion. Other languages in this group are *Elixir [Tat22]*, *Erlang [Arm13]*, *Haskell [Ski23]*, and *Prolog [Tat22a]*, to name a few. However, unlike them, m4 isn't a functional or logic language, making its case rare and possibly unique.

arguments) or changing one or more arguments until they reach the base case condition.

The following two examples illustrate the differences between the two programming styles. The first, variadic, example builds a macro that generates an HTML ordered list from the list of items. It depends on the shift() macro:

```
define(`gen_ol', <ol>`gen_li($@)'</ol>)dnl
define(`gen_li', `ifelse(`$1',,,`<li>$1</li>gen_li(shift($@))')')dnl
gen_ol(apple, banana, cherry)
dnl Output:
dnl <ol><li>apple</li><li>banana</li><li>cherry</li></ol>
```

The macro in the second example produces a list of consecutive integer numbers. It relies on the incr() macro to change the first argument:

```
define(`range', `ifelse($1,$2,,`$1,range(incr($1),$2)')')dnl
range(1,10)
dnl Output:
dnl 1,2,3,4,5,6,7,8,9,
```

Macro Stack

The built-in macros pushdef(name[,body]) and popdef(name) support a stack-like structure for each defined macro. Calling pushdef() with a name not previously defined is equivalent to defining a new macro with that name. Macro stacks allow you to redefine macros temporarily and restore their previous definitions later.

In this example, look at an m4 "implementation" of a fictional self-driving car that recognizes commands straight, left, right, and go and outputs control instructions move, keep_left, and keep_right. The script defines and then redefines, as needed, the go() macro, which, depending on the previously issued command, activates one of the forward-moving or turning actuators.

```
m4/sdc.m4
divert(-1)
define(`straight', `ifdef(`go',`popdef(`go')',`define(`go',`move')')')
define(`left',     `pushdef(`go',``keep_left'')')
define(`right',    `pushdef(`go',``keep_right'')')
divert`'dnl
```

The driving instructions are also written in m4 in the form of macro expansions.

```
m4/sdc-test.m4
straight go go go
left go go
straight go go
right go go
straight go go go
dnl Output:
dnl move move move
dnl keep_left keep_left
dnl move move
dnl keep_right keep_right
dnl move move move
```

Handling Text

m4 provides a small but useful collection of built-in text-processing macros. In addition to the format() macro previously described on page 204, and the len() macro occasionally mentioned in Macros with Arguments, on page 202, the collection includes macros translit(), index(), substr(), regexp(), and patsubst(). These macros work as follows:

The translit(str,chars[,replacement]) macro replaces (*transliterates*) every character in str that is also in chars with the corresponding (having the same index) character in replacement. Before transliteration, m4 shortens chars or replacement to the same length. If replacement isn't provided, the chars are erased from the string—that is, replaced with an empty string. You can specify a character range in either argument, similar to regular expressions.

The macro index(haystack,needle) finds the index of the first occurrence of needle in the haystack. Indexing starts at 0. If needle is not found, the macro expands to -1. If needle is empty or absent, the macro expands to 0 since any string starts with an empty string.

The substr(str,from[,count]) macro extracts the substring of str starting at index from with count characters. If count is absent, the substring extends to the end of str.

Combining these macros, the capitalize(str) capitalizes a word by converting its first character to uppercase and the rest of the word to lowercase.

```
define(`capitalize', `translit(substr(`$1',0,1),`a-z',`A-Z')'dnl
translit(substr(`$1',1),`A-Z',`a-z')')
capitalize(heLLo)
dnl Output:
dnl Hello
```

And, as a bonus, here's a very informal proof of the English language redundancy:

```
translit(`Most English sentences can be written without vowels',`aoueiAOUEI')
dnl Output:
dnl Mst nglsh sntncs cn b wrttn wtht vwls
```

The remaining two macros operate not in terms of strings but regular expressions.

The regexp(haystack,re_needle[,replacement]) macro searches for re_needle in haystack and optionally replaces it with replacement. If replacement is missing, the macro expands to the index of the first match or -1 if there's no match. Otherwise, the macro expands to replacement. Note that m4 uses GNU Emacs regular expression syntax,[1] which differs from the more common POSIX regular expressions syntax. Key differences in GNU Emacs regular expressions include the following:

1. Most operators must be prefixed with a backslash, such as \| (alternative) and \(...\) (grouping).

2. Additional operators refer to the beginning of a word \<, the end of a word \>, and other positions.

3. In the replacement string, \N refers to the Nth parenthesized group in re_needle, and \& refers to the whole matching fragment.

Mastering Emacs regular expressions calls for a separate book, so let's look only at some simple examples:

```
define(`TEST',`Mary had a little lamb. His fleece was white as snow.')dnl
dnl Find the first 4-letter word that starts with a lowercase letter
regexp(TEST,`\<[a-z]\w\w\w\>')
dnl Output:
dnl 18
dnl Report that word
substr(TEST,regexp(TEST,`\<[a-z]\w\w\w\>'),4)
dnl Output:
dnl lamb
dnl Find a word longer than five letters and abbreviate it
regexp(TEST,`\<\(\w\w\)\w+\(\w\w\)\>',`\1-\2')
dnl Output:
dnl li-le
```

Unlike regexp(), the patsubst(haystack,re_needle[,replacement]) macro substitutes all matching fragments with replacements (or an empty string if replacement isn't

---

1.   https://www.gnu.org/software/emacs/manual/html_node/emacs/Regexps.html

provided) without affecting the nonmatching text. You can use it to perform global substitution.

```
dnl Find all words longer than five letters and abbreviate them
patsubst(TEST,`\<\(\w\w\)\w+\(\w\w\)\>',`\1-\2')
dnl Output:
dnl Mary had a li-le lamb. His fl-ce was wh-te as snow.
dnl Find all words longer than five letters and eliminate them
patsubst(TEST,`\<\(\w\w\)\w+\(\w\w\)\>')
dnl Output:
dnl Mary had a  lamb. His  was  as snow.
dnl Mask all vowels
patsubst(TEST,`\([aoueiAOUEI]\)',`.')
dnl Output:
dnl M.ry h.d . l.ttl. l.mb. H.s fl..c. w.s wh.t. .s sn.w.
```

Diverting Output and Including Files

You're already familiar with the divert([N]) macro, but its concept may still be unclear.

Recall that most m4 scripts act as filters that stream data from the standard input to the standard output (first mentioned on page 199). Like a natural water stream, a data stream can be temporarily diverted and later restored. The divert([N]) macro handles this data stream diversion.

By calling divert(N), you request m4 to stream the data from the standard input to a temporary storage unit, known as a *diversion*, numbered N. A diversion can be implemented as a RAM buffer or a file, depending on how much data it needs to hold. The divert(-1) macro discards the output, which is why it was used in previous code examples. The divert(0) macro restores the default data flow, as does calling divert without arguments.

The undivert(N) macro reconnects the Nth diversion to the m4 pipeline, causing all further input to be read from that diversion until it empties. If N is not provided, all diversions are undiverted in numerical order. The divnum macro expands to the current diversion ID. To discard the already diverted text, divert the output to -1 and undivert the desired diversion (or all of them) using divert(-1)undivert.

A toy, but practical, example illustrates how diversions could be used to generate dynamic HTML pages. Suppose the page sections (for example, the body and the head) are stored in an HTML template file html-tmpl.html in no particular order but are clearly marked as BODY and HEAD. The job of the page generator is to arrange these sections in the correct order and enclose them in proper tags.

```
m4/html-tmpl.html
BODY
<h1>Welcome to The Pragmatic Bookshelf</h1>
<p>This is the main content of the website.</p>
HEAD
<title>The Pragmatic Bookshelf</title>
<link rel="stylesheet" type="text/css" href="styles.css">
```

The goal is accomplished by streaming each section into a separate diversion. The head goes into diversion 1, the body goes into diversion 2, and so on. The generator script uses another file-related macro, include(filename). Think of it as input redirection as opposed to output diversion. As m4 reads the content of the file filename, it expands the section markers and diverts the sections appropriately. At the end of the included file, m4 resumes the script execution: it formats the page and populates it with the undiverted content.

```
m4/html-gen.m4
Line 1  divert(-1)
        define(`HEAD_DIV', `1')
        define(`BODY_DIV', `2')
        define(`HEAD',`divert(HEAD_DIV)')
5       define(`BODY',`divert(BODY_DIV)')
        include(`m4/html-tmpl.html')
        divert`'dnl
        dnl Page generator
        dnl Run as `m4 -I code code/m4/html-gen.m4'
10      <html>
        <head>undivert(HEAD_DIV)</head>
        <body>undivert(BODY_DIV)</body>
        </html>
```

For include() to work correctly, the file filename should be in the same directory as the running script. If not, you should provide the full relative or absolute path to the file or call m4 with the -I (uppercase *i*) command-line option specifying the file's location, as shown on line 9 in the preceding code example.

Interacting with the System

m4 is a Turing-complete programming language, but many tasks are better left to specialized power tools. m4 designers allow you to utilize the services the host operating system provides.

The syscmd(cmd) macro executes the specified cmd—a program or a script with or without command-line options. The command may include pipes, I/O redirection, and even background execution. Anything permissible on the shell command line is permissible as an argument to syscmd(). The macro displays the output of the cmd on the screen but doesn't feed it into the m4 pipeline. For example, the following macro expands to an empty string and displays the number of files in the current working directory:

```
syscmd(ls | wc -l)
dnl Output:
dnl 41
sysval
dnl Output:
dnl 0
```

The built-in sysval macro expands to the exit status of the shell command.

Calling the System

 The syscmd() macro corresponds to the system() POSIX function in C and similar languages.

If you want to expand the output of a shell program (in other words, stream the standard output of syscmd() to m4), you must use the esyscmd(cmd) macro.

The esyscmd() macro is ideally suited for obtaining dynamic information about the host system, such as the date and time, hostname, and available disk space. Note that the shell command for the latter task, df -h / | tail -1 | awk '{print $5}', contains quotation marks, which m4 misinterprets as its own quotation marks. You must temporarily change the quote delimiters to something else, such as a pair of square brackets []. The change is done by calling the built-in changequote(start,end) macro. Use the same macro to restore the quote delimiters to `' after you're done.

```
divert(-1)
define(`DATE',`esyscmd(date)')
define(`HOSTNAME',`esyscmd(hostname)')
changequote([,])
define([DISK_USAGE],esyscmd(df -h / | tail -1 | awk '{print $5}'))
changequote(`,')
divert`'dnl
DATE`'HOSTNAME`'DISK_USAGE`'dnl
dnl Output:
dnl Fri May 31 01:08:11 AM EDT 2024
dnl leo
dnl 34%
```

This example demonstrates capturing and using dynamic system information within your m4 scripts.

Writing Something Big

Search the Web for "small-size project in m4." (Admit that any project in the "Writing Something Big" sections so far was not really *big* but *barely bigger than tiny!*) You'll find many ideas that boil down to one: using m4 to generate text in X from text in Y, where X is usually LaTeX or HTML, and Y is some other notation, such as Markdown.[2] This discovery affirms the language's preprocessing nature and makes choosing a "big" project difficult. Nobody wants yet another HTML code generator.

Fortunately, being Turing-complete, m4 can do much more. For example, it can model *finite state automata* (FSA), also known as *finite state machines* (FSM).

An FSA is a mathematical apparatus for modeling finite-state systems— systems that can be in exactly one of a finite number of states at any time. An FSA consists of a set of states (one designated the initial state), a set of external events, a set of transitions in the form <S1,E,S2,A>, and a set of final, or terminal, states.

Let's model a three-color traffic light with a pedestrian crossing option.

The traffic light can be in one of the following states: Red, Green, Yellow (in antici-pation of red), Yellow (in anticipation of pedestrian crossing), Broken (blinking), or Crossing (red for car traffic, green for pedestrians).

---

2. https://daringfireball.net/projects/markdown/

The FSA starts in the initial state. When event E occurs, the FSA transitions from the current state, S1, to another state, S2, possibly executing action A. The events in this model are as follows:

- Timer (an abstraction representing the passage of time)
- Error (something going wrong in the system, causing it to fall back to blinking)
- Maintenance (resetting the system to the initial state, Green)
- Pedestrian (someone pushing the crossing request button)

The actions associated with each transition mostly place the traffic light in the namesake physical state by sending Red, Green, Yellow, or Blink signals to the controller. A Maintenance event results in the system being reset to Green. The crossing request button instructs the main light to go Yellow and the pedestrian signal to turn to Wait. While in the Crossing state, the system displays Red and Go, respectively.

The following *state transition diagram* graphically summarizes the operation of the traffic light. The rounded rectangles represent states, and the arrows with names represent transitions. For example, the arrow from Red to Broken labeled Error implies that when the FSA is in the state Red and the system breaks, the new state of the system is Broken. The black dot in the lower-left corner is the initial state.

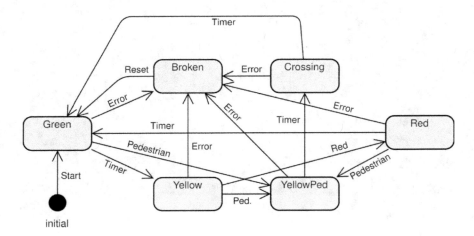

The m4 program simulates the FSA. It sends a sequence of events to the FSA and reports its reaction. The program consists of three major parts.

The first part defines macros responsible for the core functionality of the automaton. The macros whose names begin with an underscore are helper macros.

The _error(e) and _warning(e) macros report unexpected events and optionally terminate the program. The _events macro is a list of event types. It's built automatically by collecting event names from the transactions' definitions via the _addevent(e) macro. The latter uses built-ins ifelse() and regexp() to check if the name e is already on the list and add it if it's not. Note that you cannot use a comma as a list separator, because the constructed list with commas looks like more than one argument to define().

```
m4/fsa.m4
divert(-1)
define(`_error',`errprint(`[[Unexpected: $1]]')m4exit(1)')
define(`_warning',`errprint(`[[Unexpected: $1]]')')
define(`_events',`')
define(`_addevent',`ifelse(regexp(_events,\b`'$1`'\b),-1,`
                    define(`_events',_events`$1'`|')')')
define(`transition',`define($1`_'$2, `define(`STATE',$3)dnl
[ifelse(len(`$4'),0,`$3',`$4')]')
                    _addevent($2)')

define(`mkevent',
  `define($1,
    `ifdef(STATE`_'$1',
      `indir(STATE`_'$1')',
      `_warning(`$1')')')')
define(`mkevents',`ifelse(`$1',,,`mkevent($1)mkevents(shift($@))')')
```

The transition(s1,e,s2[,a]) macro describes a transition. It defines a new macro whose name is a concatenation of the origin state name and the event name (for example, Yellow_Error). When the new macro expands (when the state and the event match), it redefines the current state STATE, expands the action a or the destination state name if the action isn't defined, and attempts to add the event name to the event list.

The mkevent(e) assigns actionable behavior to the event e. If the event is allowed in the current state, the state/event name macro is expanded. Otherwise, m4 displays a warning or error message. Finally, mkevents(elist) recursively calls mkevent(e) for each collected event type—but first, you must convert the vertical bar-separated event list to an "official" comma-separated argument list, as highlighted in the following code block.

The second code block meticulously lists every possible transition in the FSA and implicitly gathers the event names. If you use a CASE (computer-aided software engineering) tool for diagramming, such as VisualParadigm,[3] you may be able to automate the transition generation process, but those techniques are outside this book's scope.

```
m4/fsa.m4
dnl Setting up the FSA
transition(Broken,Maintenance,Green,``Reset; Green'')
transition(Crossing,Error,Broken,``Blink'')
transition(Crossing,Timer,Green,)
transition(Green,Error,Broken,``Blink'')
transition(Green,Pedestrian,YellowPed,``Yellow/Wait'')
transition(Green,Timer,Yellow,)
transition(Red,Error,Broken,``Blink'')
transition(Red,Pedestrian,YellowPed,``Yellow/Wait'')
transition(Red,Timer,Green,)
transition(Yellow,Error,Broken,``Blink'')
transition(Yellow,Pedestrian,YellowPed,``Yellow/Wait'')
transition(Yellow,Timer,Red,)
transition(YellowPed,Error,Broken,``Blink'')
transition(YellowPed,Timer,Crossing,``Red/Go'')
transition(initial,Start,Green,)
mkevents(patsubst(_events,`|',`,'))

define(`STATE',`initial')
divert`'dnl
```

The block also defines the automaton's initial state and generates event-handling macros.

The last code block tests the model by feeding it legal (previously mentioned) event names. This specific example starts the traffic light, lets it operate for a while, causes an error followed by a reset, and even attempts to trigger another reset when the traffic light isn't broken. Since such behavior is undefined, the attempt leads to a warning message.

```
m4/fsa.m4
dnl Testing
Start Timer Timer Timer Pedestrian Timer
Error Maintenance
Pedestrian Timer Timer Timer Maintenance
dnl Output:
dnl [Green] [Yellow] [Red] [Green] [Yellow/Wait] [Red/Go]
dnl [Blink] [Reset; Green]
dnl [Yellow/Wait] [Red/Go] [Green] [Yellow] [[Unexpected: Maintenance]]
```

---

3. https://www.visual-paradigm.com/

Further Reading

- *GNU m4 Reference Manual [SPVB15]*

The End of Week Seven

Congratulations! You're presumably at the end of the seventh week of your computer-archeological journey. You've learned a bit of Forth, Occam, APL, Simula, SNOBOL, Starset, and m4—programming languages once cherished and expected to become successful and marketable tools but now virtually unknown to computer programmers. You just joined the cohort of software developers who know more about stack and array computing, unorthodox text and set processing, and computer modeling and simulation than your average coworker.

Bibliography

[AKW23]   Alfred Aho, Brian Kernighan, and Peter Weinberger. *The AWK Programming Language*. Addison-Wesley, Boston, MA, 2023.

[Alm18]   Ulisses Almeida. *Learn Functional Programming with Elixir*. The Pragmatic Bookshelf, Dallas, TX, 2018.

[Arm13]   Joe Armstrong. *Programming Erlang (2nd edition)*. The Pragmatic Bookshelf, Dallas, TX, 2nd, 2013.

[Bro04]   Leo Brodie. *Thinking Forth*. Punchy Publishing, USA, 2004.

[Bro87]   Leo Brodie. *Starting Forth: An Introduction to the Forth Language and Operating System for Beginners and Professionals*. Prentice Hall, Englewood Cliffs, NJ, 1987.

[BS89]   Graham Brookes and Andrew Stewart. *Introduction to occam 2 on the Transputer*. Macmillan, New York, NY, 1989.

[chr15]   chromatic. *Modern Perl, Fourth Edition*. The Pragmatic Bookshelf, Dallas, TX, 2015.

[Dij68]   Edsger Dijkstra. "Go To Statement Considered Harmful". *Communications of the ACM*. 11:147–148, 1968.

[DMN70]   Ole-Johan Dahl, Bjørn Myhrhaug, and Kristen Nygaard. *SIMULA Information: Common Base Language*. Norwegian Computing Center, Oslo, Norway, 1970.

[Fow03]   Martin Fowler. *UML Distilled: A Brief Guide to the Standard Object Modeling Language*. Addison-Wesley Professional, Boston, MA, Third, 2003.

[Gal96]   John Galletly. *Occam 2: Including Occam 1*. CRC Press, Boca Raton, FL, 1996.

[Gil83]   Leonard Gilman. *APL: An Interactive Approach*. John Wiley & Sons, New York, NY, 1983.

[Gil94]   Mikhail Gilula. *The Set Model for Database and Information Systems*. Addison-Wesley, Boston, MA, 1994.

[GPP71]   Ralph Griswold, J Poage, and Ivan Polonsky. *The Snobol4 Programming Language*. Prentice Hall, Englewood Cliffs, NJ, 1971.

[GS91]   Mikhail Gilula and Alexei Stolboushkin. *Iazyk Programmirovaniia Starset (in Russian)*. Nauka, Moscow, Russia, 1991.

[Hen09]   Sten Henriksson. "A Brief History of the Stack". *Proc. SIGCIS 2009 Workshop*. 2009.

[Hoa78]   C.A.R. Hoare. "Communicating Sequential Processes". *Communications of the ACM*. 21:666–677, 1978.

[Hoc86]   Susan Hockey. *SNOBOL Programming for the Humanities*. Oxford University Press, New York, NY, 1986.

[Hol92]   David Holzgang. *Understanding Postscript*. Sybex, Inc., Alameda, CA, 1992.

[INM84]   INMOS Corp. *Occam Programming Manual*. Prentice Hall, Englewood Cliffs, NJ, 1984.

[Ive62]   Kenneth Iverson. *A Programming Language*. John Wiley & Sons, New York, NY, 1962.

[Jon87]   Geraint Jones. *Programming in Occam*. Prentice Hall, Englewood Cliffs, NJ, 1987.

[Kat70]   Harry Katzan. *APL Programming and Computer Techniques*. Van Nostrand Reinhold, New York, NY, 1970.

[Ker75]   Brian Kernighan. "Ratfor—A Preprocessor for a Rational Fortran". *Software —Practice and Experience*. 5:395–406, 1975.

[Ker87]   Jon Kerridge. *Occam Programming: A Practical Approach*. Blackwell Scientific, Chichester, UK, 1987.

[Kir89]   Bjorn Kirkerud. *Object-Oriented Programming with SIMULA*. Addison-Wesley, Boston, MA, 1989.

[Kov10]   Balás Kovács. "A Generalized Model of Relational Similarity". *Social Networks*. 32:197–211, 2010.

[Lam83]   Günther Lamprecht. *Introduction to Simula 67*. Springer, New York, NY, 1983.

[Leg09]   Bernard Legrand. *Mastering Dyalog APL: A Complete Introduction to Dyalog APL*. Dyalog Limited, Bramley, UK, 2009.

[Leg84]   Bernard Legrand. *Learning and Applying APL*. John Wiley & Sons, New York, NY, 1984.

[LP06]   Lawrence Leemis and Stephen Park. *Discrete-Event Simulation: A First Course*. Prentice Hall, Englewood Cliffs, NJ, 2006.

[Mag83]   Nikolai Magariu. *Iazyk Programmirovaniia APL (in Russian)*. Radio i Sviaz, Moscow, Russia, 1983.

[MM80]   Richard Miller and Jill Miller. "BREAKFORTH Into FORTH!". *BYTE*. 150–164, 1980.

[Ost18]   Roberto Ostinelli. *Modern Erlang for Beginners*. The Pragmatic Bookshelf, Dallas, TX, 2018.

[Pel11]   Stephen Pelc. *Programming Forth*. MicroProcessor Engineering Limited, UK, 2011.

[PM87]   Dick Pountain and David May. *A Tutorial Introduction to OCCAM Programming*. INMOS Corp, Bristol, UK, 1987.

[Pol75]   Raymond Polivka. *APL: The Language and Its Usage*. Prentice Hall, Englewood Cliffs, NJ, 1975.

[Poo87]   Robert Pooley. *Introduction to Programming with Simula*. Blackwell Scientific, Chichester, UK, 1987.

[Rat08]   Elizabeth Rather. *Forth Application Techniques*. FORTH, Inc., Los Angeles, CA, 2008.

[RC07]   Elizabeth Rather and Edward Conklin. *Forth Programmer's Handbook*. BookSurge Publishing, Charleston, SC, 2007.

[RCM93]   Elizabeth Rather, Donald Colburn, and Charles Moore. "The Evolution of Forth". *ACM SIGPLAN Notices*. 28:177–199, 1993.

[Rei90]   Clifford Reiter. *APL with a Mathematical Accent*. Routledge and Kegan Paul, London, 1990.

[RM81]   James Ramsey and Gerald Musgrave. *APL-STAT: A Do-It-Yourself Guide to Computational Statistics Using APL*. Lifetime Learning Publications, Belmont, CA, 1981.

[Sca82]   Leo Scanlon. *FORTH programming*. Sams Publishing, Indianapolis, IN, 1982.

[SDDS86]   Jacob Schwartz, Robert Dewar, Edward Dubinsky, and Edmond Schonberg. *Programming with Sets: An Introduction to SETL.* Springer, New York, NY, 1986.

[SGG11]   Abraham Silberschatz, Greg Gagne, and Peter Galvin. *Operating System Concepts.* John Wiley & Sons, New York, NY, 2011.

[Ski23]   Rebecca Skinner. *Effective Haskell.* The Pragmatic Bookshelf, Dallas, TX, 2023.

[SPVB15]   René Seindal, François Pinard, Gary Vaughan, and Eric Blake. *GNU M4 Reference Manual.* Samurai Media, Wickford, UK, 2015.

[Tat22]   Bruce Tate. *Programmer Passport: Elixir.* The Pragmatic Bookshelf, Dallas, TX, 2022.

[Tat22a]   Bruce Tate. *Programmer Passport: Prolog.* The Pragmatic Bookshelf, Dallas, TX, 2022.

[Vic17]   Steven Vickers. *The Jupiter ACE Manual–35th Anniversary Edition: Forth Programming.* Acorn Books, New Harbor, ME, 2017.

[vT23]   Maarten van Steen and Andrew Tanenbaum. *Distributed Systems.* Maarten van Steen, Netherlands, 2023.

[Wie74]   Clark Wiedmann. *Handbook of APL Programming.* Petrocelli Books, CA, 1974.

[Wol21]   Herbert Wolverson. *Hands-on Rust.* The Pragmatic Bookshelf, Dallas, TX, 2021.

[Zin18]   Dmitry Zinoviev. *Complex Network Analysis in Python.* The Pragmatic Bookshelf, Dallas, TX, 2018.

Index

Thank you!

We hope you enjoyed this book and that you're already thinking about what you want to learn next. To help make that decision easier, we're offering you this gift.

Head on over to https://pragprog.com right now, and use the coupon code BUYANOTHER2024 to save 30% on your next ebook. Offer is void where prohibited or restricted. This offer does not apply to any edition of the *The Pragmatic Programmer* ebook.

And if you'd like to share your own expertise with the world, why not propose a writing idea to us? After all, many of our best authors started off as our readers, just like you. With up to a 50% royalty, world-class editorial services, and a name you trust, there's nothing to lose. Visit https://pragprog.com/become-an-author/ today to learn more and to get started.

Thank you for your continued support. We hope to hear from you again soon!

The Pragmatic Bookshelf

Seven More Languages in Seven Weeks

Great programmers aren't born—they're made. The industry is moving from object-oriented languages to functional languages, and you need to commit to radical improvement. New programming languages arm you with the tools and idioms you need to refine your craft. While other language primers take you through basic installation and "Hello, World," we aim higher. Each language in *Seven More Languages in Seven Weeks* will take you on a step-by-step journey through the most important paradigms of our time. You'll learn seven exciting languages: Lua, Factor, Elixir, Elm, Julia, MiniKanren, and Idris.

Bruce Tate, Fred Daoud, Jack Moffitt, Erin Dees (formerly Ian Dees)
(318 pages) ISBN: 9781941222157. $38
https://pragprog.com/book/7lang

Seven Languages in Seven Weeks

You should learn a programming language every year, as recommended by *The Pragmatic Programmer*. But if one per year is good, how about *Seven Languages in Seven Weeks*? In this book you'll get a hands-on tour of Clojure, Haskell, Io, Prolog, Scala, Erlang, and Ruby. Whether or not your favorite language is on that list, you'll broaden your perspective of programming by examining these languages side-by-side. You'll learn something new from each, and best of all, you'll learn how to learn a language quickly.

Bruce A. Tate
(330 pages) ISBN: 9781934356593. $34.95
https://pragprog.com/book/btlang

Complex Network Analysis in Python

Construct, analyze, and visualize networks with networkx, a Python language module. Network analysis is a powerful tool you can apply to a multitude of datasets and situations. Discover how to work with all kinds of networks, including social, product, temporal, spatial, and semantic networks. Convert almost any real-world data into a complex network—such as recommendations on co-using cosmetic products, muddy hedge fund connections, and online friendships. Analyze and visualize the network, and make business decisions based on your analysis. If you're a curious Python programmer, a data scientist, or a CNA specialist interested in mechanizing mundane tasks, you'll increase your productivity exponentially.

Dmitry Zinoviev
(260 pages) ISBN: 9781680502695. $35.95
https://pragprog.com/book/dzcnapy

Pythonic Programming

Make your good Python code even better by following proven and effective pythonic programming tips. Avoid logical errors that usually go undetected by Python linters and code formatters, such as frequent data look-ups in long lists, improper use of local and global variables, and mishandled user input. Discover rare language features, like rational numbers, set comprehensions, counters, and pickling, that may boost your productivity. Discover how to apply general programming patterns, including caching, in your Python code. Become a better-than-average Python programmer, and develop self-documented, maintainable, easy-to-understand programs that are fast to run and hard to break.

Dmitry Zinoviev
(150 pages) ISBN: 9781680508611. $26.95
https://pragprog.com/book/dzpythonic

Data Science Essentials in Python

Go from messy, unstructured artifacts stored in SQL and NoSQL databases to a neat, well-organized dataset with this quick reference for the busy data scientist. Understand text mining, machine learning, and network analysis; process numeric data with the NumPy and Pandas modules; describe and analyze data using statistical and network-theoretical methods; and see actual examples of data analysis at work. This one-stop solution covers the essential data science you need in Python.

Dmitry Zinoviev
(224 pages) ISBN: 9781680501841. $29
https://pragprog.com/book/dzpyds

Seven Concurrency Models in Seven Weeks

Your software needs to leverage multiple cores, handle thousands of users and terabytes of data, and continue working in the face of both hardware and software failure. Concurrency and parallelism are the keys, and *Seven Concurrency Models in Seven Weeks* equips you for this new world. See how emerging technologies such as actors and functional programming address issues with traditional threads and locks development. Learn how to exploit the parallelism in your computer's GPU and leverage clusters of machines with MapReduce and Stream Processing. And do it all with the confidence that comes from using tools that help you write crystal clear, high-quality code.

Paul Butcher
(296 pages) ISBN: 9781937785659. $38
https://pragprog.com/book/pb7con

Seven Web Frameworks in Seven Weeks

Whether you need a new tool or just inspiration, *Seven Web Frameworks in Seven Weeks* explores modern options, giving you a taste of each with ideas that will help you create better apps. You'll see frameworks that leverage modern programming languages, employ unique architectures, live client-side instead of server-side, or embrace type systems. You'll see everything from familiar Ruby and JavaScript to the more exotic Erlang, Haskell, and Clojure.

Jack Moffitt, Fred Daoud
(302 pages) ISBN: 9781937785635. $38
https://pragprog.com/book/7web

Seven Mobile Apps in Seven Weeks

Answer the question "Can we build this for ALL the devices?" with a resounding YES. Learn how to build apps using seven different platforms: Mobile Web, iOS, Android, Windows, RubyMotion, React Native, and Xamarin. Find out which cross-platform solution makes the most sense for your needs, whether you're new to mobile or an experienced developer expanding your options. Start covering all of the mobile world today.

Tony Hillerson
(370 pages) ISBN: 9781680501483. $40
https://pragprog.com/book/7apps

The Pragmatic Bookshelf

The Pragmatic Bookshelf features books written by professional developers for professional developers. The titles continue the well-known Pragmatic Programmer style and continue to garner awards and rave reviews. As development gets more and more difficult, the Pragmatic Programmers will be there with more titles and products to help you stay on top of your game.

Visit Us Online

This Book's Home Page
https://pragprog.com/book/dzseven
Source code from this book, errata, and other resources. Come give us feedback, too!

Keep Up-to-Date
https://pragprog.com
Join our announcement mailing list (low volume) or follow us on Twitter @pragprog for new titles, sales, coupons, hot tips, and more.

New and Noteworthy
https://pragprog.com/news
Check out the latest Pragmatic developments, new titles, and other offerings.

Save on the ebook

Save on the ebook versions of this title. Owning the paper version of this book entitles you to purchase the electronic versions at a terrific discount.

PDFs are great for carrying around on your laptop—they are hyperlinked, have color, and are fully searchable. Most titles are also available for the iPhone and iPod touch, Amazon Kindle, and other popular e-book readers.

Send a copy of your receipt to support@pragprog.com and we'll provide you with a discount coupon.

Contact Us

Online Orders:	*https://pragprog.com/catalog*
Customer Service:	*support@pragprog.com*
International Rights:	*translations@pragprog.com*
Academic Use:	*academic@pragprog.com*
Write for Us:	*http://write-for-us.pragprog.com*